THE COLLECTED COURSES OF THE ACADEMY OF EUROPEAN LAW

Series Editors

PROFESSOR MARISE CREMONA,

PROFESSOR BRUNO DE WITTE,

PROFESSOR FRANCESCO FRANCIONI

European University Institute, Florence

Assistant Editor

ANNY BREMNER

European University Institute, Florence

VOLUME XXI/2

EU Migration Law

THE COLLECTED COURSES OF THE ACADEMY OF EUROPEAN LAW

Each year the Academy of European Law in Florence, Italy, invites a group of outstanding lecturers to teach at its summer courses on Human Rights law and European Union law.
A 'general course' is given in each of the two fields by a distinguished scholar or practitioner, who examines the field as a whole through a particular thematic, conceptual, or philosophical lens, or looks at a theme in the context of the overall body of law.
In addition, a series of 'specialized courses' brings together a group of highly qualified scholars to explore and analyse a specific theme in relation to Human Rights law and EU law.
The Academy's mission, to produce scholarly analyses which are at the cutting edge of these two fields, is achieved through the publication of this series, the Collected Courses of the Academy of European Law.

EU Migration Law

Legal Complexities and Political Rationales

Edited by
LOÏC AZOULAI
and
KARIN DE VRIES

OXFORD
UNIVERSITY PRESS

OXFORD
UNIVERSITY PRESS

Great Clarendon Street, Oxford, OX2 6DP,
United Kingdom

Oxford University Press is a department of the University of Oxford.
It furthers the University's objective of excellence in research, scholarship,
and education by publishing worldwide. Oxford is a registered trade mark of
Oxford University Press in the UK and in certain other countries

First Edition published in 2014

Published in the United States of America by Oxford University Press
198 Madison Avenue, New York, NY 10016, United States of America

British Library Cataloguing in Publication Data
Data available

Library of Congress Control Number: 2013950749

ISBN 978–0–19–870853–7

Contents

Table of Cases

COURT OF JUSTICE OF THE
EUROPEAN UNION

EUROPEAN COURT OF HUMAN RIGHTS

Australia

Committee Against Torture

Table of Legislation

Directives

Regulations

INTERNATIONAL TREATIES AND CONVENTIONS

Notes on Contributors

Loïc Azoulai holds the Chair of European Union Law at the European University Institute in Florence, Italy. He is co-Director of the Academy of European Law and of the Centre for Judicial Cooperation, both hosted at the European University Institute. He is on leave from University of Panthéon-Assas Paris II, where he is a Professor of Public Law. From 2003 to 2006, he was a *référendaire* at the European Court of Justice, working with Advocate General Poiares Maduro. He is a member of the Editorial Boards of various law journals, including *Common Market Law Review, Revue trimestrielle de droit européen*, and *European Journal of Legal Studies* (*EJLS*). He has published on a wide range of questions of European Union Law.

Christina Boswell is Professor of Politics at the University of Edinburgh. Her research focuses on European immigration and asylum policy, theories of public policy, and the relationship between knowledge and policy.

Sergio Carrera is Senior Research Fellow and Head of the Justice and Home Affairs Research Programme at the Centre for European Policy Studies (CEPS) in Brussels. He regularly acts as an external expert for European institutions and has cooperated in various European research networks and projects dealing with the relation and tensions between human mobility, frontiers, and fundamental rights. He holds a PhD on immigration and citizenship law from the University of Maastricht, The Netherlands.

Karin de Vries is Assistant Professor of Constitutional and Administrative Law at the VU University, Amsterdam. In 2011–12 she was a Max Weber Fellow at the European University Institute in Florence. She is the author of various publications on international and European migration law and citizenship and integration policies. Her dissertation, *Integration at the Border. The Dutch Act on Integration Abroad and International Immigration Law*, was published in 2013.

Bernd Martenczuk holds a doctoral degree in law from Frankfurt University. He also holds a Master of Public Administration from the Kennedy School of Government (Harvard University). He has been a Member of the Legal Service of the European Commission since 1999, where he has worked in the areas of external relations, trade, state aid, and institutional matters. In the External Relations Team of the Legal Service, he has in particular been responsible for the external aspects of justice and home affairs. He is currently working in the institutional team of the Legal Service. Bernd Martenczuk has represented the Commission in numerous cases before the WTO, the General Court and the Court of Justice of the European Union, and the EFTA Court. He is also Professor in the LL.M. Program on International Legal Co-operation (PILC) of the Vrije Universiteit Brussels and has published widely on questions of European and public international law.

Thomas Spijkerboer is Professor of Migration Law at VU University Amsterdam. His research interests lie in the areas of gender and sexuality, women and immigration law, migrant deaths, and the role of courts in migration law. His publications include a monograph, *Women and Refugee Status* (2000), edited volumes, *Fleeing Homophobia* (2013), *Women and Immigration Law* (with Sarah van Walsum, 2007), and many articles and book chapters.

Helen Toner is Dean of Students at Warwick Law School. She has worked in the area of EU citizenship and migration law for a number of years, obtaining her DPhil in this area from Oxford in 2003. She is the author of *Partnership Rights, Free Movement and EU Law* (2004) and co-editor of *Whose Freedom, Security and Justice?* (2006) as well as a number of articles and chapters.

Seline Trevisanut is Marie Curie Fellow and Assistant Professor at the Netherlands Institute for the Law of the Sea of Utrecht University. Her publications include a monograph on *Irregular Migration by Sea in International Law and EU Law* (2012, in Italian), and several articles and contributions on migration control at sea.

1

Introduction

Loïc Azoulai and Karin de Vries

1. The European Union as an Area of Migration

Migration constitutes a physical and social reality within the European Union (EU). Millions of persons circulate within Europe every year and millions cross the EU's external borders and seek to access the European territory. More importantly, migration has become a special feature of the self-understanding of the EU: the constitution and the very existence of the EU depends upon a continuing flow of persons crossing the borders of the member states (establishing an activity in another member state, studying abroad, travelling, or residing in another member state) and upon the management of the flows of third-country nationals (TCNs) knocking at the doors of the EU. This feature clearly appears in paragraph 2 of Article 3 of the Treaty on European Union (TEU) which sets out: 'The Union shall offer its citizens an area of freedom, security and justice without internal frontiers, in which the free movement of persons is ensured in conjunction with appropriate measures with respect to external border controls, asylum, immigration and the prevention and combating of crime'. Noteworthy in this formulation is the dichotomy between citizens and persons: Union citizens are offered an area where both Union citizens and certain non-citizens are conferred facilities to move within an area where access is placed under constant surveillance[1]. A European polity is made possible and tangible by the individual acts of migrants crossing the internal borders, developing a transnational life, and integrating into European societies. It is made tangible to the same extent by the individual or collective initiatives to cross the external borders and by the operations of control to which these initiatives are subject.

EU migration policy is the result of this definition and of these concrete actions. One might discern a double rationale at the basis of this policy. The first one is to be found in the first part of Article 3 of the TEU, which originates in a provision introduced by the Single European Act (now Article 26 of the Treaty on the Functioning of the European Union (TFEU)) which says: 'The internal market shall comprise an area without internal frontiers in which the free movement of goods and persons is ensured'. Legal guarantees have been created to ensure

[1] On the question of access, see P. Dumas, *L'accès des ressortissants des pays tiers au territoire des Etats membres de l'Union européenne* (2013).

freedom of movement, thus enabling intra-EU migration. In particular, Article 20 of the Schengen Borders Code provides: 'Internal borders may be crossed at any point without a border check on persons, irrespective of their nationality, being carried out'.[2] In reality, this liberty is nothing but the mere consequence of the programme initiated in the 1980s to complete the establishment of the internal market through the abolition of internal borders. This programme was the trigger for the development of common controls at the external borders of the EU, as well as European cooperation in the fields of asylum and immigration.[3] This rationale has been crudely put by the Commission in *Wijsenbeek*:

> [A]bolition of [internal] controls concerns all persons, since the maintenance of controls for nationals of non-member countries at internal frontiers would mean that they would have to be distinguished from nationals of the Member States and that the latter would therefore also have to undergo controls. Consequently, special Community measures at the external borders would be necessary in order that no Member State has to deal with undesirable foreigners from non-member countries entering via another Member State.[4]

It is in this correlation between the abolition of internal borders and the loss of control over migration flows that the necessity originated to develop 'flanking policies' on migration (Amsterdam, Article 61(a) of the Treaty Establishing the European Community (TEC)), soon to become 'common' European migration policies (Lisbon, Articles 77, 78, and 79 of the TFEU). Alongside the establishment of a single European area without internal frontiers, the member states have increasingly sought to harmonize the conditions under which TCNs are granted access to their territories. Although Europeanization in the area of migration has been relatively recent, migration is today firmly established as part of the administrative and regulatory framework of the EU and there has been a gradual but certain growth of legislative and policy measures in this field.[5]

A second rationale driving the Europeanization of migration policies has emerged more recently. The Treaty of Amsterdam has introduced the EU objective of creating an 'Area of Freedom, Security, and Justice' (AFSJ) which is protective of TCNs. This was first expressed in Article 61(b) of the TEC: 'In order to establish progressively an area of freedom, security and justice, the Council shall adopt ... other measures in the fields of asylum, immigration and safeguarding the rights of nationals of third countries'. Now, Articles 67(2) and 79(1) of the TFEU provide that the common migration policies of the EU must be 'fair' towards TCNs and have the

[2] Regulation 562/2006, [2006] OJ L105/1. See also Cases C-188/10 and C-189/10, *Melki and Abdeli*, [2010] ECR I-5667. However, TCNs are only allowed to circulate freely for a maximum of three months within a period of six months.

[3] Cp. Art. K.1 of the Treaty of Maastricht, stating that policies on asylum, external border controls, and immigration shall be regarded as matters of common interest 'for the purposes of achieving the objectives of the Union, in particular the free movement of persons'.

[4] Case C-378/97, *Wijsenbeek*, [1999] ECR I-6207, Rec. 28.

[5] Visa procedures; the granting and withdrawing of asylum and other protection statuses; the admission of family members and highly qualified workers; and the return of irregularly staying migrants are but several examples of areas where there has been at least partial harmonization of national rules through EU legislation. The scope of EU migration policy stretches even wider, including issues such as the integration of TCNs, extraterritorial protection, and migration and development.

purpose of ensuring the 'fair treatment' of TCNs legally residing in the territories of the member states. These treaties not only require that EU policies on migration comply with fundamental rights standards, but in addition provide the Union with a competence to *act* in order to safeguard TCNs' rights and fair treatment. It follows that the common European migration policy must provide standards for the entry and residence of TCNs in the member states that are adequate to meet the increasing demands deriving from fundamental rights norms in relation to immigration law. Although a definition of 'fair treatment' is not provided in the TFEU it can be assumed that this includes, at a minimum, compliance with the fundamental rights that are protected under the European Convention on Human Rights (ECHR).[6] Whereas existing standards are most developed in relation to the fields of asylum and family reunification, there is growing evidence of the pertinence of fundamental rights norms to other topics of migration policy including, for example, access of TCNs to social security and other benefits and the treatment of irregular migrants.[7]

The 'fair treatment' or 'fundamental rights' rationale of EU migration law can be seen to have gained strength through the adoption of the Tampere Conclusions in 1999, which called, inter alia, for the approximation of the legal status and rights of long-term resident TCNs to those of nationals of the member states and for measures to combat discrimination. Ten years later, the objective of ensuring respect for the rights of TCNs was further strengthened through the entry into force of the Lisbon Treaty which granted legally binding force to the EU Charter of Fundamental Rights. It has not, however, obtained the same impetus as the internal objective of promoting the social integration of Union citizens. According to this objective, all the obstacles Union citizens may encounter when invoking their rights of free movement and residence within the territory of the member states should be lifted. Moreover, by virtue of their status of Union citizens conferred by the Treaty, which is deemed to be 'the fundamental status of the nationals of the Member States',[8] Union citizens enjoy the right to equal treatment with the nationals of the host member state and a series of 'second-order rights' forged by the European Court of Justice (ECJ) followed by the EU legislator.[9] In fact, Union citizens and their family members are granted a constitutional right to carry out a transnational life. There is no doubt that, in this respect, the situation of the

[6] Relevant international norms also include the provisions of the 1951 Refugee Convention; compliance with this is expressly required in Art. 78(1) TFEU in relation to the EU policy on asylum.

[7] See, eg Case C-329/11, *Achughbabian*, judgment (GC) of 6 December 2011, not yet published, Rec. 49 and Case C-571/10, *Kamberaj*, judgment (GC) of 24 April 2012, not yet published. The issue of non-discrimination of aliens as regards access to social benefits has been addressed in several recent judgments by the ECtHR, eg *Ponomaryovi v. Bulgaria*, ECHR (2011) Appl. No. 5335/05, 21 June 2011 and *Bah v. UK*, ECHR (2011) Appl. No. 56328/07, 27 September 2011.

[8] Case C-184/99, *Grzelczyk*, [2001] ECR I-06193, Rec. 31.

[9] The expression is from Dougan, 'Judicial Activism or Constitutional Interaction? Policymaking by the ECJ in the Field of Union Citizenship', in H.-W. Micklitz and B. De Witte (eds), *The European Court of Justice and the Autonomy of the Member States* (2012) 113. These rights cover fields as diverse as the language in which criminal proceedings are conducted, the individual's freedom of choice over her name, the right to benefit from an education grant, the right to welfare benefits and tax advantages, and the right to organize one's succession.

TCNs stands in sharp contrast. As stated by the Court, the fundamental principle of non-discrimination on the ground of nationality 'is not intended to apply to cases of a possible difference in treatment between nationals of Member States and nationals of non-member countries'.[10] Equal treatment and residence rules for TCNs, when they exist, are entirely governed by regimes of secondary law and the facilities conferred on TCNs are subject to strict conditions and limitations.[11] Moreover, member states are granted considerable discretionary powers. Many of the migration measures adopted at the European level provide for derogations and exceptions to the general rules and the common standards.[12] Examples include the Family Reunification Directive (2003/86), the Long-term Residents Directive (2003/109), and the Blue Card Directive on the admission and conditions of residence of highly qualified third-country workers (2009/50). Under the latter Directive, the discretionary power of the member states to decide on the admission of TCNs remains so extensive that it would seem difficult to qualify such admission in terms of an individual 'right'. Quite apart from secondary legislation, Carrera's contribution in this volume describes how the reluctance of member states to cede competence to the EU in the field of TCN integration has led to the creation of a set of soft law and policy tools with limited transparency and accountability (see further section 3).

It must be noted that the combination of these two potentially conflicting rationales is likely to generate tensions within the structure of EU migration law. The complex interaction of protection against 'undesirable foreigners' with the objective to establish an internal area of prosperity, freedom, security, and justice has led to a structuration of the field which is very much organized around the distinction between legal and illegal migration. Whilst the fight against illegal migration has become a clear objective of the Union, legal migration is seen as an asset for Europe, taking into account in particular the fact that the EU population is growing older. In the long run, the integration of TCNs who are long-term residents in the member states is even said to be 'a key element in promoting economic and social cohesion' at the EU level.[13] This dichotomy unquestioningly endorsed by the European institutions as well as by the member states seems to work as a correlation according to which fighting illegal migration would be the only way to facilitate legal migration. However, in practice the distinction between illegal and legal migrants is not as clear-cut as one would assume. First of all, the conditions of illegality as well as the ability to receive legal migrants still very much depend on the legal framework of each member state and vary from one to the other. Secondly, there are limbo situations in which individuals, whilst being regarded as illegal migrants, cannot be removed from the European territory for

[10] Cases C-22/08 and C-23/08, *Vatsouras and Koupatantze*, [2009] ECR I-04585, Rec. 52.

[11] See, eg the Long-term Residents Directive: Council Directive 2003/109, [2004] OJ L16, Arts. 5 (right to long-term resident status, but conditional) and 11 (equal treatment conferred for certain purposes).

[12] De Bruycker, 'L'émergence d'une politique européenne d'immigration', in P. De Bruycker (ed.), *L'émergence d'une politique européenne d'immigration* (2004) 351.

[13] Long-term Residents Directive, *supra* n 11, Rec. 4.

some compelling legal reasons.[14] Furthermore, despite the introduction of the 'fundamental rights' rationale, EU migration policy appears to be predominantly characterized by controls and obligations. A clear example of this can be found in the Return Directive where the language of obligations prevails. Obligations are imposed on member states to issue a return decision or to issue an entry-ban decision under certain circumstances. The obligation to return imposed on individuals is balanced by a few procedural rights. Also illustrative are the border control operations carried out by Frontex (see the chapter by Trevisanut) and the asylum regime, the latter granting a right to access to procedures but without a right to access the European territory. All of these drawbacks reflect constitutive tensions in the development of EU migration law.

2. The Structure of EU Migration Law and Policy

Compared to the broader body of EU law and policies, the field of migration has a number of specific characteristics. Since Toner further elaborates on some of these in her contribution to this volume, we will content ourselves with stating the most salient features.

First, migration law and policy fall under the EU competence to establish the AFSJ. Article 4(2)(j) of the TFEU specifies that, in establishing the AFSJ, the Union acts on the basis of a shared competence with the member states. Compared to the TEC, the Lisbon Treaty has slightly expanded the areas in which the EU is allowed to act within the migration field.[15] However, the AFSJ is a very peculiar field of shared competence. First, it works on the premise that the member states enjoy a large discretion in relation to immigration control—in particular with regard to the conditions of admission to the national territory—and remain exclusively responsible with regard to the maintenance of law and order and the safeguarding of internal security (Article 72 of the TFEU). Moreover, it is a field of 'differentiation'. The UK, Ireland, and Denmark do not fully participate in these common policies, while third countries are associated with the development of the AFSJ (namely Iceland, Norway, Switzerland, and Liechtenstein). It is also well known that the UK, Ireland, Bulgaria, Romania, and Cyprus are not parties to the Schengen agreements, hence intra-EU migration to these countries continues to be subject to border controls.

[14] See European Commission, Study on the situation of third-country nationals pending return/removal in the EU Member States and the Schengen Associated Countries, Home/2010/RFXX/PR/1001, March 2013.

[15] New competences include the adoption of measures for the establishment of an integrated management system for external borders (Art. 77(2)(e) TFEU); for defining the rights of TCNs other than the right to free movement (Art. 79(2)(b) TFEU); for combating trafficking in persons (Art. 79(2)(d) TFEU); and for supporting member state action to promote the integration of TCNs (Art. 79(4) TFEU). In the field of asylum, the TFEU now provides a legal basis for the establishment of a truly 'Common' European Asylum System, going beyond the enactment of minimum standards (Art. 78). Lastly, the expansion of the external dimension of the EU's immigration policy is backed up by new competences to cooperate with third countries for the purpose of managing the inflows of people seeking protection (Art. 78(2)(g) TFEU) and to conclude readmission agreements (Art. 79(3) TFEU).

Secondly, as already mentioned, EU migration law is essentially a regime of secondary law. The position of individuals derives from EU secondary legislation and national law, rather than from the Treaties. There has not been a tendency towards constitutionalization comparable to that driving the law on the free movement of EU citizens. Following the Treaty of Amsterdam, decision-making procedures in the field of migration moreover reflected a high level of inter-governmentality. The point of departure was that the legislative measures required by Articles 62 and 63 of the TEC were to be adopted unanimously by the Council with only a consultative role for the European Parliament. It is here that the Lisbon Treaty has introduced some important and often-mentioned institutional changes. Subject to only a few limited exceptions,[16] EU measures on immigration are now to be adopted by means of the ordinary legislative procedure, requiring agreement from the European Parliament and qualified majority voting in the Council. Nevertheless, Union legislation remains the product of programmes[17] which lead to institutional battles.[18] National parliaments have, moreover, emerged as new potentially important actors after Lisbon, as illustrated by the high number of reasoned opinions issued in relation to the proposed directive on seasonal employment.[19]

A third important feature of this field is the emergence of a body of global and European norms that may be classified as 'international migration law'. This is the result of the growing movement of people across national borders that has occurred in the course of the past decades. The development of international norms generally predates the enactment of EU legislation in various fields of migration policy (including asylum, family reunion, and labour migration) and thus serves as a source of reference for EU law. Importantly, the fact that certain aspects of migration policy are now also governed by EU law does not absolve the member states from the obligation to respect their commitments under international law. This means that the international treaties to which the member states are parties do not serve only as a source of inspiration, but also as a set of standards that they must adhere to including when implementing or acting in accordance with EU law.[20] The EU legal framework takes this into account most explicitly in Article 78(1) of the TFEU, which states that the measures constituting the Common European Asylum Policy must be in accordance with the 1951 Refugee Convention and its 1967 Protocol. Not surprisingly, EU migration regulations make frequent reference to international law.[21] Additionally, as mentioned above, international

[16] See Arts. 77(3) and 78(3) TFEU on measures concerning passports, identity cards, and similar documents and provisional measures to deal with sudden inflows of TCNs in emergency situations.

[17] J.-Y. Carlier and F. Crépeau, 'Le droit européen des migrations: exemple d'un droit en mouvement?' 57 *Annuaire français de droit international* (2011) 674.

[18] S. Carrera and E. Guild, 'Does the Stockholm Programme Matter? The Struggles over Ownership of AFSJ Multiannual Programming' (2012) CEPS Policy Paper 51.

[19] COM (2010) 379. According to a report issued by the Commission itself, this proposal attracted the highest overall number of opinions from national parliaments, with as many as nine chambers claiming that it breached the principle of subsidiarity (COM (2011) 345 final, at 7).

[20] On the relationship between EU law and international law, see H. Battjes, *European Asylum Law and International Law* (2006).

[21] See, eg Art. 1 of the Return Directive (EP and Council Directive 2008/115, [2008] OJ L348/98): 'in accordance with' and Art. 27 of the Procedures Directive (Council Directive 2005/85, [2008] OJ L239/6) on the application of the safe third country concept.

law norms on migration derive from the provisions of the ECHR which must be respected as part of the general principles of EU law (Article 6(3) of the TEU) and, in the not too distant future, as treaty obligations that are binding not only on the member states but also on the EU itself (Article 6(2) of the TEU).

Another feature of EU policy on migration is externalization. Immigration is, by definition, a topic that touches upon both the internal and the external policy of the EU and its member states. It is, therefore, not surprising that the extension of EU legislative and policy-making activity into new sectors of the migration field has been accompanied by the expansion of the external dimension of EU migration policy.[22] This externalization has, first of all, a physical or territorial dimension: the operations carried out by Frontex take place at, but also beyond, the external borders of the EU, where immigrants are intercepted at sea. Another example concerns the introduction, by individual member states but within the confines of the EU migration directives, of integration tests and programmes in countries of origin. Externalization also has a legal and political dimension, which concerns the conclusion of agreements and cooperation between the EU and third countries. Since the Treaty of Amsterdam, the need for such cooperation, including in the field of immigration, has been consistently stressed by the European Council in its Tampere Conclusions and in the multi-annual programmes adopted in The Hague and Stockholm. In the meantime, the scope of EU immigration policy has expanded beyond the regulation of visa policies and border controls and into the domains of long-term migration and the combating of irregular migration. As demonstrated by Martenczuk in this volume, in each of these fields cooperation with third countries can be instrumental to achieving the EU's immigration objectives. Examples include agreements on visa waivers and visa facilitation, on local border traffic, on the readmission of TCNs who are not entitled to residence within the EU, and on migrant smuggling and trafficking in persons. It follows that, at the EU level, the policy fields of migration and external relations are becoming increasingly intertwined.

Finally, a word must be said about the role of the ECJ. The Court is not absent from this field. However, its positioning does not seem to be clearly settled yet and varies according to the instrument at issue. On the one hand, it tends to rely strongly on the aim of the various migration directives, as formulated by the Union legislator, rather than on constitutional principles derived from the Treaties.[23] On the other hand, it relies on respect for fundamental rights and the principles of proportionality and effectiveness to impose obligations on the member states and circumscribe the amount of discretion left to them. Illustrations of this dynamic can be found in the field of family reunification, where the Court was asked to

[22] On the broadening scope of this external dimension see F. Trauner and H. Carrapiço, 'The External Dimension of EU Justice and Home Affairs after the Lisbon Treaty: Analysing the Dynamics of Expansion and Diversification' 17 *European Foreign Affairs Review* (2012) Special Issue, at 1.

[23] See, eg Case C-578/08, *Chakroun*, [2010] ECR I-1839; Case C-61/11, *El Dridi*, [2011] ECR I-3015; Case C-329/11, *Achughbabian*, judgment (GC) of 6 December 2011, not yet published; and Case C-430/11, *Md Sagor*, judgment of 6 December 2012, not yet published.

interpret the Family Reunification Directive (2003/86), and where it was asked to rule on the conditions of residence for long-term resident TCNs under the Long-term Residents Directive (2003/109).[24]

Arguably, the Court's role will be further strengthened in the future. One step in this direction is that, since the entry into force of the Lisbon Treaty, the possibility to refer preliminary questions is no longer limited to national courts of last instance. This change provides an important opening for increased judicial scrutiny at the European level. The post-Lisbon EU legal order is moreover characterized by a strengthened commitment to the protection of fundamental rights, as evidenced through the binding character attributed to the EU Charter of Fundamental Rights and the prospect of EU accession to the ECHR (Articles 6(1) and (2) of the TEU). The relevance of the fundamental rights framework to the area of immigration and asylum, which often involves human beings in very vulnerable situations, was already stated above. Case-law shows that the Court is under pressure from both NGOs and national courts to adopt a constitutional approach based on fundamental rights. Thus far the Court has shown a tendency to delegate the burden of 'constitutionality review' to the national courts, which are required to interpret EU legislation in conformity with EU fundamental rights.[25] This has allowed the ECJ to protect EU legislation from annulment, while at the same time acknowledging the importance of fundamental rights.[26] However, where national courts take their role in protecting fundamental rights seriously there is a risk that the integrity of EU legislation will be undermined. Hence, the importance of the Court stepping in. The accession of the Union to the ECHR will probably trigger this development with the 'prior involvement' of the Court on questions relating to the validity of EU acts.

3. A Selection of Current Issues

The purpose of this volume is not to cover in its entirety the rapidly growing field of EU law and policy on migration in the post-Lisbon era. Instead, the six chapters included in this book focus on a number of current issues that together, nevertheless, address many of the developments outlined above.

It has been observed that the emergence of agencies at the European level illustrates the EU's moving away from 'a mere law-making community—with the European

[24] Case C-540/03, *Parliament v. Council*, [2006] ECR I-5769; Case C-578/08, *Chakroun*, [2010] ECR I-1839; Case C-571/10, judgment (GC) of 24 April 2012, not yet published; and Case C-508/10, *Commission v. The Netherlands*, judgment of 26 April 2012, not yet published. See also, in the field of asylum, Case C-465/07, *Elgafaji*, [2009] ECR I-921. For further analysis, see the case-law review by Steve Peers in 50 *Common Market Law Review* (2013) 529.

[25] See, eg Joined cases C-411/10 and C-493/1, *N.S. and M.E. and others*, judgment (GC) of 21 December 2011, not yet published; and Case C-540/03, *Parliament v. Council*, [2006] ECR I-5769.

[26] L. Azoulai, 'The Case of Fundamental Rights: a State of Ambivalence', in H.-W. Micklitz and B. De Witte (eds), *The European Court of Justice and the Autonomy of the Member States* (2012) 207, especially at 213.

institutions legislating and the Member States' authorities implementing'.[27] In the field of immigration policy, the clearest example of this development is the establishment of Frontex, the European agency responsible for the management of the EU's external borders. Frontex coordinates and supports the operational activities of the member states with regard to the management of the external borders of the EU. Like other regulatory agencies, Frontex acts as a specialized body providing technical expertise and assistance to aid the implementation of EU policy in a particular field. In the case of Frontex, however, such implementation includes the coordination of so-called Joint Operations, whereby migrants are intercepted at sea, and the deployment of Rapid Border Intervention Teams (RABITs) to deal with exceptional migrant inflows.[28] It follows that Frontex is closely involved with the physical protection of the EU's borders, which can include the use of force and have a direct impact on migrants' safety and well-being.

The legal and political settings of Frontex are examined in this volume by Trevisanut. The author notes that Frontex was created at a time when the control of irregular migration became part of a set of security concerns, also including terrorism and organized crime, in the aftermath of the terrorist attacks in New York, Madrid, and London. Although Trevisanut observes that the existence of these concerns facilitated European integration in the field of border management, she argues that Frontex has remained, in essence, a forum for intergovernmental cooperation. This follows, in particular, from the agency's composition, which guarantees a central role for the member states in the decision-making process, and from the fact that the means for operational activities are to be provided by the member states on a voluntary basis. Both factors are perceived as obstacles to the achievement of an effectively functioning system for integrated border management. While the Regulation establishing Frontex has recently been amended with the aim of strengthening the agency's independence, Trevisanut points out that the member states remain the primary actors to decide on its activities.

Another institutional complexity concerns the involvement of national border guards in Frontex operations. These operations engage national border guards from different member states and are governed by a complex legal framework, determining whether the guards' actions are subject to the law of the home or the host state. In addition to this, Frontex can conclude 'working arrangements' with third countries. Such arrangements are, however, not public or at least hard to find. The issue of transparency and the lack of operational procedures have been picked up by the European Commission and the Council, the latter having called, in the Stockholm Programme, for the enactment of 'clear rules of engagement'. Trevisanut asks, however, whether such rules, having a military connotation, could be established as part of the EU's policy on border controls rather than under the European Security and Defence Policy. It follows that Frontex is faced with a dual challenge of improving both its capacity for effective implementation of

[27] S. Griller and A. Orator, 'Everything under Control? The "Way Forward" for European Agencies in the Footsteps of the Meroni Doctrine' 35 *European Law Review* (2010) 3.

[28] See S. Trevisanut, in this volume, sections 7 and 11.

the management of the external borders, ensuring that its actions are sufficiently transparent and allowing for accountability in cases of human rights violations.

Lastly, the Joint Operations conducted by Frontex raise the question of compatibility with fundamental rights norms. As these operations entail physical restriction of the movement of migrants coming to the EU by sea, they affect migrants' rights to emigrate and to enjoy liberty and security of the person as well as the application of the principle of *non-refoulement*. Trevisanut argues that international asylum and fundamental rights norms contain sufficiently clear rules regarding the treatment of migrants who are intercepted or returned at sea. What is needed, however, is the consistent application of these norms by member states, in particular when cooperating through Frontex. Trevisanut observes that the need for Frontex operations to conform to fundamental rights standards has been recognized in the recently amended Frontex Regulation.[29] Nevertheless, as explained above, these operations remain subject to a lack of transparency that makes it hard to identify responsible actors where human rights violations do occur.

The institutional forms and modes of cooperation shaping EU law and policy on immigration also come to the fore in Carrera's contribution, which considers the domain of immigrant integration. As observed above, integration has only been added to the list of EU competences in the Treaty of Lisbon (Article 79(4) of the TFEU). Nevertheless, action had already been undertaken in this field, including through the adoption of the EU Framework on Integration (EFI). As Carrera notes, the Framework is in some ways similar to the Open Method of Coordination (OMC) but has its own specific features. It came into being after a proposal from the European Commission for an OMC on immigration proved too ambitious, due to the limited willingness of member states to coordinate their policies on the sensitive topic of integration. It is, therefore, perhaps not surprising that the EFI functions largely as an exchange platform for national policy-makers, with very little involvement from the EU institutions and a mostly coordinating role for the European Commission.

Emerging from Carrera's careful description of the EU Framework on Integration are not only the lack of Europeanization but also its strong technocratic character. The Framework is built on four pillars: the National Contact Points on Integration, the establishment of Common Basic Principles of Integration, financial support from the European Integration Fund, and the involvement of experts and civil society through the European Integration Forum and the European Website on Integration. Actors within these pillars include national policy-makers as well as academics and civil society. Important functions of the EFI are to facilitate the sharing of knowledge and best practices and to develop benchmarks for integration policies, resulting in outputs such as the *Handbook on Integration for Policy Makers and Practitioners*, the Migrant Integration Policy Index, and, more recently, the European Modules for Migrant Integration, which are to serve as 'building blocks' for national integration policies. As Carrera notes, these outputs promote

[29] Council Regulation 2007/2004, [2004] OJ L349/1, as amended by EP and Council Regulation 1168/2011 [2011] OJ L304/1.

certain strategies or best practices in the field of integration without, however, touching upon fundamental debates about the underlying values or objectives of integration policies, let alone about the contours of a European understanding of what integration means. It thus appears that the way to move forward with EU policy in the field of integration has been largely through depoliticization.[30]

Although the EFI produces 'soft law and policy' tools which lack a legally binding nature, Carrera nevertheless warns against underestimating its effects on national integration policies and—directly or perhaps more indirectly—on the legal position of TCNs residing in the EU. He argues that the EFI has contributed to the spread of an integration paradigm focused on immigration and identity control rather than the inclusion of immigrants through the promotion of equality and security of residence. While the standards developed in the context of the CFI, such as the Common Basic Principles on Integration, are not legally binding, they are used by the Commission to allocate funding for national integration programmes under the European Integration Fund. Considering the potential impact of the EFI on the integration and legal position of immigrants, Carrera argues that the procedures and policy tools developed within the Framework lack transparency, democratic accountability, and the possibility of judicial control. He suggests that Article 79(4) of the TFEU may partly remedy this situation, as it provides a treaty basis for the EFI and specifies that measures to support national integration policies shall be adopted according to the ordinary legislative procedure. As the experiences in several member states show, the fact that integration laws are enacted through democratic and transparent procedures does not always correlate with an inclusive or rights-based approach to integration.[31] Nevertheless, as Carrera stresses, such procedures will create a forum for critical and public reflection on the added value, necessity, and possible negative effects of particular integration measures.

The above examples illustrate how the expansion of EU immigration policy into new areas and the strengthening of its operative dimension have given rise to the establishment of new institutional actors and venues of cooperation. Despite the very different contexts and levels of harmonization, both Frontex and the EFI show how practical responses to events, such as the arrival and settlement of immigrants, often precede the formulation of adequate legislative and administrative frameworks to guarantee their legality and democratic control. As cooperation in the field of immigration moves forward, the development of such frameworks is one of the challenges facing both the EU and the member states.

The theme of externalization is picked up again in Martenczuk's contribution, this time from the perspective of legal competence. Besides showing how cooperation with third countries serves to meet the objectives of the EU migration policy, for example through visa waivers and readmission agreements, the author observes

[30] See also P. Scholten, *Framing Immigrant Integration: Dutch Research-Policy Dialogues in Comparative Perspective* (2011).

[31] E. Guild, K. Groenendijk, and S. Carrera (eds), *Illiberal Liberal States: Immigration, Citizenship and Integration in the EU* (2009).

that the regulation of immigration may also be instrumental to the realization of foreign policy objectives. Examples of the latter include the refusal of entry to TCNs to implement sanctions against other countries or organizations (travel bans), or the facilitation of trade in services through free movement of service providers. Through an examination of the above measures, adopted both within and outside the context of the EU's immigration policy, Martenczuk sets out to demarcate the scope and the nature of the EU's external competence in immigration matters. As mentioned earlier, the Lisbon Treaty has introduced express competences for the EU to manage the inflows of asylum seekers in cooperation with third countries and to conclude readmission agreements. Nevertheless, a general and exclusive external competence to regulate immigration remains far off. Whereas a more or less exclusive competence pertains in the area of visas and border controls, member states retain room to act independently within the fields of long-term and irregular migration. The lack of exclusive competence in the latter domains is related to the lower levels of harmonization which, given the politically sensitive nature of the issues at stake, are likely to persist for a while. Lastly, where immigration measures are adopted for foreign policy purposes, the question of legal competence will depend on the prior identification of the correct legal basis for such measures.

Whereas the existence of legal competence is a necessary factor for the EU to act externally, it does not as such provide a motive. From a political perspective, it may be asked what the incentives and mechanisms are that drive the EU to cooperate with third countries. This question is explored by Boswell in relation to the control of irregular migration. Engaging with different theories that have been put forward to explain why irregular migration is a structural feature of liberal welfare states, Boswell analyses which of these theories is most helpful in explaining EU policy measures in this area. As she observes, the larger share of the policy measures adopted to combat irregular migration—including notably readmission clauses and agreements, but also development funding—belong to the external dimension of the EU immigration policy.

The three theories analysed by Boswell—the liberal constraint, political economy, and social systems theories—explain how, at both the national and the European level, policies to control irregular migration are impeded by liberal constraints (commitments to free movement and the abolition of EU internal border controls), by the demands of the business lobby, and by the existence of social and economic structures (such as welfare and education systems) that have internal dynamics favourable to irregular entry and residence. From the perspective of liberal constraint theory, EU external cooperation in the field of irregular migration has been explained as a way to avoid democratic and judicial scrutiny after the communitarization of EU immigration policy. This raises the question of what will happen in this area after the Lisbon Treaty, which has strengthened the role of the European Parliament and the ECJ, and whether the EU and the member states will tend towards those measures that are not subject to democratic or judicial scrutiny or where such scrutiny is hard to apply (eg in the case of Frontex operations involving both member states and third countries).

Alternatively, political economy theory could help to explain why member states choose to highlight European external cooperation against irregular migration, while at the same time internal policies tolerate such migrations so as not counteract the business sector's need for labour. Looking at systems theory, however, Boswell warns that the EU may have only a limited capacity to influence the actions and policies of third countries and to ensure their cooperation. Whereas irregular migration is, in itself, a highly complex process that is inherently difficult to regulate, the management of such migration through third country cooperation offers very few prospects for success.

Lastly, the legal dynamics of EU migration law and fundamental rights norms are examined, in this volume, by Spijkerboer. Spijkerboer starts his contribution from the premise that the content of legal norms, including fundamental rights norms on migration, is not fixed and that their interpretation by the courts can result in different outcomes. The possible variety of such outcomes can be classified through four ideal typical political positions on migration issues, resulting from the intersection between two axes: left/right and libertarian/statist. According to Spijkerboer, legal interpretations constructed by lawyers to criticize court decisions will mostly, if not always, reveal a preference for one of these positions and a desire to make the case-law correspond to that position. Nevertheless, many lawyers will be tempted to present a particular outcome of legal interpretation as 'legally correct' rather than just 'politically preferable', because this gives that outcome legal authority. Lawyers can, however, use different strategies within legal discourse to criticize judicial reasoning and to steer such reasoning into different directions.

Spijkerboer explores three ways in which critical lawyers can navigate the terrain between the 'freedom and constraint' that are both present in legal reasoning. They can demonstrate inconsistency in the case-law (and argue for consistency along a particular line), expose the legal choice available to judges (and challenge the choice that was made), or question an unspoken or seemingly evident rule or factual assumption standing at the basis of a judgment or line of case-law. These options are illustrated through analyses of case-law of the European Court of Human Rights (ECtHR) and the ECJ on the level of scrutiny to be applied in asylum cases, the right of European workers to family reunification with TCNs, and the expulsion of people suffering from HIV/AIDS. At the same time as 'adding to the arsenal of critical lawyers', as Spijkerboer aims to do, awareness of the above strategies also helps to understand how judges and other lawyers engage with the evolving legal framework of EU migration law.

2

The Lisbon Treaty and the Future of European Immigration and Asylum Law

Helen Toner

This chapter introduces and discusses the most significant issues arising from the Lisbon Treaty and their likely impact in the area of Immigration and Asylum law in the next few years. The chapter will focus mainly on issues directly linked to changes brought about in December 2009 by the Lisbon Treaty (particularly Chapter III (on Immigration, Asylum, Borders, and Visas) of Title V (on the Area of Freedom, Security, and Justice)), but will of course also integrate some significant element of discussion about the way these treaty changes have been used and the direction that can be discerned in the Stockholm Programme[1] and the so-called 'European Pact on Immigration and Asylum',[2] although there is too much in these programmes to make much detailed analysis of them in their own right. There are, therefore, several themes to address. Decision-making changes and competences will be addressed first: these are two major issues of the Lisbon Treaty. Changes are also made to the opt-out arrangements, but they still remain, so the continuation of the fragmentation of the 'area' of freedom, security, and justice is another theme to be examined. Other issues to be covered include the possibility of a renewed focus on fundamental rights; the emphasis on monitoring, evaluation, and updating of the legislative *acquis*; the continued tension between the competing forces of inter-governmentalism and nationalism and supranationalist Europeanization and integration; and the emerging and increasingly important role of the Court of Justice in the development and enforcement of European Union (EU) Immigration and Asylum law. Guild and Carrera suggest that the Lisbon Treaty introduces a 'new supranational setting that is characterised by stronger democratic accountability, judicial control, efficient evaluation mechanisms for the full application of the rule of law and an ambitious, fundamental human rights strategy'[3] —we shall see the extent to which this analysis is substantiated in the course of this chapter. Is this

[1] Council Document 17024/09. [2] Council Document 13440/08.

[3] Guild and Carrera, 'The EU's Area of Freedom Security and Justice Ten Years On', in E. Guild and S. Carrera (eds), *The Area of Freedom Security and Justice Ten Years On: Successes and Failures under the Stockholm Programme* (2010) 12.

indeed a treaty which ushers in profound positive institutional and constitutional changes, or is a more cautious assessment justified, especially in the light of subsequent developments?

1. Decision-making Changes

The first change to examine is the decision-making process. This is crucial as it affects the institutional dynamics of decision-making. There has been plenty of research concerning the possible effect of these institutional arrangements on the negotiation of the various legislative instruments and the shape of the EU's immigration and asylum *acquis* in its early years.[4] It is commonly assumed that the relative strengths of the various institutional parties have a significant impact on their ability to influence the final outcome of legislative texts. The term 'negotiating in the shadow of the veto' is one way of expressing this: the fact that one party (whether that be a member state in the Council of Ministers, or the European Parliament) *has to* agree to the final form of a text considerably increases its bargaining power during negotiating processes if no resort is had to formal votes, and conversely the fact that one party may be outvoted does significantly affect its negotiating and bargaining power, even if consensus is usually sought first without resorting to formal votes. Initially in Amsterdam, there was much that was to be decided by unanimity and by merely consulting the European Parliament. This drew significant criticism from those who were convinced that this was constraining the development of immigration and asylum policy and preventing agreement on anything other than 'minimal' standards that were riddled with compromises to accommodate particular elements of national immigration and asylum systems that the member states were not willing to give up. It has been described as the 'good' (Parliament), the 'bad' (Council), and the 'ugly' (Commission),[5] with the influence of the member states still very strong and that of the European Parliament weak.

Decision-making prior to the Lisbon Treaty had developed in stages. From Amsterdam, there was a complex transitional structure whereby some decision-making procedures were due to change automatically after a period of time, whereas others would change once the basic general outline had been put in place.

Immediately before the Treaty of Lisbon, therefore, Steve Peers[6] identifies a threefold classification.

[4] G. Papagianni, *Institutional and Policy Dynamics of EU Migration Law* (2006); Peers, 'The EU Institutions and Title IV', in S. Peers and N. Rogers, *EU Immigration and Asylum Law: Text and Commentary* (2006) 47; A. Geddes, *Immigration and European Integration: Towards Fortress Europe* (2000) and (2nd edn, 2008); A. Geddes, *The Politics of Migration and Immigration in Europe* (2003).

[5] Acosta, 'The Good, the Bad and the Ugly in EU Migration Law: Is the European Parliament Becoming Bad and Ugly? (The Adoption of Directive 2008/15: The Returns Directive)' 11 *EJML* (2009) 11, at 19.

[6] Peers, 'EU Immigration and Asylum Competence and Decision Making after the Treaty of Lisbon' 10 *EJML* (2008) 219.

1. *Qualified majority voting (QMV) in Council and Co-decision with EP*: border controls under Article 62(1) and some visa issues under Article 62(b), third-country nationals (TCNs) travel under Article 62(3), asylum under Article 62(1), and irregular migration under Article 62(3)b.
2. *QMV in Council and consultation with EP*: administrative cooperation, common visa format, and common visa list under Article 62(b).
3. *Unanimity and consultation*: legal migration under Article 64(3)a.

In terms of the *proposal of legislation*, the usual position of the Commission's monopoly on legislative proposals had already been established at the end of the transitional period of five years from the coming into force of the changes agreed by the Treaty of Amsterdam.[7] In fact, even before the deadline and abolition of the member states' power of initiative, the Commission in practice proposed most measures in a number of areas and the areas in which the member states did in fact make use of this right of initiating proposals were somewhat limited.[8] The significance of this is that the Commission acts as a 'neutral broker' pursuing compromise and the Community interest at the earliest stage of legislative proceedings, rather than initiatives emanating from a particular member state or group of states. Although this role was diluted in the transitional period, the reality reflected this somewhat less than the treaty structure might indicate.

In the Treaty of Lisbon, most decision-making, including in the 'Area of Freedom, Security, and Justice' (AFSJ), moves to the 'Ordinary Legislative Procedure', that is qualified majority voting and co-decision. The major move here is the provision in Article 79 of the Treaty on the Functioning of the European Union (TFEU) that matters of *legal migration* will now be decided by this method, with greater participation by the European Parliament and moving away from the individual member state 'veto' effect of unanimous voting. Visa lists and formalities would also move to the ordinary legislative procedure. One exception to this (noted further below) is the competence to enact monitoring procedures in Article 70 of the TFEU from which the European Parliament remains excluded from co-decision.

Will the future shape of immigration and asylum law be significantly changed by this? Undoubtedly the increased power of the European Parliament must be welcomed and the removal of the veto of individual member states will mean that they are in a less strong position to push forward their individual interests and views originating in national discourse 'up' to influence law and policy at the regional EU level if these are not shared by at least some others. But there are two significant points to note, both with the same underlying thrust: not to hastily overestimate the beneficial changes that may be brought about. The move from unanimity to QMV does not necessarily mean that every measure will be voted on, nor that member states will be outvoted with great regularity. It may be easy to underestimate the pressure that may be brought to bear on member states to agree

[7] What was Art. 67(2) EC Treaty. See discussion in Peers, 'Transforming Decision-Making on EU Immigration and Asylum Law' 30 *European Law Review* (2005) 285.

[8] Peers, *supra* n 6.

to a measure even when they have a veto, despite the fact that this negotiation is carried out 'in the shadow of the veto'. Naturally, there is and will be a continuing pressure to reach as wide a consensus as possible rather than to rush to use the qualified majority methodology to bind member states to particular provisions, or compromises on the overall shape of legislation with which they are not happy. There is, however, no doubt that the gradual removal of the unanimity 'veto' is widely seen to have been a necessary and welcome progression over the years, and the completion of this process is certainly to be welcomed. The other significant change is the greater input of the European Parliament, but again some caution is required to ascertain the extent to which this really will make a difference. It is widely held common ground that the European Parliament, championed by the work of its LIBE (Civil Liberties and Fundamental Rights) Committee, takes a more migrant-friendly approach than the Council,[9] but has struggled to make its more liberal rights-based voice heard in the absence of co-decision. The co-decision power will certainly give the EP potential to make its voice heard more effectively but how this will be used in practice will take some time to emerge.

Evidence is now emerging of the extent to which these changes will influence the shape of immigration and asylum law: whether the final move away from unanimity will speed up and ease the passage of helpful measures that were previously being held up by the requirement of unanimity, and whether the greater powers of the European Parliament will result in greater influence and a more migrant-friendly approach actually having a real impact on law and policy.[10] Some early tentative conclusions may be discerned. The Returns Directive and the extension of the Long-term Residence Directive to beneficiaries of the Qualification Directive must be considered, as well as the wider record of reaching deals at first reading, which is certainly a source of some concern.

A. Returns Directive

The Returns Directive[11] was proposed in 2005[12] as part of the Hague Programme.[13] It was to be adopted under the co-decision procedure as this had applied since the beginning of that year. Thus, although not passed under the Treaty of Lisbon procedures itself, it was an early indication of the use of the QMV/co-decision procedure. Acosta[14] pinpoints six issues that were discussed at length and were contentious: the scope of the Directive, issues of voluntary departure, re-entry bans, remedies, detention, and unaccompanied minors. In respect of all of these

[9] Hence Acosta's characterization of the European Parliament as the 'good' rather than the 'bad' or 'ugly'.

[10] Note the ambivalent response of Commissioner Cecilia Malmström, giving evidence to the House of Lords EU Committee for its report on 'Implementing the Stockholm Programme: Home Affairs' (9th Report of 2010/11), at 11 stating 'But the involvement of the European Parliament so far has not made anything more complicated', and suggesting that any complications arise from the complexity of the issues.

[11] Directive 2008/115, [2008] OJ L348/98. [12] COM (2005) 391.

[13] Council Document 16054/05. [14] Acosta, *supra* n 5.

issues, the Council Working Party discussions following on from the Commission's Proposal 'tended towards a dilution of the relevant provisions with an increase of the prerogatives that Member States could keep' yet the European Parliament consistently proposed its extension and greater protection.[15] This divergence of views was evident in relation to the scope of protection and whether the individuals could be turned back at the border without the protection of the Directive. The voluntary return period was similar but the Council proposed a maximum period and only on the application of the migrant, rather than a minimum period. Re-entry bans became optional under the European Parliament's proposal but the Council wanted them to be compulsory. Procedural rights also diverged. Perhaps the most startling divergence was detention, the Council making it obligatory and potentially indefinite where necessary to prepare the return or carry out the removal, whereas the European Parliament's draft made this optional and limited to a maximum of 18 months. The Parliament also wanted a specific provision to deal with minors. The process of 'trilogues' (informal three-way discussions between representatives of the Council, Commission, and Parliament) then proceeded in 2008, during which compromises were struck on a number of these issues at first reading. Most of them were resolved in favour of the Council's position, with the notable exception of detention and unaccompanied minors. The position here resembles much more the position of the European Parliament, with detention being optional and limited to 18 months. Thus Acosta's questioning of whether the Parliament has gone 'bad' and/or 'ugly', abandoning its previous 'good' position as the rights champion.

B. Extending the Long-term Residence Directive

The exclusion of refugees and beneficiaries of subsidiary protection from the Long-term Residence Directive[16] (which, after a period of time, gives settled third country nationals certain rights within the member state of long residence and certain rights to move to a second member state) has been criticized as one of its significant limitations.[17] A proposal to amend the legislation to bring this about was published by the Commission, an agreement was reached at first reading,[18] and the Directive has now been amended.[19] The proposal does not touch on

[15] Acosta, *supra* n 5, at 28. [16] Directive 2003/109, [2004] OJ L16/44.

[17] Some of the literature on the Directive includes Boelaert-Suominen, 'Non-EU Nationals and Council Directive 2003/109/EC Concerning the Status of Third-Country Nationals who are Long-Term Residents: Five Paces Forward and Possibly Three Paces Back' 42 *Common Market Law Review* (2005) 1011; Halleskov, 'The Long-Term Residents Directive: A Fulfilment of the Tampere Objective of Near-Equality?' 7 *EJML* (2005) 181; and Peers, 'Implementing Equality? The Directive on Long-Term Resident Third Country Nationals' 29 *European Law Review* (2004) 437.

[18] Peers, 'Statewatch Analysis: Extending EU Long-term Resident Status to Refugees and Persons with Subsidiary Protection Status' (2010), available at <http://www.statewatch.org/analyses/no-114-ltr.pdf>. See also Peers, 'Legislative Update EU Immigration and Asylum Law 2010: Extension of Long-term Residence Rights and Amending the Law on Trafficking in Human Beings' 13 *EJML* (2011) 201.

[19] See Directive 2011/51, [2011] OJ L132/1, amending Directive 2003/109, [2004] OJ L16/44.

the transfer of refugee status and protection as such, but rather the benefits of long-term residence status for those who have been resident for sufficient periods of time. Steve Peers' analysis notes the fairly limited, although useful, input of the European Parliament's new co-decision procedure, mainly in the area of the length of the waiting period stipulated in the text, but the absolute centrality of the switch to qualified majority voting in getting agreement to the measure at all in the Council. Prior to this change, the unanimity requirement was blocking progress with one objecting state, but once this was removed the Council could forge ahead on the basis of a widespread even though not unanimous agreement: certainly a positive step.

C. First reading deals

The wider record of first reading deals is also troubling to many. The Returns Directive and amending the Long-term Residence Directive were not isolated cases, but part of a fairly large number of other cases which have also taken a similar approach.[20] This has led to calls for greater transparency and openness, and a more democratic approach to the law-making process on the part of the European Parliament, its Committees, and their Rapporteurs. Perhaps the Parliament is coming up against the harsh reality of what it means to have not just the power to protest but the obligation to reach solutions which can attract sufficient consensus to survive the legislative process in the context of migration law issues. Playing the role of 'rights champion' perhaps becomes increasingly problematic as the role of relatively powerless 'outside' critic gives way to real power which has to be shared with others despite some deep disagreements, as the experience of the Liberal Democrat party joining with the Conservatives in the first coalition government in the UK since the 1970s is illustrating clearly in domestic UK politics.

D. Recasting the asylum *acquis*

The process of reviewing and recasting the initial directives will now take place under the altered decision-making competences under the Treaty of Lisbon. Only one of these Directives (the recast Qualification Directive) has yet been passed,[21] although political agreement has now been reached on two others (Reception conditions and Dublin recast), formal publication is still pending at the time of writing.[22] Initial indications suggest that while there may indeed be some progress and positive

[20] Bunyan, 'Statewatch Viewpoint: Secret Trilogues and the Democratic Deficit' (2007), available at <http://www.statewatch.org/analyses/no-84-ep-first-reading-deals.pdf>; Bunyan, 'Statewatch Analysis: European Parliament: Abolish 1st [and 2nd] Reading Secret Deals—Bring Back Democracy "Warts and All"' (2009), available at <http://www.statewatch.org/analyses/no-84-ep-first-reading-deals.pdf>; Acosta, *supra* n 5, at 24–5.

[21] Directive 2011/95, [2011] OJ L337/9.

[22] See Council Document 16853/12 and Press Release 17315/12, indicating political agreement on both Reception and Dublin Proposals, and continued progress on Eurodac and the Procedures Directive.

influence from the altered decision-making procedures, this is likely to be relatively modest and critical voices will undoubtedly remain.[23]

2. Competences

The other, and more complex, thing that changes in the AFSJ as a result of the Treaty of Lisbon is the scope of the EU's *competences*. Steve Peers gives a good and more detailed overview of this area.[24] This may seem something of a dry and technical area, yet it is of importance. The delimitation of the outer edges of EU competences generally has always been a contested issue, and remains thus after the Lisbon Treaty. The national court decisions regarding the Lisbon Treaty's compatibility with national constitutions,[25] and the continuing dynamic of unresolved tension between different views of the relationship between EU and national law from the national and EU/Court of Justice of the European Union (ECJ) perspectives are ample evidence of this. In particular, a new perspective has arisen questioning not just the issue of protecting those competences which have not in fact been transferred to the EU, but a more fundamental questioning of whether there may be some competences that the German Constitutional Court at least would view as too fundamental to the nature of the nation state to be transferred. The criminal law competences were amongst those that troubled the Constitutional Court most, but there was nothing in the new competences in the Lisbon Treaty nor the Court decision that would cast any doubt on any of these competences, so it is only of indirect relevance to the migration issues in question here. Alongside the delay in the Single Permit Directive[26] and discussion over the Commission's 2011 Schengen Governance Package[27] surrounding issues of competences and proper legal base, it is, however, a timely reminder that these questions are still very much live issues.

There are a number of changes made by the Treaty of Lisbon, which can be split into a number of categories. General provisions are followed by a number of more

[23] NGOs continue to raise some concerns, see eg the Analysis by AEDH, 'Analysis of the Forthcoming Common European Asylum System' (2012), available at <http://www.aedh.eu/The-AEDH-publishes-an-analysis-of.html>. For an early analysis of the Qualification Directive, see Peers, 'Legislative Update 2011, EU Immigration and Asylum Law: The Recast Qualification Directive' 14 *European Journal of Migration and Law* (2012) 199.

[24] Peers, *supra* n 6.

[25] Especially that of the German Federal Constitutional Court, *Gauweiler v. Treaty of Lisbon*. Pliakos, 'Who is the Ultimate Arbiter? The Battle over Judicial Supremacy in EU law' 36 *European Law Review* (2011) 109; Mayer, 'Rashomon in Karlsruhe: A Reflection on Democracy and Identity in the European Union: the German Constitutional Court's Lisbon Decision and the Changing Landscape of European Constitutionalism' 9 *IJCL* (2011) 757; and Doukas, 'The Verdict of the German Federal Constitutional Court on the Lisbon Treaty: Not Guilty, but Don't Do it Again!' 34 *European Law Review* (2009) 866.

[26] See further Pascouau and McLoughlin, 'EU Single Permit Directive: A Small Step Forward in EU Migration Policy', EPC Policy Brief, January 2012.

[27] See Carerra, 'An Assessment of the Commission's 2011 Schengen Governance Package', CEPS Policy Paper 47/2012; Pascouau, 'The Schengen Evaluation Mechanism and the Legal Basis Problem: Breaking the Deadlock', EPC Policy Brief, January 2012.

detailed issues concerning the specifics of immigration and asylum competences (namely: borders and visas, asylum, legal migration, irregular migration).

A. General provisions

Previously Article 61 of the Treaty Establishing the European Community (TEC), Article 67 of the TFEU now contains the general provisions, and the term '[a]n Area of Freedom, Security and Justice' is central to Article 67(1). Later, in Article 67(2)–(4), there are three further 'general' provisions. The first is specifically focused on immigration and asylum, the second starts with mentioning 'security' and focuses on crime, and the third is concerned with justice and focuses on civil justice. It is interesting to see the admittedly imperfect mapping of security to crime, and justice to civil proceedings, without the perhaps obvious corresponding direct mapping of freedom (of movement) that might have introduced the title on Immigration and Asylum, although this connection does appear much more clearly later in Article 79 of the TFEU regarding the common immigration policy, including a reference to 'freedom of movement and residence' of third country nationals in other member states.

In terms of immigration and asylum, the TFEU now states that the EU 'shall ensure the absence of internal border controls for persons and shall frame a common policy on asylum, immigration and external border control, based on solidarity between member states, which is fair towards third country nationals. For the purpose of this title, stateless persons shall be treated as third country nationals'. The previous terminology of 'flanking measures' therefore falls away in favour of 'common policies', and the direct causative link of other 'flanking measures' implicitly or explicitly being made *necessary* by the abolition of internal border controls is diminished. The 'common' policy on immigration, asylum, and external borders here gains something more of a self-standing justification, not just as a necessary corollary of the coming down of internal borders.

The European Council is now referred to in Article 68 of the TFEU, but as Steve Peers notes, the role indicated there for it (it 'shall define the strategic guidelines for legislative and operational planning within the area of freedom, security and justice') is largely a repetition in the specific context of what it has already been doing for years in the multi-annual programme under the old TEU provisions of general application concerning the European Council, the 'Tampere Conclusions', and the 'Hague Programme'.

Finally, one other new general competence is the provision in Article 70 for adoption by the Council of measures for member states collaborating with the Commission to conduct 'impartial and objective' evaluations of policies by member states. The striking issue here is the exclusion of the European Parliament from this procedure, which has given rise to some difficulties in making progress on an early Proposal for a Schengen evaluation mechanism.[28]

[28] See Pascouau and McLoughlin, *supra* n 26.

B. Borders and visas

Here, we have to compare the provision of Article 77 of the TFEU with the previous Article 62 of the TEC.[29] The provisions on border controls are the same, those on crossing external borders are nearly the same. There is an extended competence on visas, dropping the existing limitation of the competence to visas for only three months and now, therefore, covering longer visas. Steve Peers doubts whether the wrapping up of the policy into the simple formulation of the 'common policy on visas' rather than the four sub-categories previously in Article 62 of the TEC extends the policy much further, arguing that the four categories are already quite extensive—it is indeed difficult to envisage much that would not already be covered by this. As regards the 'intensity' of the move to a 'common policy' as opposed to the rules on a 'uniform' visa, again Peers argues that it is difficult to discern any clear advancement on what competence had already been provided. The competence regarding rules on freedom to travel now extends beyond three months to an indeterminate 'short period', allowing greater flexibility, although how this is to be determined, let alone whether it might ultimately prove to be any kind of justiciable concept, is an interesting question! There is a new competence relating to the 'gradual establishment of an integrated border management system for external borders'. Here, Peers suggests a distinction would have to be drawn between the customs cooperation powers, not subject to the AFSJ opt-out, and the 'regulation of the synergy between the different borders administrations' which would be covered by this new competence and would be subject to the opt-out. Finally, the last power relates to passports and other documents, the exception to the general move to QMV and co-decision. This applies not just to passports but to other residence documents as well. Peers[30] suggests (drawing on Case C-137/05, *United Kingdom v. Council*) that the *security* features of EU citizen passports (and other documents used to cross external borders) could still fall under the general external borders legal base, but that any harmonization of the *format* of these documents facilitates free movement within the EU rather than more efficient crossing of external borders and would be dealt with differently.

C. Asylum

Here we have to compare Article 78 of the TFEU with the previous Article 63(1) of the TEC, and also Article 64(2) of the TEC. The main changes would be to competence rather than decision-making, as the switch to Qualified Majority Voting and co-decision had already largely taken place. The first and main general point to note, in line with what we have seen elsewhere, is the reference in Article 78(1) of the TFEU to developing a 'common policy on asylum' rather than the less ambitious and more modest wording of the previous Article 63(1) of the TEC which focused on the adoption of 'minimum standards'. Of course the

[29] For more details on visa policy under this Article, see Meloni 'The Development of a Common Visa Policy under the Treaty of Amsterdam' 42 *Common Market Law Review* (2005) 1357.
[30] Peers, *supra* n 6.

political commitment to a Common European Asylum System (CEAS) was always there, from the Tampere Conclusions setting the agenda for the development of immigration and asylum and the exercise of the new Amsterdam competences in 1999. Yet the competences in relation to specific measures refer consistently time and again to 'minimum standards'. Peers comments that 'it is difficult to see how a genuinely "common" system could ever be established pursuant to the current [pre-Lisbon] framework'.[31] The restriction of competences in this field to nationals of third countries, and consequent exclusion of nationals of any EU member state from the scope of EU asylum law, is now more comprehensive and all-embracing, although as Peers notes 'this would not constitute a change in practice'[32] as competences throughout this field have in fact only be used in relation to third country nationals.

The shift in Article 78(2)(a) of the TFEU from mentioning 'qualification' to 'status' as a refugee is potentially significant in regulating not just the requirements for an individual to be recognized as a refugee but the legal rights and status of individuals once they are so recognized. The streamlining of the decision-making process will make differences between immigration and asylum competences largely academic now that the same procedures are used throughout, but recourse to multiple legal bases (as in the Qualification Directive)[33] may not be necessary in the future to deal with such matters. It is hardly appropriate to say that this is a radical shift in the substantive content of competences conferred, but they will be streamlined and rationalized.

In comparison to the status of subsidiary protection which would only be uniform (but conferred upon and enjoyed within separate member states), we see in Article 78(2)(b) of the TFEU that provision could be made for the status of asylum to be 'valid throughout the Union'. Peers suggests a range of different approaches here from recognition simply of the non-refoulement obligation being transferred to other member states, to a more formal recognition of a right of residence and other benefits (welfare, housing, and employment) valid in each and every member state once granted in one. This certainly opens the door to possible future development of provisions which could be highly significant to the individuals concerned, especially if they have aspirations of onward movement within the EU territory once granted protection. A tension may arise which will not be easy to reconcile. Such provisions could in fact operate to minimize the possible 'pull' effect between member states of actually seeking to process an asylum claim in a particular preferred destination (due to perception or reality of better conditions) rather than in the first country of entry to the EU. On the other hand, others may perceive a risk of making the EU as a whole a more attractive destination for asylum seekers. The argument that easily transferable onward migration rights makes the EU as a whole a more attractive destination for highly skilled migrants is certainly

[31] *Ibid.* [32] *Ibid.*, at 234–5.

[33] This Council Directive 2004/83, [2004] OJ L304/12, refers to the old Arts. 62(1)(c), 62(2)(a), and 62(3)(a).

a common theme and has resulted in the passage of the so-called 'Blue Card' Directive. The prospect of easily transferable rights for refugees would certainly be a problematic and controversial development in some quarters.[34] Opposition to overly extensive measures might conceivably be based on competence limitation, especially if the member states opposed were about to be or had been outvoted[35] but although this argument may have something to it, it would be far from certain to succeed.

Temporary protection competence in Article 78(2)(c) in the Lisbon Treaty is both expanded in intensity (in that there is now provision for a 'common system', not just minimum harmonization) but also limited in scope (only to situations of 'mass influx' which was not necessary to trigger the competence before, although the Directive does comply with the new Treaty framework, as it does already contain such a limitation).[36] The previous specific burden-sharing power Article 63(2)(b) of the TEC which provided for measures 'promoting a balance of effort between Member States in receiving and bearing the consequences of receiving refugees and displaced persons' is now gone in the new Article 78 of the TFEU—but the new Article 80 of the TFEU (see further below) provides an underlying guiding principle of solidarity and fair sharing of responsibility. The provision dealing with measures for the benefit of individual member states faced with a mass influx (Article 78(3) of the TFEU) is carried over from Article 64(2) of the TEC with some changes. The temporal limitation is lifted so measures need no longer be for six months only, although they are still referred to as 'provisional', and the European Parliament must simply be consulted rather than the co-decision that is normal under the Ordinary Legislative Procedure, so this is another minor departure from the general rule of the normal legislative procedure.

Finally the provision on partnership and cooperation with third countries in Article 78(2)(g) of the TFEU is a clearer and more comprehensive competence than before. It is also, according to Peers, a stronger potentially exclusive competence that could pre-empt the member states' positions, in contrast to development policy which remains shared.

D. Immigration

Here, Article 79 of the TFEU has to be compared to the previous Article 63(3) and (4) of the TEC. Again, and on a similar note to the immigration competences, Peers suggests a more 'intensive' competence, given the introduction of the

[34] Note the sensitivity already expressed regarding the difference between the Stockholm Programme and the Action Plan implementing it on this point in the House of Lords EU Committee 9th Report of 2010/11, *supra* n 10.

[35] The Tobacco Advertising case, Case C-376/98, *Germany v. Council and Parliament*, [2000] ECR I-08419, is a classic example of that, and a rare one of the lack of competence argument succeeding, as is the second Tobacco Advertising case, Case C-380/03, *Germany v. Parliament and Council*, [2006] ECR I-11573, an example of how such a challenge will not necessarily succeed.

[36] See the Directive on Temporary Protection, Council Directive 2001/55, [2001] OJ L212/12, which even in its title and also in Arts. 1 and 2 makes clear that a 'mass influx' as necessary to trigger the Directive's provisions.

terminology of 'common' policy in Article 79(1) and the removal of the explicit provision at the end of Article 63(3) of the TEC referring to the retention of national measures which are compatible with the EU Treaty and other international agreements. Guiding principles are also found in Article 79(1) of the TFEU referring to 'efficient management', 'fair treatment' of those residing lawfully, and 'prevention of' and 'enhanced measures to combat' illegal immigration and trafficking.

E. Legal migration

Legal migration is dealt with in Article 79(2)(a) and (b) and Article 79(4) with an important limitation in Article 79(5) of the TFEU. As regards Article 79(2)(a) of the TFEU, this largely repeats the existing competence relating to regulating conditions of entry and residence. As regards the rights of those resident there is a wider power expressed. In particular, the framework now presumptively includes rights within the first member state, and includes, almost as a secondary issue, the regulation of movement (now called 'free movement') to another member state. As Peers points out, the current powers have been used in the Directive on Long-term Residence[37] to regulate the status in the first member state, and also in the Highly Skilled Workers or 'Blue Card' Directive,[38] albeit both of these directives also regulate to some degree movement to further member states as well, so this appears to be a consolidation of something already implicitly accepted in the previous treaty framework. The Single Permit Directive[39], however, was held up until the passage of the Lisbon Treaty itself due in part to issues of legal base and competence to act.[40]

Article 79(5) of the TFEU provides that '[t]his Article shall not affect the right of Member States to determine volumes of Third Country Nationals coming from third countries to their territory in order to seek work, whether employed or self-employed'. This does appear as a new restriction, although nothing proposed so far under the previous Treaty arrangements would prevent member states from doing this. Peers[41] looks in some detail at overlapping competences and concludes that now Article 79 is a clear competence to regulate economic migration regardless of Article 46, and this is subject to two things—first, the limitation in Article 79(5) of the TFEU and secondly, the overlap between this and Article 153 regulating 'conditions of employment'. In regard to the overlap he suggests that if regulating conditions of employment is ancillary to general regulation of conditions of TCNs, the immigration power in Article 79 of the TFEU would apply, whereas if a measure only concerns the regulation of conditions of TCN employment, then Article 153 of the TFEU would apply. The Single Permit Directive only mentions Article 79 of the TFEU as its legal base.

[37] Directive 2003/109, [2004] OJ L16/44.
[38] Directive 2009/50, [2009] OJ L155/17.
[39] Directive 2011/98, [2011] OJ L343/1.
[40] Pascouau and McLoughlin, *supra* n 26.
[41] Peers, *supra* n 6.

So what is the extent of the exclusion in Article 79(5)? Peers makes four points. (1) it is only relevant for limiting competence under Article 79, not other Treaty articles of relevance to economic migration; (2) it 'only concerns volumes of admissions' and would not cover rights once admitted or the procedures for admissions; (3) it appears not to cover the issue of *intra-community* migration of TCNs from one member state to another; and (4) it applies only to those who *seek* employment, although Peers' suggestion that it could be interpreted to extend only to 'workseekers' rather than those coming to take up confirmed and established work contracts or business arrangements does seem rather far-fetched. It is also worth noting that it applies not just to employed activity (as did the transitional restrictions on A8 and A2 nationals, from the eight new member states in 2004 and two in 2009 that were subjected to phasing in of free movement rights over a period of several years) but also to self-employed activity. Nonetheless, the argument over the scope of this exception has been raised surprisingly quickly (in the context of a subsidiarity review of the Seasonal Workers Directive)[42] so we may well expect to hear more of this as further measures in the field of economic migration are proposed.

Finally, a further addition in Article 79(4) of the TFEU is the provision for establishing 'measures to provide incentives and support for the action of Member States with a view to supporting integration of third country nationals residing legally in their territories'. It is, however, important to note both that some EU activities in the field pre-date this[43] and that this precludes 'any harmonisation of the laws and regulations of the Member States'.

F. Irregular migration and other related issues

Here we compare Articles 79(2)(c)(d) and 79(3) of the TFEU with Articles 63(a)(c), 63(d), and 63(3) of the TEC. There are few changes of substance regarding irregular migration—the use of the term 'unauthorised' still sits alongside a reference to 'illegal' immigration and the addition of 'removal' alongside 'repatriation' does not seem to change a great deal of much real substance. Implied competence to conclude readmission treaties has already been exercised on a number of occasions,[44] so adding this is confirming explicitly what had already been recognized in practice. Trafficking is now dealt with in its immigration law aspects but there is also a criminal law aspect to this, which, as Peers notes, would be dealt with under criminal law competence. This would therefore be subject to the so-called 'emergency brake' in Article 83(1) of the TFEU.[45]

[42] See House of Lords, EU Committee Report 1, 'Subsidiarity Assessment: Admission of Third Country National Seasonal Workers' (November 2010).

[43] See the discussion of the development of EU involvement in this area in S. Carrera, *In Search of the Perfect Citizen? The Intersection between Integration, Immigration and Nationality in the EU* (2009).

[44] See Commission Communication, 'Evaluation of EU Readmission Agreements', COM (2011) 76.

[45] Arts. 83(1) and 83(2) TFEU. Human trafficking is dealt with in Art. 83(1) as one of the particular cross-border serious issues. Other issues regarding illegal migration facilitation, employer sanctions, etc., are found in Art. 83(2).

G. Subsidiarity, proportionality, and solidarity in the development of a truly 'common' policy?

In developing a truly 'common' policy, the extent and pace of developments will be important. The 'Stockholm Programme' and the 'Action Plan' for implementing it are going to be crucial in shaping the agenda. Some tension has arisen surrounding the relationship between these two, and areas in which the Action Plan does not match the Stockholm Programme.[46] A comparison of the two suggests that these issues are in fact to a large extent not in the immigration and asylum area, but the issue of transfer of recognition of refugee status is one such issue that has been mentioned as potentially troublesome. The concepts of subsidiarity and proportionality also represent significant conceptual tools that might be employed to balance the harmonizing impetus towards the use of the competences to create truly 'common' immigration and asylum policies, and this has already happened with the Proposed Directive on Seasonal Workers.[47] The UK Parliament is not the only one to have concluded that there are sufficiently serious subsidiarity concerns over this Directive to send a reasoned opinion to the Commission,[48] rebutting and contesting all four of the reasons given in the Commission's Proposal in favour of action at Community level. Nothing formal happened, however.[49] This leads on to the next theme to be addressed, that of the continued tension between nationalism and Europeanization. Solidarity is another underlying theme from Article 80 of the TFEU. It now covers the entire field, not just asylum, and is couched in the language of 'Solidarity and the fair sharing of responsibility, including its financial implications, between Member States'. However, it is not clear what this means or how it might be put into effect throughout the area of migration, borders, and visas.[50] Refugee resettlement priorities were introduced in March 2012 in relation to financial support for resettled refugees from outside the EU, but the ongoing concern surrounding the Greek asylum system[51] certainly indicates that concerns remain about the effectiveness of solidarity arrangements that may be necessary to ensure the effective implementation of the asylum *acquis* in some member states where pressing logistical and financial constraints remain.

[46] See the discussion in the House of Lords EU Committee 9th Report of 2010/11, *supra* n 10.

[47] See *supra* n 42.

[48] The 'Subsidiarity Review' report, *supra* n 42, served as a reasoned opinion to be forwarded to the Commission: see House of Lords EU Committee 9th Report of 2010/11, *supra* n 10.

[49] See the Commission Report on Subsidiarity and Proportionality, COM (2011) 344.

[50] See DG for Internal Policies, *The Implementation of Article 80 TFEU on the principle of solidarity and fair sharing of responsibility, including its financial implications, between Member States in the field of border checks, asylum and immigration* (2011), PE 453.167, commissioned by the European Parliament Committee on Civil Liberties, Justice, and Home Affairs, exploring in some detail the possibilities and complexities involved.

[51] Which has given rise to litigation both in the ECtHR and the ECJ, Case C-411/10, *N.S. v. Secretary of State for the Home Department*, judgment of 21 December 2011, not yet published, and *M.S.S. v. Belgium and Greece*, ECHR (2011) Appl. No. 30696/09, 21 January 2011.

3. Continued Tension between Nationalism and Europeanization

There is a continued tension between nationalism and Europeanization which seems not to have been dispelled by the planning or coming into force of the new institutional framework of the Lisbon Treaty, and which will continue to influence the future directions in which the EU's immigration and asylum law develops as the competences and decision-making powers are put into action.

A. Pact on immigration and asylum

The European Pact on Immigration and Asylum[52] agreed in 2008, which influenced and fed into the development of the Stockholm Programme[53] are two key documents here. Guild and Carrera helpfully draw out some of the issues involved.[54] The extent to which various French national initiatives made their way into the Pact, strongly in early stages but less so in later drafts, is striking. It is also worth noting the 'inherently intergovernmental nature'[55] of the Pact and the language used at times. In particular, the emphasis on member states' competences, and the curious silences regarding both the EU's competences and the measures so far adopted which certainly question the extent of the member states' continuing unlimited control over immigration and asylum issues and are critical to a balanced understanding of the extent to which these issues have over recent years become matters for the shared responsibility and competence of both the EU and the member states. Guild and Carrera conclude that the thinking behind the Pact, apparent in the way it is presented, demonstrates a persistence of nationalism and intergovernmentalism to a degree that they view as surprising at this stage in the integration process and which they think will be likely to foreshadow continued tensions.

Several other issues underline this theme. The use (to be discussed further below) of the 'opt-outs' by the UK in relation to the development of the second stage of the legislation making up the Common European Asylum System (CEAS) is also pertinent here, the UK's perceived national interest being pursued by opting out of many of these second wave measures as the second stage of the CEAS takes shape. A number of issues which have also become quite highly visible in public discourse also serve to highlight this continued tension. We might consider the tensions between France and the Commission relating to the 'expulsion' (or 'voluntary removal') of Roma (even though this relates to EU citizens' free movement law), recent comments by Angela Merkel on multiculturalism in 2011

[52] Council Document 13440/08. [53] Council Document 17024/09.

[54] Guild and Carrera, 'The French Presidency's European Pact on Immigration and Asylum: Intergovernmentalism vs Europeanisation? Security vs Rights?', CEPS Policy Brief 170, September 2008, available at <http://www.ceps.be>.

[55] *Ibid.*, at 5.

and Sarkozy on the number of immigrants in France in 2012, and the restrictive immigration agenda of the Dutch coalition government as further evidence of these ongoing tensions, fuelled by something of a resurgence of national governments dominated or influenced by migration-sceptic and/or right-wing (sometimes radical right-wing) parties. Carrera[56] also highlights the tensions that have arisen between nationalism/intergovernmentalism and Europeanization/supranationalism surrounding the reinstatement of internal border controls within the Schengen area and the Commission's Schengen Governance Package. Clearly the Lisbon Treaty has not yet signalled a retreat from the complex interplay between the forces of national interest and a more cooperative supranational Europeanized approach to these matters, and indeed the complexities of understanding the interplay between national or European-level approaches, and more liberal/restrictive immigration policies. Most often these tensions seem to play out between national-level authorities pressing for or wanting to maintain greater restrictions in the face of European-level norms seeking to impose more liberal policies that would challenge these restrictions.

4. Renewed Emphasis on Fundamental Rights?

There are two major issues, brought about by Article 6 of the TEU, and underlined specifically in relation to the AFSJ in Article 67(1).

A. Charter of Fundamental Rights

Since the Lisbon Treaty, the Charter of Fundamental Rights has had the same legal effect as the main Treaties. Its provisions are divided into a number of different areas: dignity, freedoms, equality, solidarity, and citizens' rights. It has the potential to have a significant impact in rights-sensitive areas, of which of course immigration and asylum law is one. The change in legal status in itself is perhaps not very likely to have a fundamental effect on the legislative processes as such, as the Charter has already been used for some time as a benchmark in 'rights-proofing' new EU legislation and policy initiatives through the 'Impact Assessment' process.[57] The effectiveness of this process can certainly be questioned and challenged from a rights perspective,[58] yet it seems unlikely that a change in the formal legal status of the Charter will enhance it very substantially. It is more likely that increasing the visibility of fundamental rights issues within the impact assessment process may have just as much impact, at least in cases where the (lack of) visibility of rights issues alongside others may give rise to a risk of them being overlooked or their

[56] Carrera, *supra* n 27.

[57] Commission Communication, 'Compliance with the Charter of Fundamental Rights in Commission Legislative Proposals', COM (2005) 172.

[58] Toner, 'Impact Assessments and Fundamental Rights Protection in EU law' 31 *European Law Review* (2006) 316.

importance underestimated. This has not been included as such in the redesigned Impact Assessment guidelines published in 2009, although the Commission and the Council have both recently restated the importance of the Charter and their determination to see it applied at all stages of the legislative and policy process.[59]

It seems more likely that key issues concerning the Charter will emerge at a later stage when its meaning and legal effect is interrogated and elaborated by the Court of Justice when cases are referred to it. Some of these questions have already been raised,[60] so the Court has already had an opportunity to begin to address these issues. The *N.S.* case came from the UK, and so also raises directly the question of the status of the Protocol relating to the application of the Charter.[61] The case involves the failure of protection of asylum seekers in Greece, and the responsibilities of other member states when faced both with evidence that Greece is responsible under the provisions of the Dublin Convention (it often is as a first port of entry to the EU) but also with a request to resist return to Greece on the basis of the systemic failures of the system giving rise to a risk both of *refoulement* back to countries of persecution and inhuman and degrading treatment during the asylum process in Greece. The referring court had asked in particular whether EU fundamental rights, interpreted in the light of the Charter, provide a level of protection additional to that under the European Court of Human Rights (ECtHR) in the context of protection provided by Article 3 in 'Dublin' asylum transfer cases. This was potentially a significant issue in the light of cases in the Strasbourg Court (*T.I. v. UK*[62] and *K.R.S. v. UK*[63]) which had both denied responsibility for transfer on the facts. However, in the more recent case *M.S.S. v. Belgium and Greece*, it proved unnecessary to answer this particular question very directly, the responsibility of the member state being established along comparable principles. The Court did not consider that other provisions of the Charter were of particular significance in altering its conclusions. Nonetheless, the other questions dealt with by the ECJ—making clear that the exercise of the *discretion* to hear an asylum case remains an option even though another state was initially responsible, the fact a sending state may be liable for abuses of human rights in a destination state where there is clear evidence of systemic and serious failure, and that any presumption of safeness of another EU member state must be rebuttable both in law and in practice—are all underpinned by the Charter and follow closely the conclusions of the ECtHR in Strasbourg in the *M.S.S.* case brought under the Convention itself. The question of whether the Charter might point towards particular distinctive interpretations of rights that might differ from that coming from Strasbourg in its interpretation of the European Convention on Human Rights (ECHR) has been

[59] Commission Communication, 'Strategy for the effective implementation of the Charter of Fundamental Rights by the European Union', COM (2010) 573, draft Council Conclusions of 11 February 2011, Council Document 6387/11.

[60] *N.S supra* n 51.

[61] Protocol on the Application of the Charter of Fundamental Rights to the UK and Poland.

[62] *T.I. v. UK*, ECHR (2000) Appl. No. 43844/98, 7 March 2000.

[63] *K.R.S. v. UK*, ECHR (2008) Appl. No. 32733/08, 2 December 2008.

raised again, however,[64] and another case[65] raises very directly the meaning of the right to asylum under Article 18 of the Charter.

B. Accession to the ECHR

Accession to the ECHR is also a significant issue taken to a new level by the Treaty of Lisbon. The EU is now given explicit competence to accede to the Convention, and not only that but the wording implies an *obligation* to accede. The nature of this obligation and whether or not and if so how it might ever be legally enforced in the absence of agreement is a more complex question which we will not address here, but suffice it to say that discussions have continued quickly towards a draft agreement for Accession.[66] This means that in time, the EU itself and its legislation and legally effective acts will be challengeable before the Court in Strasbourg, and possibly that the EU could be added as a co-defendant in cases involving EU legislation which make their way to Strasbourg. In itself this may not add significantly to the apparent content of the rights protection offered through the Charter in EU law—after all, there is often discussion of how the Charter might add rights to the ECHR regime or point towards a more generous interpretation of commonly held rights rather than the other way round. The key addition of ECHR accession will be of an additional element of transparency and accountability to an *external* human rights court concerning the standards enshrined in EU legislation itself. It will be interesting to see how this system develops and, for example, whether such external scrutiny will eventually place responsibility quite so squarely on the member states alone in terms of implementation as we see, for example, in *Parliament v Council*,[67] (concerning the Family Reunification Directive and emphasizing the member states' responsibility for compliance in individual decisions) and in *N.S.* (concerning responsibility for the member states' use of discretion to deal with an asylum application despite another state in principle being 'responsible'), or whether it will enhance scrutiny with Fundamental Rights of the compatibility of the supranational EU regime of EU law under which the member states implement individual decisions.

[64] Case C-245/11, *K v. Bundesasylamt*, judgment of 6 November 2012, not yet published.

[65] Case C-528/11, *Halaf*, judgment of 30 May 2013, not yet published.

[66] Lock, 'Walking on a Tightrope: the Draft ECHR Accession Agreement and the Autonomy of the EU Legal Order' 48(4) *Common Market Law Review* (2011) 1025; Lock, 'A Critical Account of the Accession of the European Union to the European Convention on Human Rights' 8 *Justice Journal* (2011) 11; Lock, 'EU Accession to the ECHR: Implications for the Judicial Review in Strasbourg' 35 *European Law Review* (2010) 777; White, 'Accession of the European Union to the European Convention on Human Rights' 8 *Justice Journal* (2011) 58; Jacque, 'The Accession of the European Union to the European Convention on Human Rights and Fundamental Freedoms' 48 *Common Market Law Review* (2011) 995.

[67] Case C-540/03.

C. Pre-legislative scrutiny, the Fundamental Rights Agency, and other fundamental rights issues

It is also worth considering the increasing role of the Fundamental Rights Agency (FRA), and the effectiveness of the pre-legislative scrutiny under the 'impact assessment' programme. Although the changed legal status of the Charter in and of itself may have a relatively modest effect here, there are other changes of more significance. One of the weaknesses of the process is the relative lack of visibility of fundamental rights issues. Although integrated into the process, there is not a separate 'fundamental rights impact' section in the same way as there is for economic, social, and environmental impacts. There is a danger that a culture of trading off rights too easily may emerge, and that some less obvious rights issues may suffer for lack of visibility.[68] These may, however, be in the process of changing: as noted above, the splitting of the Freedom, Security, and Justice portfolio in two has already given rise to some optimism in thinking that there may be a sharper, more focused, and perhaps more effective advocacy for fundamental rights within the Commission. The FRA is also increasingly having opportunities to contribute to the monitoring and development of immigration and asylum law, and it is one of the thematic priorities that the FRA has on its current agenda. Several of its projects involve immigration and asylum issues and these may increasingly have a useful role in influencing the ongoing development of the EU's law and policy.[69]

D. The implementation challenge: falling at the first hurdle? The judgments in *M.S.S. v. Belgium and Greece* and *N.S.*

As noted above, one of the most serious challenges to the actual 'on the ground' implementation of the asylum legislation in terms of human rights has been the operation of the Dublin system, particularly in relation to transfers to member states where there remained serious questions about asylum systems and their compliance with both EU standards laid down in directives, and with fundamental rights. Greece is the member state whose asylum system has caused the most concern, with reasoned opinions and enforcement action by the Commission. Parallel to this, however, individual cases have been lodged in the Strasbourg European Court of Human Rights (ECtHR) and referred to the Luxembourg Court of Justice, which has raised sharply the issue of the obligations of the member states in their implementation of EU law. Two earlier ECtHR cases demonstrated the potential issues for sending states in such cases but in one, *T.I. v. UK*,[70] it was held that there was no real risk of Germany returning the applicant to his country of origin in violation of Article 3 and in the other, *K.R.S. v. UK*,[71] it was held that with no proof to the contrary it must be assumed that Greece would comply with its

[68] Toner, *supra* n 58.

[69] See the projects and publications on the FRA website, <www.fra.europa.eu>, including those on irregular migrants returns, migrants at sea, separated minor asylum seekers, amongst others.

[70] *T.I. v. UK, supra* n 62. [71] *K.R.S. v. UK, supra* n 63.

obligations to returnees. In neither case then was the UK held to be in breach of its ECHR obligations in seeking to return, and returning, the applicants to Germany, and Greece. By 2011, however, concern at conditions in Greece had not abated but rather had continued to mount. In *M.S.S. v. Belgium and Greece*[72] the Strasbourg Court had another opportunity to consider the positions of both sending and receiving countries under the ECHR, and *N.S.*[73] was an opportunity for the Luxembourg Court to consider the position under EU law. In *M.S.S.*, the ECtHR found violations by Greece in the applicants' case in respect of the detention, conditions of destitution the applicant faced, and its failure to provide an adequate asylum procedure. All of these perhaps may be regarded as relatively unsurprising and flowing essentially more from the failure of Greece to implement its obligations effectively than defects in the relevant EU law instruments themselves. More crucially for the purposes of the EU's entire asylum system, and the Dublin Regulation in particular, are two comments made by the Court. The first, very damning both for Greece and the EU itself, is the Court's acceptance of the widespread degrading treatment of asylum seekers and ineffective asylum procedures in Greece, a background of which it takes note and which persuades it (unlike previously in *K.R.S. v. UK*) to lend credence and credibility to the applicant's version of events in the specific case. These are clearly accepted to be not just isolated cases but systemic failures. The second set of comments, directed at Belgium and highly damaging to the 'automatic' transfer system in place under the Dublin Regulation, involve the consideration of Belgium's position. It is held that it (the sending state) is under no fixed and inflexible *obligation* to return under the Dublin Regulation, given the 'enabling' or 'sovereignty' clause in Article 3(2) of the Regulation permitting Belgium to decide to hear the case anyway even if Greece is the responsible member state. This then allows Belgium to be held responsible for its decision to decline to halt the transfer on these grounds (both risk of indirect *refoulement* through Greece, and direct *refoulement* to unacceptable conditions in Greece itself) and to send the applicant back to Greece. This possibility was clear in the previous two cases, but they were both admissibility decisions which went against the applicant on the facts. In the *M.S.S.* case a sending state was made responsible clearly for the first time for its willingness to trust the procedures and reception conditions in another member state, where that trust was manifestly misplaced.[74] This approach was picked up and repeated clearly by the ECJ in the *N.S.* case,[75] and several other cases are pending to clarify when exactly the presumption of adequate compliance by possible destination member states may be rebutted and whether, and to what extent, the 'enabling' clause may more clearly assume the character of an obligation on the part of the state in question, or indeed give rise to some kind of individual

[72] *M.S.S. v. Belgium and Greece, supra* n 51. [73] *N.S., supra* n 51.

[74] Although note the dissenting judgment in relation to Belgium, questioning whether, in the light of the previous judgment in *K.R.S.* and the reticence of the Court in granting interim measures, Belgium should be criticized at the relevant point (in 2009) for not concluding on the evidence then available that there was a risk of violation of the applicant's convention rights in Greece.

[75] *N.S. supra,* n 51.

right of the applicant.[76] This certainly poses serious challenges for the future of the Dublin system, especially in the situation where a member state's asylum system is struggling, for infrastructure and/or resource reasons, to cope with the caseload it has to deal with. It will also pose serious questions about the future of the Dublin Regulation[77] as the proposal to recast it[78] is considered, including a mechanism to suspend transfers to member states and mandatory suspensive appeals against transfers. Steve Peers asks whether this heralds the 'death of mutual trust'[79] and Moreno-Lax[80] refers to the 'dismantling' of the system. While details remain to be clarified further in subsequent cases, it is indeed a salutary reminder that mutual trust, whilst it remains the starting point on this matter, should not blind member states to clear evidence of serious and systemic failures in asylum protection elsewhere in the EU. If they do, they continue returns to such countries at the risk of being held responsible for violations themselves, both under the ECHR and EU law. In summary, although the judgment is a significant victory for human rights protection within the EU asylum system and the Charter has played a significant role in this, it highlights in a more than slightly embarrassing way the inadequacy of the existing EU legislation and enforcement system which allowed this situation to develop and (thus far) seems to have failed to provide a truly effective remedy. The final compromise text addresses the issues arising regarding 'early warning, preparedness, and crisis management' instead of the original temporary suspension mechanism, and provisions to address suspensive effects of appeals and for the determination of responsibility where transfer is impossible due to a real risk of violation of fundamental rights.[81] The European Council on Refugees and Exile (ECRE)[82] acknowledges some improvements in the scheme, but fuller analysis and experience of whether these solutions, together with resources and effective practical implementation, will effectively address the problems at hand will emerge in time. As at the beginning of 2013, the UK will participate in the Recast Dublin Directive,[83] and Eurodac,[84] but not the recast Reception Conditions and Procedures Directives.[85]

[76] See, eg Case C-4/11 *Puid*, (no judgment yet); Case C-245/11, *K v. Bundesasylamt*, judgment of 6 November 2012, not yet published; and Case C-528/11, *Halaf*, judgment of 30 May 2013, not yet published, all of which tackle Dublin transfers in one way or another. When the first draft of this chapter was completed, the ECJ had only given judgment in one of these, *K*, but has clearly stated that under Art. 15(2) a state may indeed in certain circumstances become responsible for hearing the claim.

[77] Council Regulation 343/2003, [2003] OJ L50/1.

[78] COM (2008) 243.

[79] Peers, 'Analysis. Court of Justice: The *NS* and *ME* Opinions: The Death of "Mutual Trust"?' (2011), available at <http://www.statewatch.org/analyses/no-148-dublin-mutual-trust.pdf>.

[80] Moreno-Lax, 'Dismantling the Dublin System' 14 *EJML* (2012) 1.

[81] See Council Document 15605/12, ADD 1 and Arts. 3, 27, and 33 of the text.

[82] ECRE, 'Dublin II Regulation: Lives on Hold' (2013), available on the ECRE site at <http://www.ecre.org/>.

[83] See Council Document, *supra* n 81.

[84] See UK Home Office statement, available at <http://www.homeoffice.gov.uk/publications/about-us/parliamentary-business/written-ministerial-statement/eu-opt-in-eurodac-regulation/>.

[85] See announcement of intention by the UK Home Office, available at <http://www.homeoffice.gov.uk/media-centre/news/EU-asylum>.

5. Continued Fragmentation?

The story of fragmentation begins in the 1980s. Aiming to complete the internal market as an area in which border controls on persons within the EU were abolished, it quickly became clear that this was not going to be an easy task. The awkward partners were the UK, with Ireland following along on its coat-tails in the interests of maintaining the 'Common Travel Area', and Denmark. The UK had, and still has, a basic deep-seated opposition to lifting border controls. The basic leap of faith to give up sovereignty, even with the promise of 'flanking measures' to compensate for the lifting of border controls, was just not possible for the UK. Denmark stayed out of the original intergovernmental cooperation but joined in 1996—but has a particular arrangement in respect of later measures within the Community framework after the Amsterdam Treaty.

Alongside the basic removal of checks on persons at the internal borders, a host of other 'compensatory' measures were agreed to make this possible. These included: a common set of rules applying to people crossing the external borders of the EU member states; harmonization of the conditions of entry and of the rules on visas for short stays; enhanced police cooperation (including rights of cross-border surveillance and hot pursuit); stronger judicial cooperation through a faster extradition system and transfer of enforcement of criminal judgments; and the establishment and development of the Schengen Information System (SIS).

In Maastricht, alongside the cooperation taking place *outside* the framework of EC law, the pillar structure of the EU was being constructed. Again, in the second and third pillars, this focused on *intergovernmental* rather than supranational cooperation. The pillar we are concerned with of course is the 'Third Pillar' entitled 'Justice and Home Affairs'. This fell far short of full communitarization but did tackle visas, immigration, and asylum as well as criminal justice cooperation. No opt-out was negotiated here although unanimity was the rule and directly effective 'hard law' was not the order of the day—so perhaps it is hardly surprising that this was not perhaps thought to be necessary at this stage of the integration process.

Fragmentation really came into its own, however, in Amsterdam. A number of issues—visas, immigration, and asylum—in the previously intergovernmental 'Third Pillar' were transferred to the First Pillar. This had profound implications for the way the EU would deal with these areas. Qualified majority voting and full participation of the European Parliament were still some way off, with transitional arrangements in a number of areas to introduce these over time, an initially weaker than normal role for the Commission, and a limited role for the Court of Justice. So it cannot be said that this was full communitarization. Two things must be separated—Title IV on Immigration and Asylum, which gave new competences to enact new legislation, and the integration of the Schengen *acquis* which was brought in from outside the EU Framework. *Some* of these existing Schengen measures were allocated to the Third Pillar, others to the First, depending on whether they were concerned with immigration or criminal justice. In relation to Title IV, the UK and Ireland negotiated a protocol which enabled them to decide within three months whether to opt in to any proposed legislation. Other member states would then go ahead with negotiations without them if no positive opt-in was forthcoming. Rules were also in place to protect the position of the other member states in the event that the UK or Ireland indicated an intention to opt in but then vetoed it against the will of all the other member states. The Schengen opt-in and opt-out is rather more complicated. Denmark has yet a different set of opt-ins and opt-outs. The main pattern has been that the UK has tended to opt into most of the measures relating to illegal immigration and asylum, but out of most of the measures on legal migration (ie family reunification, long-term residence, highly skilled workers, etc).

A. The Lisbon Treaty and the continuation of fragmentation

The Lisbon Treaty continues the opt-outs but alters them slightly.[86] The first major difference is that, in fact, following the collapsing of the pillar structure, the opt-outs cover not just the area of immigration and asylum but all of the rest of the 'Area of Freedom, Security and Justice'. This means that criminal and civil justice cooperation will also be subject to these potentially 'fragmenting' provisions. Other than this, the UK and Ireland keep the existing opt-out, but with an additional clarification concerning *amending* measures. They are bound by the existing measures already opted in to and would be bound by the new amending measure if they opt in. But if they decide that they do not wish to assume the obligations, as has been the case with several new asylum measures, the position is more complex. A new Article 4a of the Protocol clarifies. The Council may determine that the non-participation makes the new amended legislation 'inoperable' and urge participation. If the UK or Ireland decides not to do so the Council may decide that the existing original and amended measure will cease to apply to the UK or Ireland. The position is not clear, however, if this mechanism is not invoked. This is not just a hypothetical example, as there is significant ongoing discussion in the next stage of the CEAS. The recast Refugee Qualification Directive raises this, as do the Reception Conditions[87] and Asylum Procedures[88] Directives, unlike the proposal to amend the Dublin Regulation, which the UK has indicated its intention to opt in to. There seems to be a difference of opinion depending on whether the amending measure simply amends the existing measure or repeals and replaces it. The UK's view initially seemed to be that if the new amending Proposal operates simply by amending, it would remain bound by the existing legislation, but if it operated by way of *repeal-and-replace* this would mean that the entire original measure would fall and not be applicable to the UK. In other words, it argues that the *repeal* part of the amending measure enacted by the other states would be operational in relation to it, while the *replacement* part would not.

[86] Peers, 'In a World of Their Own: Justice and Home Affairs Opt-outs and the Treaty of Lisbon' 10 *CYELS* (2007–8) 383.

[87] Council Directive 2003/9, [2003] OJ L31/18.

[88] Council Directive 2005/85, [2005] OJ L326/13.

The Commission was not impressed with this distinction and argued against it.[89] As the House of Lords EU Committee points out,[90] two of the recast Directives raise this question, as in contrast with the Dublin Regulation which arguably *does* become problematic to operate if member states are operating different regimes, there is far less obvious reason why a somewhat amended regulation on Reception Conditions (or Procedures) could not operate for most member states alongside the original directive applicable in the UK. Another question to consider raised by Peers is whether there are linkages between different Directives that are so strong that one would become unworkable without the other—it has been suggested that without the Reception Conditions Directive the new Dublin regime (in which the UK has indicated it will participate) might be unworkable. Yet this suggestion seems odd and unconvincing. It is when non-participation of the UK in amended measure A makes *that amended measure* unworkable that the UK can be excluded, whereas the scenario envisaged here is the non-participation in amended measure A (Reception) makes *not that measure itself* unworkable but another one, amended measure B (Dublin). It is not clear in that scenario that, under the terms of the Protocol, the UK can be prevented from exercising its right to participate in the amended measure B (Dublin, there seems to be no way to *prevent* participation as of right), nor its right to remain outside the amended measure A (as this itself *standing alone* is operable, the inoperability affects a different measure). Despite all of these complexities, it appears now to be accepted that the UK remains bound by the first phase of the Asylum *acquis* as the second phase of 'recast' directives are passed, if it does not opt in.[91] No serious issue seems to have arisen yet regarding 'inoperability' due to UK non-participation. The current position is that the UK has decided to opt in to the Eurodac and recast Dublin Regulations but out of the Recast Reception Conditions and Procedures Directives.

6. Monitoring, Reviewing, Updating

The other themes for discussion here, but only very briefly, are the ongoing evaluation and monitoring of the legislation, linked to the second wave of legislative activity, the 'recast' asylum Directives and the possibility foreshadowed in the Stockholm Programme of recasting or consolidating the immigration Directives into an EU Immigration code alongside any revision of the first wave of these Directives.[92] As noted above, only one of the Asylum Recast Directives has so far

[89] See the Commission's views, reported in the House of Lords EU Committee, n 90 below.

[90] House of Lords EU Committee, Report 1 of 2008/2009, 'Asylum Directives: Scrutiny of the Opt in Decisions'.

[91] EU Scrutiny Committee, 41st Report of 2010–12. See also Peers, 'Statewatch Analysis: The Revised Directive on Refugee and Subsidiary Protection Status' (2011), available at <http://www.statewatch.org/analyses/no-141-qaulifications-directive.pdf>.

[92] See Peers, 'An EU Immigration Code: Towards a Common Immigration Policy' 14 *EJML* (2012) 33.

been agreed,[93] and the process of reviewing the Directives on legal migration is at an even earlier stage. This will be an opportunity to take stock of the legislative achievements of the past few years as well as evaluate how the new *acquis* is operating 'on the ground' and being applied by member states.

It is clear that many significant issues remain on the ground. Recognition rates for those seeking refugee status, even of those from the same country of origin, still vary very substantially from state to state.[94] Contentious issues of interpretation have of course not been eliminated and can sometimes lead to wide divergences of practice in critical matters. Some member states remain far from able to meet the standards required. An example combining these last two concerns can be seen in the application of the Dublin Convention in cases of transfer to Greece. The Greek asylum system, including the treatment of Dublin Returnees, has been very heavily criticized and many applicants have resisted transfer to Greece on the basis that this would breach their fundamental rights due to the lack of a fair asylum hearing and wholly inadequate reception conditions. Reports from Greece are indeed troubling,[95] and different member states have taken quite different views on how to respond to these concerns. Some have halted most or all transfers to Greece, others have been slower to do so and their courts have not been willing to accept many challenges to the transfers that have come before them. This has left both a state of considerable uncertainty and serious concerns about the adequacy of the Greek asylum system.

Finally, it is worth noting that although the Lisbon Treaty offers a competence for enacting specific monitoring and evaluation processes, one early attempt to use this competence has run into controversy, inter alia on the grounds of what legal base should be used,[96] especially in the light of the exclusion of the European Parliament from the process under the specific 'monitoring' Article 70.

7. Greater Legal Accountability through ECJ Litigation

The final theme mentioned earlier is that of legal accountability and the growing role of the European Court of Justice (ECJ). This is an important issue because of the changes brought about by the Lisbon Treaty. In earlier years, the jurisdiction

[93] There was an initial consultation on the Family Reunification Directive in 2012, the Green Paper COM(2011) 735, which is likely to be part of a larger process of consolidation and consideration of an EU Immigration Code—see the discussion in Peers, *supra* n 86. This development is not due to get under way properly until 2013 and is still at the roadmap stage. The roadmap is available online at <http://ec.europa.eu/governance/impact/planned_ia/docs/2011_home_007_eu_immigration_code_en.pdf>. There has also been an initial consultation on the rules relating to third country national researchers, students, school pupils, unremunerated trainees, and volunteers: see <http://ec.europa.eu/dgs/home-affairs/what-is-new/public-consultation/2012/consulting_0024_en.htm>.

[94] See the news release from Eurostat 96/2012, 'Asylum Decisions in the EU 27', 19 June 2012, documenting statistics and varying recognition rates, although this is not specifically broken down *both* by country destination and country of origin.

[95] See the extensive list of reports outlined in the ECtHR judgment in the *M.S.S.* case, *supra* n 51, para. 160.

[96] See Carrera, *supra* n 27.

of the ECJ was significantly curtailed, but has been normalized under the Lisbon Treaty, principally by removing the restriction that prevented 'lower' courts (ie those against whose decision there was a legal remedy) from referring cases for preliminary rulings from the ECJ. This was intended to avert the commonly perceived danger of 'overloading' the ECJ with an excessive burden of cases with which it could not easily cope without long delays. Measures taken to control the Court's caseload have undoubtedly succeeded, resulting in a notably slow start. Yet some years after the transposition of the first wave of legislation, and with the removal of the limits on the ECJ's jurisdiction by the Lisbon Treaty in 2009, the pace of work has now begun to speed up and the Court is beginning to make a real contribution to shaping EU Immigration and Asylum law. Cases have arisen across a number of areas, including family reunification,[97] long-term residents,[98] asylum,[99] borders,[100] detention,[101] and procedures.[102] Sensitive issues such as the scope of the exclusion from refugee protection of those guilty of serious crimes,[103] the interaction of asylum procedures and transfer pursuant to arrest warrants,[104] the status of the Charter of Fundamental Rights,[105] and effective remedies within the framework of the heavily criticized Asylum Procedures Directive[106] have all been raised. Cases raising serious allegations of defaults in fundamental rights protection within member states have arisen, particularly in the context of Dublin transfers[107] as have cases in which member states have engaged in what seems on one view to be blatant denial of rights clearly conferred under the Directive or, at the least, quite inadequate transposition.[108]

A brief summary rather than a detailed analysis of these cases will suffice. While it is still early days, we can be optimistic about the Court's contribution, but modestly so.[109] The *N.S.* case has been critical in exposing the flaws both in Greece's implementation of the asylum *acquis* and in the rigid persistence in maintaining 'mutual trust' in assuming compliance with EU law and safety of asylum seekers in Greece in the face of clear evidence that this trust was not well-founded. There

[97] Case C-540/03, *European Parliament v. Council*, [2006] ECR I-5769; Case C-578/08, *Chakroun*, [2010] ECR I-1839.

[98] Case C-502/10, *Singh*, judgment of 18 October 2012, not yet published; Case C-508/10, *Commission v. Netherlands*, judgment of 26 April 2012, not yet published; Case C-571/10, *Kamberaj*, judgment of 24 April 2012, not yet published.

[99] Case C-465/07, *Elgafaji*, [2009] ECR I-921; Case C-31/09, *Bolbol*, [2010] ECR I-5539; Case C-175/08, *Abdulla*, [2010] ECR I-1493; Joined Cases C-57/09 and C-101/09, *B and D*, judgment of 9 November 2010, not yet published; *N.S. supra*, n 51.

[100] Joined Cases C-188/10 and C-189/10, *Melki and Abdeli*, [2010] ECR I-5667; Case C-261/08, *Zurita García*, [2009] ECR I-10143.

[101] Case C-357/09 PPU, *Kadzoev*, [2009] ECR I-11189.

[102] Case C-19/08, *Petrosian*, [2009] ECR I-495.

[103] *B and D, supra* n 99.

[104] Case C-105/10 PPU, *Gataev*.

[105] *N.S. supra* n 51.

[106] Case C-69/10, *Diouf*, [2011] ECR I-7151.

[107] *Gataev*, *supra* n104 and *N.S.*, *supra* n 51.

[108] *Kadzoev*, *supra* n 101.

[109] For further discussion of the emerging role of the ECJ, see Acosta Arcarazo and Geddes, 'The Development, Application and Implications of an EU Rule of Law in the Area of Migration Policy' 51 *Journal of Common Market Studies* (2013) 179. See also the discussion of the possible role of the ECJ in Carrera, De Somer, and Petkova, 'The Court of Justice of the European Union as a Fundamental Rights Tribunal Challenges for the Effective Delivery of Fundamental Rights in the Area of Freedom, Security and Justice' (2010), available at <http://www.ceps.eu/>.

is still scope, for example, for increased engagement with international law and cases, and with literature. While some more blatantly objectionable behaviour of member states has been condemned, and a hearteningly rights-based approach can be seen in several cases, other potentially problematic issues have not been challenged effectively,[110] and this has even been noted in the recent draft recasting of the legislation, with no plans to amend this particular point and the European Parliament's suggestion rejected. It remains to be seen how far the Court will be willing to go to develop a strong proactive role to 'correct' or make up for deficiencies in legislation.

8. Conclusion

What conclusions the can be drawn from this? Legal and political accountability have certainly increased and the framework put in place under the Treaty of Lisbon is indeed more democratic, streamlined, and potentially more effective in vindicating fundamental rights and the rule of law. This is indeed a welcome positive step in the next stage of the EU's journey towards a common immigration and asylum policy as part of its AFSJ; as the second stage of the Common European Asylum system is put in place and policies and legislation are implemented, monitored, and reviewed; and as the Court of Justice becomes a significantly more important presence in shaping the law and its implementation. Yet there are also some more troubling signs that the struggle between the impulses of nationalism and Europeanization has not dissipated; that there are limits to what the Court of Justice can do to deal with deficiencies in the first wave of legislation; and that there remains much to play for in the next stage of development of the EU's immigration and asylum *acquis*. Alongside this, Peers notes that many of the issues remaining are now less directly linked to the 'distinctiveness' of the matters dealt with in the AFSJ—immigration and asylum being key issues here—and are now far more clearly manifestations of *general* issues of transparency, legitimacy, and democracy within the EU law-making processes, or the structure of fundamental rights protection and vindication of the rule of law through legal accountability in the Court of Justice. Thus, as the Lisbon Treaty has largely completed the process of 'normalization' of the AFSJ, attention inevitably shifts to a more general, less 'immigration-specific', and more wide-ranging critique of the EU legal order.

[110] The concept written into the Qualification Directive that international agencies and multinational forces could provide effective protection against feared persecution to make the country of origin sufficiently safe for the individual claiming protection to be refused or required to return by cessation of protection.

3

The Politics of Irregular Migration

Christina Boswell

The bulk of chapters in this book are devoted to legal analyses of immigration. So what can political science and political theory contribute to such discussions, and in what sense is a political perspective different from that of law? To put it in the simplest terms, the legal system considers social phenomena in terms of their relevance to law: is this action or behaviour legal or illegal, and how can one justify such an assessment? Legal analysis can also address second order questions about whether the norms that categorize certain behaviours as 'legal' and 'illegal' are themselves appropriate or correct. As a result, one might expect the issue of illegal migration to be most appropriately addressed by a legal specialist, who is best qualified to define the circumstances under which a person may be deemed to be an illegal immigrant, and whether such norms are appropriate.

The political system is also preoccupied with questions about how to steer social action, including through laws about what sorts of behaviour are permitted and which discouraged or forbidden (other common means are through market mechanisms, information, or prompts). But what makes the question of illegal migration so interesting for a political scientist is that it goes to the heart of the role and functions of modern nation states. Decisions about whether to treat immigrants as legal or illegal are essentially decisions about who is to be treated as an authorized resident, and thus subject to the various rights and responsibilities attached to residency or citizenship in that territory. The criteria for deciding who is illegal and who legal will therefore hinge on what the state expects and desires from its population. Which sorts of people, with which sorts of backgrounds or characteristics, are desirable residents for the state? What are the consequences of authorizing or forbidding the entry and stay of those the state does not want as residents? And what sorts of mechanisms does the state employ to tackle illegal immigration?

There is a further aspect of illegal migration that raises even more intriguing questions for political science. This is the idea that, far from being an anomaly or marginal problem to be addressed through control measures, illegal migration is in fact a structural feature of the liberal welfare state. In other words, it is not simply an undesirable side effect of the state's attempts to control who enters and resides in its territory. Rather, there are a range of pressures and interests that imply that illegal migration is a desirable, perhaps even necessary, element of contemporary politics and political economy.

In this chapter, I would like to unpack some of these questions, through examining two central themes. First, I will consider three different ways of theorizing illegal migration as an unavoidable structural feature of contemporary liberal welfare states. These three perspectives can be labelled the liberal constraint, political economy, and social systems accounts. Secondly, I build on these accounts to explore the more practical question of how states and the EU go about attempting to prevent or control irregular migration. If illegal immigration is indeed a structural feature of liberal states, what are the prospects for managing it?

The first section outlines the three theories accounting for why illegal migration is a structural problem for welfare states. The second section applies these theories to help understand national European responses to illegal migration over the past two decades. In the third section, I analyse cooperation to combat illegal migration at the European Union (EU) level. I explore how far these three theories can help shed light on the pace and direction of EU cooperation, and explore the plausibility of the three theories through an analysis of the key areas of EU policy. The chapter concludes with an overview of the merits of each of the three theories as an explanation of both national and EU policy on illegal immigration.

1. Illegal Immigration as a Structural Feature of Liberal Welfare States

Irregular or illegal migration can be defined as the crossing of borders without proper authority, or the violation of conditions for entering another country.[1] Article 36 of the EU Return Directive, agreed in June 2008, defines illegal stay as the presence, on the territory of a member state, of a third country national who does not fulfil or no longer fulfils the conditions of entry as set out in Article 5 of the Schengen Borders Code or other conditions of entry, stay, or residence in that member state.[2] Estimates of the scale of illegal immigration are notoriously difficult to provide. A European Commission report back in 2003 estimated that around 500,000 illegal migrants entered the EU each year. It suggested that there were around 300,000 illegal residents in Germany, 200,000 in the UK, and up to 800,000 in Italy.[3] Of these, it has been estimated that around 70 per cent are illegally employed.[4]

Since scholars first began writing about illegal migration in Europe in around the 1980s, it has been commonplace to stress that the problem is a function of restrictive immigration policies. The typical account is that prior to the 1970s,

[1] B. Jordan and F. Düvell, *Irregular Migration: The Dilemmas of Transnational Mobility* (2002), at 15.

[2] Directive 2008/115 of the EP and the Council, [2008] OJ L348/98.

[3] Communication from the Commission to the European Parliament and the Council in View of the European Council of Thessaloniki, on the Developments of a Common Policy on Illegal Immigration, Smuggling and Trafficking of Human Beings, External Borders and the Return of Illegal Residents (2003).

[4] Djajić, 'Illegal Immigration Trends, Policies and Economic Effects', in S. Djajić (ed.), *International Migration: Trends, Policies and Economic Impact* (2001) 137.

and especially in the 1960s, many West European countries offered quite liberal conditions allowing the entry of labour migrants and asylum seekers. Germany, France, the Netherlands, Belgium, Switzerland, and Austria all introduced guest-worker programmes through which they recruited hundreds of thousands of labour migrants. The UK, meanwhile, accepted immigrants from former colonies. With increasingly restrictive measures on labour migration from 1972–3, and the subsequent tightening of provisions on family reunification and asylum seeking in the 1980s and 1990s,[5] the legal options for entering European countries were substantially reduced. As a result, so the account runs, many would-be migrants began to either travel into European countries clandestinely or without valid documents, or they entered as tourists, temporary workers, or asylum seekers and then overstayed their authorized period of stay.

The problem of illegal migration from the 1970s onwards was further compounded by 'push' factors in a number of developing countries, with civil conflict and organized violence driving refugees to seek protection in Europe. The expansion of cheap travel routes and communication and the availability of information about opportunities in Western countries facilitated travel, thus making it a viable option for more people to travel to destinations outside of their regions of origin. By the early to mid-1980s, illegal immigration had become an acknowledged problem in France, Belgium, Italy, and Spain. By the end of the 1980s, it was affecting most West European countries. The problem was exacerbated in the early 1990s because of increased possibilities for free movement from the former Soviet Bloc following the fall of the Iron Curtain. Instability in the Western Balkans, notably the conflict and the difficult transition to peace in the former Yugoslavia, also created more pressures and opportunities for irregular migratory flows. This period also saw the emergence of increasingly nefarious practices of smuggling and trafficking.

This classic account of the rise of illegal migration to Europe also suggests that European states are to a large degree responsible for more sinister developments, namely the rise in migrant smuggling and trafficking. Attempts by European states and the EU to combat illegal migration through imposing visa conditions, tighter border controls, carrier sanctions, or maritime patrols since the 1990s, have simply driven the problem further underground. The more sophisticated the controls, the more organized—and potentially hazardous—the smuggling routes for entering Europe. As a UNHCR report of 2000 argued, migration control had effectively spawned a huge industry in migrant smuggling and trafficking.[6]

The notion that illegal migration is a by-product of state and EU policies is, therefore, quite widely accepted. But a number of political scientists and sociologists have gone a step further in tying illegal migration to state actions. They have identified a number of pressures and interests in European countries that perpetuate

[5] S. Castles and M. Miller, *The Age of Migration: International Population Movements in the Modern World* (1998); Joppke, 'Immigration Challenges to the Nation-State' in C. Joppke (ed.), *Challenge to the Nation-State: Immigration in Western Europe and the United States* (1998) 5.

[6] J. Morrison and B. Crosland, *The Trafficking and Smuggling of Refugees: The End Game in European Asylum Policy?* (2000).

flows of illegal immigration; and, further, they have suggested that these pressures and interests are a structural feature of liberal welfare states. So states contribute to the problem not just through attempts to control their borders and limit the entry of unauthorized residents, but also because key features of their political systems and/or economies encourage the persistence of the problem. Indeed, there are three rather different, but overlapping, accounts of how states might help create this problem. Although these accounts share a number of ideas about the relationship between states and illegal migration, each of the three is premised on a rather different theory of the state, so it is worth considering each in turn.

A. The politics of restriction and the liberal constraint

Perhaps the most influential perspective on the politics of illegal migration is what can be labelled the structuralist account of the state.[7] Such accounts often draw on historical sociology, tracing the role of the state in regulating migration back to the historical emergence and consolidation of the modern nation-state system. Modern states are defined—indeed they receive their identity—through governing a fixed and bordered state territory. Unlike other organizations such as universities, or businesses, their whole identity as states is contingent on the fixed nature of territory, and also the fixed nature of the population inhabiting that territory.[8] Their decisions are legally binding on that particular population, and that population alone.

Now why would this population agree to be subject to binding rules? Those trying to govern face the persistent problem of political obligation, or how to guarantee the loyalty of their citizens. How does the state secure its own legitimacy, and thus the obedience of its population? To put it very simply, nation-states have received support and loyalty from their populations through making a deal, or social contract: citizens receive a range of goods in exchange for their loyalty. Thus the state promises to provide security, voting rights, and (in the case of modern welfare states) universal education, employment rights, welfare support, and so on. In return, citizens agree to comply with laws, pay taxes, and be conscripted to fight wars. Of course, the idea of a contract is more metaphorical than literal: governments never actually sat down to bash out a contract with their citizens. However, European history offers numerous examples of social movements mobilizing to secure greater rights or benefits from the state, with governments often reluctantly acquiescing in order to quell violence or mobilize support.[9] So to put it crudely, loyalty was bought through offering a range of rights and benefits to citizens.

[7] For classic structuralist accounts in political science, see Skocpol, 'Bringing the State Back In: Strategies of Analysis in Current Research', in P. B. Evans, D. Rueschemeyer, and T. Skocpol (eds), *Bringing the State Back In* (1985) 3; E. A. Nordlinger, *On the Autonomy of the Democratic State* (1981). For a discussion and overview of different perspectives, see J. Bartelson, *The Critique of the State* (2001).

[8] Halfmann, 'Welfare State and Territory', in M. Bommes and A. Geddes (eds), *Immigration and the Welfare State: Challenging the Borders of the Welfare State* (2000) 34.

[9] C. Tilly, *The Formation of National States in Western Europe* (1975); A. Giddens, *The Nation-State and Violence* (1985).

The implication of this contract was that members benefited from a superior set of entitlements in relation to non-members. And this privileged status was contingent on the fixity of the population. Access to security, voting rights, welfare, and social services were dependent on being resident in the territory. Moreover, many of these goods were finite, implying that the population had an interest in their being limited to a given number of people. So what happens to this contract once the fixity of the population is challenged? More specifically, how does the state respond when people enter from other states, and attempt to avail themselves of these privileges (whether as asylum seekers, labour migrants, or irregular migrants)?

Not surprisingly, one would expect public consternation that the privileges of members are now being extended to outsiders. Citizens are likely to—and indeed often do—complain about the resulting burden on the welfare state, social services, and jobs. They may also be concerned that newcomers do not sufficiently understand or respect the norms and values underpinning civic and political life. The challenge is even greater in the case of illegal immigrants. Because their entry and/or stay is irregular, illegal migrants do not enter any sort of contractual arrangement with the authorities, so their obedience is not assured. Indeed, they attempt to remain invisible to the state, avoiding taxes and evading the law.[10]

Governments (and most political parties) have tended to respond to public concerns by attempting to limit immigration, and especially illegal migration. However, as many scholars have pointed out, they have limited success in restricting migration.[11] Indeed, states face a number of constraints in their attempts to control. While public opinion may, by and large, support restriction, other forces militate against restrictive measures. One of these constraints derives from international legal commitments.[12] Most liberal democratic states are signatories to a number of international treaties and conventions, including the 1951 Geneva Convention on refugees, and international human rights instruments. EU states are also signed up to the European Convention on Human Rights, as well as a number of EU instruments on asylum seekers and refugees, as well as provisions on the free movement of EU citizens. These commitments are not just legal, but arguably also impose a strong normative pressure to comply with widely accepted human rights norms. States risk losing international credibility if they are not seen to be acting in accordance with such provisions. It is, therefore, useful to distinguish between formal legal norms, and more informal normative pressures deriving from concerns about losing legitimacy in the eyes of sections of public opinion or other EU states. Both kinds of pressure can limit the margin of manoeuvre of states when it comes to measures to combat illegal migration.

[10] Boswell, 'The Elusive Rights of an Invisible Population' 22 *Ethics and International Affairs* (2008) 187.

[11] Cornelius, Martin, and Hollifield, 'Introduction: The Ambivalent Quest for Immigration Control', in W. A. Cornelius, P. L. Martin, and J. F. Hollifield (eds), *Controlling Immigration: A Global Perspective* (1992) 3; Castles, 'The Factors that Make and Unmake Migration Policies' 38 *International Migration Review* (2004) 852; Joppke, *supra* n 5.

[12] R. Bauböck, *Transnational Citizenship. Membership and Rights in International Migration* (1994); Y. N. Soysal, *Limits of Citizenship: Migrants and Postnational Membership in Europe* (1994).

A good example of an EU member state which faced this kind of normative constraint is Italy, whose government found itself under acute pressure from the EU when it introduced stringent measures against its Roma population in 2007. The government declared a 'Roma emergency', shutting down unauthorized Roma camps and deploying 3,000 soldiers around stations and tourist spots in Rome to crack down on Roma crime.[13] The government also introduced controversial measures involving photographing and fingerprinting all Roma over 14 years of age.[14] The measures were strongly criticized by the European Parliament, which adopted a resolution in 2008 condemning the government for measures that violated numerous human rights and anti-discrimination provisions, as well as provisions on free movement in the EU. The European Commission also approached the Italian government to criticize the provisions, and received a report from the Italian government at the beginning of August reassuring them that the exercise would be carried out in conformity with relevant laws.[15] This case show how informal international norms invoked to criticize governments on human rights or humanitarian grounds can constrain efforts at domestic migration control.

The second constraint derives from domestic constitutional and judicial considerations.[16] Most European states have incorporated international refugee law and human rights considerations into their constitutions, or at least into their legislation on the treatment of refugees and those resident on their territory. Such provisions are often interpreted and applied in an expansionist way by court rulings. For example, a famous series of constitutional court rulings in Germany extended a range of constitutional rights to guest workers who had been resident a long period, notably protection against deportation and entitlement to family reunion.[17] Similarly, domestic constitutional constraints often mean that governments cannot be as stringent controlling irregular migration as they might otherwise like. For example, an attempt by the French government to tighten rules on deportation in the early 1990s was overturned by a 1993 ruling of the *Conseil Constitutional*, which ruled that a one-year ban on the re-entry of those deported from France was not constitutional.[18]

Thirdly, capitalist states have a number of economic interests which further militate against restricting migration. They have an interest in keeping borders open for business, tourism, and students, all of which are an important source of revenue. And, more importantly, they may consider that they can best secure economic growth through allowing the admission and employment of (certain

[13] Meo, 'Italians Welcome Army on Streets as Anti-gipsy Sentiment Sweeps Country', *The Telegraph*, 9 August 2008, available at <http://www.telegraph.co.uk/news/worldnews/europe/italy/2529024/Italians-welcome-army-on-streets-as-anti-gipsy-sentiment-sweeps-country.html>.

[14] Pisa, 'Italy Declares State of Emergency over Roma Immigrants', *Daily Telegraph*, 25 July 2008.

[15] Barrot, 'Intervention du M Barrot, Vice-président de la Commission Européenne, au Sommet Européen sur le Peuple Rom', SPEECH/08/435 (2008).

[16] Joppke, *supra* n 5. [17] *Ibid.*, at 284–5.

[18] Hollifield, 'Ideas, Institutions, and Civil Society: On the Limits of Immigration Control in France', in G. Brochmann and T. Hammar (eds), *Mechanisms of Immigration Control: A Comparative Analysis of European Regulation Policies* (1999) 59, at 78.

categories of) foreign labour. Thus states recognize the business case for a more liberal immigration policy, even if such a policy is not popular with the bulk of the electorate.[19]

Taken together, these three explanations of how liberal democratic institutions can constrain more restrictive approaches have been termed the 'liberal constraint'.[20] The core idea is that—despite popular demands for restiction—liberal democracies simply cannot be as restrictive as they might like. They are constrained by a range of international and domestic norms, as well as business interests.

What are the implications of the liberal constraint account for illegal immigration? States tend to be pulled in two different directions on immigration policy. They need to strike a difficult balance between, on the one hand, meeting domestic and international normative requirements and business interests, while at the same time mollifying public concerns about immigration. In many cases, the implication is some form of dualism in immigration policy: a split between what governments promise in their rhetoric and formal decisions, and what really happens on the ground.[21] Thus, for example, governments frequently make quite bold rhetorical claims about what they are doing to reduce immigration. But in practice, they keep open a number of routes to ensure that certain sectors are guaranteed a supply of foreign labour. Alternatively, they may introduce quite draconian legislation that ostensibly cracks down on illegal immigration and illegal employment. But in practice, such provisions are only patchily implemented, and large numbers of irregular migrants are able to live and work on their territory.

This form of toleration of irregular migration is quite widespread in many European countries, notably those with relatively informal employment markets, such as Italy.[22] In this case, the Berlusconi government has adopted a highly restrictionist rhetoric, whilst tolerating substantial numbers of irregular migration and employment, and even encouraging these through periodic regularizations. Italy is an extreme case, but there are elements of this approach in many other countries, including in north Europe. Many governments, for example, have been relatively lax in enforcing legislation to prosecute employers who hire migrants on an illegal basis.[23]

In sum, the structuralist account suggests that illegal immigration is not simply an unfortunate by-product of restrictive migration policies. Rather, it is a structural feature of liberal democratic states. The toleration of substantial levels of illegal migration is part of a strategy pursued by governments to reconcile conflicting pressures: the need to demonstrate a commitment to restricting migration, whilst

[19] J. F. Hollifield, *Immigrants, Markets and States: The Political Economy of Postwar Europe* (1992).

[20] *Ibid.*, 94.

[21] Boswell, 'Theorizing Migration Policy: Is There a Third Way?' 41 *International Migration Review* (2007) 75.

[22] Baldwin-Edwards and Arango, 'Where Free Markets Reign: Immigrants in the Twilight Zone', in M. Baldwin-Edwards and J. Arango (eds), *Immigrants and the Informal Economy in Southern Europe* (1999) 1, at 2; Sciortino, 'Between Phantoms and Necessary Evils: Some Critical Points in the Study of Irregular Migrations to Western Europe' 24 *IMIS-Beiträge* (2004) 17.

[23] P. Martin and M. J. Miller, *Employer Sanctions: French, German and US Experiences* (2000).

at the same time conforming to judicial and economic considerations militating against restrictive approaches. So governments maintain a gap between restrictive rhetoric and lenient practice, implying that immigration policies are often, to a large extent, symbolic.[24]

B. Political economy and the pluralist state

A second account of illegal migration focuses on some of the economic interests outlined above. It emphasizes how the state is keen to respond to the business lobby in developing its immigration policy. However, this political economy account has a rather different theory of the state, and—flowing from this—a different way of conceiving the relationship between restrictive and liberal forces influencing policies on irregular migration. As in the discussion of the liberal constraint, it is worth starting by setting out this school's theory of the state.

The most influential application of the political economy approach to immigration policy has been developed by Gary P. Freeman.[25] On his account, migration policy is essentially determined by the content and relative power of organized interests. The state is conceptualized as a broker, which is preoccupied with mollifying a range of different organized interests. It is continually lobbied by interest groups such as employers associations, trade unions, NGOs, and professional groups, all of which are keen to impose their preferences. The state juggles these different interests, and finds a course of policy that appeases the most powerful groups. In fact, the more strongly a group's interests are affected, the more resources it is likely to invest in lobbying, and thus the more influence it will have on the government. And interest groups are likely to perceive their interests to be most affected where the costs and benefits of pursuing a particular policy are very concentrated and tangible. By contrast, where the costs or benefits of a particular policy are diffuse and vague, groups will have less interest in devoting resources to lobbying the government.[26]

What are the implications of the political economy account for immigration? Freeman argued that in industrial countries, the availability of cheap foreign labour brought concentrated benefits to both employers and immigrant groups. Employers clearly had an interest in securing an abundant supply of low-cost labour, and thus lobbied the government hard to ensure policies did not overly restrict this flow. Meanwhile, immigrant groups had a strong interest in lobbying to defend the rights and welfare of their extended family and kin, placing pressure on policy-makers to ensure liberal terms of entry, stay, and employment. By contrast, any costs associated with immigration tend to be far more diffuse and

[24] Cornelius, Martin, and Hollifield, *supra* n 11.

[25] Freeman, 'Modes of Immigration Politics in Liberal Democratic States' 24 *International Migration Review* (1995) 881.

[26] Freeman, 'National Models, Policy Types, and the Politics of Immigration in Liberal Democracies' 29 *West European Politics* (2006) 227; Freeman and Hill, 'Disaggregating Immigration Policy: The Politics of Skilled Labor Recruitment in the US' 19 *Knowledge, Technology and Policy* (2006) 7.

difficult to quantify. Even if certain employment sectors are adversely affected by immigrant labour, any effect on their salaries or prospects for employment are difficult to measure. Moreover, such workers often will not have the resources to mobilize and lobby the government—for example those working in sectors such as tourism and catering or domestic work are not typically unionized. Similarly, those living in neighbourhoods that might be affected by large-scale immigration do not tend to be the most organized or well resourced when it comes to mobilization and lobbying.

The result, according to Freeman, is that employers and immigrant groups will have incentives to lobby more intensively to promote a liberal immigration policy, while those negatively affected by the policy will have fewer incentives to lobby against such an approach. The outcome will be a liberal policy. Indeed, Freeman argued that this theory was confirmed in the US case, where there was a history of liberal policies despite the apparently negative impact of immigration on low-skilled workers.

This account, therefore, has a somewhat different theory of the state. Rather than acting as a gatekeeper, trying to restrict immigration to mollify public opinion, the state acts as a broker between organized interests. It is keen to maximize support through introducing the policies that best satisfy powerful lobby groups. So rather than being constrained by business interests and seeing the relationship between politics and the economy as one of conflict, on the political economy account the state is simply acting as a broker to business interests. Given the emphasis on business interests in this account, it is worth unpacking why liberal immigration policies might be so appealing in certain sectors. And in particular, given the focus of this article, we should explore why businesses would be keen to ensure that the state did not interfere with their ability to employ illegal immigrants.

Certain industries in highly developed economies—such as agriculture, construction, hotel and catering, tourism, or cleaning—tend to face shortages of indigenous workers willing to do low-satus, low-paid, or seasonal work. Since at least the 1960s—and in many cases much earlier than that—they have been dependent on foreign workers to meet demand for labour. Yet with the restriction of legal possibilities for low-skilled immigration in many industrialized countries from the 1970s onwards, in many countries employers in these sectors have resorted to hiring illegal immigrants. It should be stressed that the employment of illegal labour is not always an existential necessity for businesses. In many cases it simply reflects the advantage for employers of minimizing costs through employing workers on an irregular basis. By employing workers illegally, firms may avoid paying social contributions, paying minimum wages, or conforming to health and safety regulations. Irregular migrants may also be willing to work more flexible hours or with substandard working conditions.

Some economists see this trend as a product of increased global competition, which forces many small and medium-sized firms to draw on a supply of cheap, flexible labour in order to stay competitive. On this account, the persistence of an interest in illegal labour reflects structural features of the global capitalist economy. Others locate the problem in the rigidity of European labour markets: in some countries, the costs of employing workers are more than double what they actually receive in wages. On this argument, more efficient labour markets would eliminate the need to employ people outside of regular employment.[27] Thus the scale of illegal immigration is a result of structural features of domestic economies, which could in principle be reformed to reduce the incentives to employ irregular labour. Whatever the causes, employing migrants on an illegal basis is—from an economic perspective—a rational strategy for many businesses. If we take this account as correct, then it would suggest that states are under pressure from business not only to sustain liberal labour migration policies, but also to tolerate significant levels of illegal immigration. And, moreover, this interest in illegal labour stems from structural features of these economies, rather than being a side effect of restrictionist policies.

C. Illegal immigration and functionally differentiated systems

The third account I would like to explore draws on Niklas Luhmann's systems theory. It has been most systematically applied to analyse immigration policy by Michael Bommes.[28] This account focuses on the causes and persistence of illegal migration, locating these in structural features of liberal welfare states. Emigrants tend to migrate to another country in order to improve their life chances, principally through employment, but also through access to services such as education, housing, health, and welfare.[29] And they are willing and able to reside illegally in other countries because these social and economic systems tend to be quite accessible to migrants. Despite attempts by the state to restrict immigration, most social systems—such as health, education, housing, and labour markets—are not interested in excluding people from participation based on factors such as ethnicity, citizenship, or country of origin. Instead, they tend to operate on an inclusive basis, accepting as participants those who are considered relevant to their particular function. Thus the labour market operates according to a logic that selects workers based on their skills and price. The health system includes people based on whether they are in need of medical treatment. Education selects participants based on their life stage (primary, secondary school age) or their need of qualifications, while welfare institutions tend to include participants based on their welfare needs. Such systems will only reluctantly impose restrictions based on nationality, ethnicity, or legal status.[30] The ease with which immigrants can and do participate in these

[27] Jahn and Straubhaar, 'A Survey on the Economics of Illegal Immigration' 3 *South European Society and Politics* (1998) 16.

[28] Bommes, 'National Welfare State, Biography and Migration: Labour Migrants, Ethnic Germans and the Re-Ascription of Welfare State Membership', in A. Geddes and M. Bommes (eds), *Immigration and Welfare: Challenging the Borders of the Welfare State* (2000) 90; Bommes, 'Transnationalism or Assimilation?' 4 *Journal of Social Science Education* (2005) 14; Bommes, 'Illegale Migration in der Modernen Gesellschaft—Resultat und Problem der Migrationspolitik Europäischer Nationalstaaten' (2008), unpublished paper; C. Boswell and G. D'Amato (eds), *Immigration and Social Systems: Collected Essays of Michael Bommes* (2012).

[29] This section draws on Bommes, 'Illegale Migration', *supra* n 28.

[30] Consider, eg, how public health services and schools tend to resist government attempts to deny access to services by rejected asylum seekers or irregular migrants.

systems helps explain why illegal migration continues to remain high, despite attempts to restrict it.

Clearly, this account again adopts a rather different theory of the state to those employed in the previous two sections. The liberal constraint account assumed that the government was in some sense at the apex of the various institutions comprising the welfare state. The government and the various ministries and departments responsible for public policy were the main locus for decision-making not just on rights of entry, residence, and employment, but also access to the labour market, welfare, and a range of social services. By contrast, the social systems account theorizes states as composed of functionally differentiated systems. On this account, society is divided into increasingly complex, autonomous, and functionally differentiated spheres, such as the economy, legal system, welfare system, education, health, and so on. In order to deal with complexity, each social system develops its own codes for making sense of itself and its environment. These codes are based on communicative selections specific to the system, so that each system becomes self-referential, operating according to its own logic or system of communication.[31]

On this account, it does not make sense to think of a hierarchy of authority, with the government or state at the apex, and various parts of the economy or welfare system guided by its decisions. Indeed, those politicians leading the government are simply part of a different system—the political system—which has its own internal system of communication and is preoccupied with its own internal tasks.

Systems are not closed, however, but are more or less preoccupied with reading signals from their environments. Indeed, many systems are engaged in reading signals from the political system or the legal system concerning government regulation. In the area of illegal migration, the economic or education systems may be aware of government attempts to limit the participation of illegal migrants in that particular system. And, insofar as they are dependent on the political or legal systems for resources, or to avoid sanctions, they may be keen to ensure their system complies with the requirements imposed from these regulatory systems. However, there is no guarantee that such attempts at regulation will be fully understood, let alone incorporated into the relevant social system. Thus it does not make sense to think of the political leaders of government—the Prime Minister, President, the Cabinet, or the legislative—as in some way the apex of authority in the state. Rather, there is a range of largely autonomous social systems, each of which operates according to its own logic, and which may, or may not, successfully incorporate the regulatory demands of the political system. This creates huge impediments to attempting to control irregular migration through 'steering' different systems through, for example, imposing employer sanctions or limiting access to health systems.[32]

Systems theory provides a good perspective for trying to make sense of the causes and persistence of illegal immigration. In particular, it suggests that illegal

[31] Luhmann, 'Limits of Steering' 14 *Theory, Culture and Society* (1997) 41.

[32] Boswell, *supra* n 10.

Table 3.1 Theories of the state and the regulation of illegal immigration

Theory of the state	Cause of illegal immigration	Impediment to regulation
Stucturalist	Liberal constraint	Judiciary, international norms, economic interests
Pluralist	Business lobby	Economic interests
Systems	Inclusionary logic of social systems	Inability to steer social systems

immigration can be considered as a quite normal and predictable part of modern welfare states, for two reasons. The first is that migrants (like any residents) are generally concerned to improve their life chances through integrating into systems relevant to their well-being. The second is that in modern, functionally differentiated societies, the systems relevant to this project tend to be inclusive, making it possible for them to participate despite their illegal states. This explains why illegal migration is likely to be a structural feature of modern welfare states.

We have now looked at three different theories, each explaining immigration as a structural problem for modern liberal democratic states. Each one is based on a rather different theory of the state. And, as a corollary, each has a rather different account of the challenges faced by governments in trying to regulate states. Table 3.1 summarizes the three accounts, and their views of the causes of illegal immigration, and the main impediments to regulating it.

2. European Responses to Illegal Immigration

Thus far we have considered three different theories of the state's role vis-à-vis illegal immigration. Each has a different account of why states are unwilling or unable to eliminate the problem. In this second section of this chapter, we will analyse what European countries and the European Union have done to attempt to combat the problem, and consider how far these attempts have been successful. We shall then return to the three theories, and consider how they can shed light on these approaches, and the various impediments to combating the problem. We start by considering domestic European responses, followed by a brief overview of EU responses. In the third section, we return to the theoretical discussion.

A. Domestic European responses to illegal migration: Italy and Germany

As we saw earlier, the phenomenon of illegal immigration was being increasingly recognized as a problem in most West European countries from at least the late 1980s onwards. However, there were considerable variations in how the problem was experienced and constructed between different countries. These differences were in part

Table 3.2 Detections of illegal entry in key EU states 2007

	Total	Land	Air	Sea
France	5,748	690	4,199	909
Greece	73,194	62,475	1,377	9,342
Italy	21,650	Not available	1,195	20,455
Spain	27,910	4,080	12,709	11,751
Total EU	163,903	82,371	20,748	48,696

Adapted from FRONTEX, General Report (2007) 15

due to the very different geographical situation of European countries. For example, some—such as Greece, Spain, or Italy—had extensive and very porous sea borders. Others, such as Germany and Austria, shared extensive land borders with Central European countries, which appeared to be a major source of illegal emigration in the 1990s. The UK, by contrast, was an example of a state with relatively tight external borders but rather limited capacity for internal checks and controls on those resident on its territory (unlike most European countries, the UK still has no ID card system for residents). Table 3.2 provides some examples of the levels of detection of illegal entry at land and sea borders, or at airports.

However, as suggested in the first section of this chapter, there are other possible reasons for variations in the scale of illegal immigration in different countries. For example, the structuralist account would argue that the main reason states are unable to control unwanted immigration is because of the liberal constraint. Thus we would expect that countries with strong judicial systems and human rights commitments, and who are bound by various regional and international commitments, might have less capacity to control illegal immigration. For example, they may find themselves constrained in the use of detention or in limiting the free movement of asylum applicants; or they may face obstacles to stringent border controls which are seen to prevent bona fide refugees from accessing their territory. The pluralist account, meanwhile, would emphasize the business lobby as one of the main reasons why states would be prepared to tolerate illegal migration. On this account, we would expect less regulated free market economies and pluralist political systems to be more lenient towards immigrant labour. The systems theory approach, on the other hand, would emphasize the inclusive and functionally differentiated nature of the social systems relevant to immigrants' life chances. Thus the more autonomous and inclusive the labour market, education, health, or welfare systems, the less scope the political and legal systems will have to steer them towards excluding illegal migrants.

Let us consider two countries—Italy and Germany—to see how far their experiences with illegal immigration conform to one of these accounts.

i. Italy

Italy provides a classic example of a government talking tough on illegal migration, but tolerating widespread infringement of its migration rules in practice. Silvio

Berlusconi's *Casa delle Libertà* coalition led the country between 2001 and 2006, and over this period was characterized by unusually restrictive rhetoric. The goal of restricting illegal migration was a prominent part of the coalition's election campaign, and was especially prominent in the rhetoric of Umberto Bossi, head of the *Lega Nord*, and Gianfranco Fini, head of the *Alleanza Nazionale*. After the election, these politicians were responsible for drafting the 2002 Bossi–Fini immigration law, which introduced stricter rules on admission, entry, and residence. However, under the coalition, Italy saw the largest ever increase in the legally resident foreign population in Italian history—from around 1.3 million to 2.67 million. It also saw the most generous regularization of illegal migrants in European history—around 650,000 people were entitled to have their status regularized (see Table 3.3 for a comparison of regularizations in Italy, Greece, and Spain).[33]

The government did not just oversee an increase in legal migration—it also appeared to fail to reduce the level of illegal immigration. Despite a number of high-profile measures to crack down on illegal entry—including declaring a state of emergency in March 2002, and introducing maritime patrols off the coast—Italian industry continues to employ hundreds of thousands of irregular migrants. As Sciortino has argued, the persistence of irregular migration reflects a number of structural features of the Italian situation, including the long history of an informal labour sector, the lack of adequate administrative infrastructure, and above all general public and business acceptance of the benign impact of illegal employment.[34]

Which of the three theories best explains this apparent paradox? The structuralist account would explain the Italian government's failure to restrict immigration in terms of the liberal constraint. Domestic and international norms and judicial institutions limit the government's margin of manoeuvre in controlling unwanted migration. Yet in this case, there appears to be limited support for this thesis. The Italian government has shown itself to be relatively immune to international criticism. For example, it has been the object of substantial criticism for its cooperation

Table 3.3 Regularizations in Greece, Spain, and Italy

Greece		1997	1998	2001	2005	2007	
	Applicants	371,941	282,000	367,504	No data	No data	
	Accepted	No data	219,000	341,278	185,800	20,000	
Italy		**1982**	**1986–8**	**1990**	**1995–6**	**1998**	**2002**
	Applicants	5,000	113,349	234,841	258,761	250,747	702,156
	Accepted	5,000	105,000	222,000	246,000	217,000	650,000
Spain		**1985**	**1991**	**1996**	**2000**	**2001**	**2005**
	Applicants	38,181	130,406	17,676	245,598	351,269	691,655
	Accepted	34,832	109,135	21,382	199,296	232,674	578,375

Adapted from M. Baldwin-Edwards and A. Kraler (eds), *REGINE: Regularisations in Europe* (2009) 68, 81, and 87

[33] C. Boswell and A. Geddes, *Migration and Mobility in the European Union* (2011), at 137.
[34] G. Sciortino, *Fortunes and Miseries of Italian Labour Migration Policy* (2009).

with Libya to reduce transit migration via that country into Italy. In August 2010 Italy celebrated the two-year anniversary of its Treaty of Friendship, Partnership, and Cooperation with Libya, which included agreements that Libya would accept migrants intercepted on the high seas while seeking to enter Italy. Between May and September 2009, 1,000 individuals were accepted by Libya, a country which is not a signatory to the UN Convention on the Status of Refugees and is not considered by UNHCR, Amnesty International, or the European Council for Refugees and Exiles to be a 'safe' country for the return of refugees. These groups have roundly condemned the Italian government.[35] Yet the government appears to be impervious to such criticism, continuing to strengthen bilateral cooperation with Libya.

The pluralist account may be more plausible as an explanation. There is a clear business interest in ensuring an abundant supply of cheap foreign labour in Italy, especially in the country's industrial northern regions. The business lobby manifested itself strongly in opposition to the 2002 Bossi–Fini Law's measures to restrict illegal and legal labour migration. The head of Italy's main employers' organization, Confindustria, protested that 'Italian industry can't survive without the help of immigrant workers', while the president of the parliamentary industrial committee argued that the new law would lead to a 'haemorrhage' of the workforce required for ecomonic growth.[36] Business and employer groups also criticized the 2002 regularization for not going far enough. These objections prompted the Berlusconi government to revise a clause excluding those facing a deportation order from the scheme.

Equally persuasive, though, is the systems theory approach. As a number of authors have shown, large segments of the Italian economy, welfare system, and housing market are characterized by a high degree of informality. The existence of these informal structures makes it easier for irregular migrants to reside and work in Italy.[37] Since these systems have their own internal rationale for selecting who should participate, it is difficult for the systems of politics or law to steer their behaviour. This is especially true in the case of the Italian state, which has traditionally been weak in implementing migration controls. As Sciortino writes on the question of employer sanctions:

> Although employer sanctions schemes have appeared often in the political debate, they have never been systematically implemented, both for the lack of an adequate administrative infrastructure and, above all, for the fear of the political backlash they would trigger. Labour inspections in Italy are scarce in number and geared only toward the most exploitative situations. The police forces do not pay particular attention to labour irregularities, staying focused nearly only on irregular residence status. And even trade-unions have often

[35] See, eg, Amnesty International, 'Libya/Italy: Bilateral Cooperation Should Not be at the Price of Human Rights' (2010).

[36] C. Boswell, *European Migration Policies in Flux: Changing Patterns of Inclusion and Exclusion* (2003), at 49.

[37] Baldwin-Edwards and Arango, *supra* n 22, at 2; Sciortino, 'Between Phantoms and Necessary Evils: Some Critical Points in the Study of Irregular Migrations to Western Europe' 24 *IMIS-Beiträge* (2004) 17.

to mediate between the rights of irregular care-workers and the expectations of their retired, card-carrying, members.[38]

In conclusion, it appears that the Italian government's ambivalence in relation to the control of illegal immigration may be best explained by a combination of two theories. The pluralist theory may help explain the government's susceptibility to pressure from the business lobby. The government is keen to turn a blind eye to infringements which are in the clear interest of an influential business lobby. While systems theory may help account for the state's incapacity to steer systems such as the labour market to exclude illegal immigrants. In this case, the impediment is not so much linked to the government's interest in complying with the business lobby, but to the inherent incapacity of the state to steer behaviour in the labour market system.

ii. Germany

The German case has rather different features from that of Italy. From 1989 onwards, with the fall of the Berlin Wall, there were considerable concerns about rising illegal entry from east Europe. However, large-scale illegal cross-border movements did not materialize, and a combination of readmission agreements and tough border controls appeared to allay public worries about a mass influx from the east. However, there was an increase in the incidence of overstay: typically, Central and east European nationals entering Germany on three-month tourist visas and then overstaying their visa. Particularly in the 1990s, this phenomenon was linked with the problem of illegal labour, and the fear that foreign labour would undercut the German workforce. Such concerns were particularly prominent in the construction industry, which was active in a September 2004 joint initiative with the Federal Ministry of Finance to tackle illegal working in this sector.

German governments have introduced a range of measures to try to combat illegal residence and employment. These measures have tended to target access to the labour market and to the welfare system.[39] For example, legislation that came into effect in 2007 stepped up the penalties to employers for employing illegal migrants, including tougher implementation of these employer sanctions through fines of up to €50,000 and a maximum prison sentence of five years. Employer sanction enforcement rates are relatively high compared to many other European countries. For example, in 2003 there were 11,052 cautions and fines against illegal employment, and 6,355 criminal charges brought.[40]

Unlike in Italy, illegal migration is not a significant issue in mainstream party politics. Indeed, debates on legal migration programmes and, more recently, on immigrant integration have overshadowed the question of illegal immigration in the 2000s. However, current estimates of the number of illegal migrants in

[38] Sciortino, *supra* n 34, at 14.

[39] Vogel, 'Migration Control in Germany and the United States' 34 *International Migration Review* (2000) 390, at 391.

[40] A. Sinn, A. Kreienbrink, and H. Dietrich von Loeffelholz, *Illegally Resident Third-country Nationals in Germany: Policy Approaches, Profile and Social Situation* (2005).

Germany do suggest it is a significant problem.[41] Does this suggest that it is a structural feature of German society, as seems to be the case in Italy? And, if so, in what sense is this the case? Certainly, the structuralist/liberal constraint argument does seem to carry some weight in the German case. Germany is most vulnerable to illegal migration from Central and eastern Europe, and especially overstay from those entitled to three-month visas. Such provisions are common to all Schengen countries, so it could be argued that Germany's commitment to Schengen and the EU hamper its capacity to control its borders. Meanwhile, a substantial proportion of illegal entry is assumed to come from other EU countries, including those to the south. It is thought that many illegal migrants enter the EU via porous sea borders in the south, and then cross through Italy, Spain, or Greece into north European countries where they are likely to find employment or may link up with friends or family already resident. Insofar as this is the case, again, Germany's commitment to free movement provisions—and especially the abolition of internal checks within the Schengen area—could be said to impede the state's capacity to limit illegal immigration.

The pluralist argument appears less persuasive in the case of Germany. To be sure, certain sectors of the German economy have an interest in employing migrants on an irregular basis. But German trade unions are well organized and well represented in the state through Germany's corporate structure. The unions have lobbied hard to restrict forms of immigration that would mean German workers are undercut by cheap immigrant labour. For example, they were instrumental in lobbying the government to crack down on the practice of construction firms subcontracting cheap foreign labour (as codified in the EU 1996 Posted Workers Directive). Moreover, unlike its Italian counterpart, the German electorate has high expectations about what its government can and should do to combat illegal migration. Governments are likely to be reluctant to bow to business pressures and tolerate illegal migration, given the high electoral costs that are likely to ensue.

Finally, the systems theory approach may have some traction in this case. Even assuming the government is intent on reducing illegal immigration, this theory suggests that there are quite profound structural impediments to steering social systems. In order to eliminate illegal stay, for example, the government would need to crack down on the labour market, housing, and health systems, to ensure these did not allow the participation of illegal migrants. If we take employer sanctions as an example, we can see how challenging these provisions are to implement rigorously.[42] First, employer sanctions raise the question of how to deal with the problem of inadvertent employment of migrants without a permit. Regulations and courts have had a difficult time determining how far employers should be liable for failing to detect forged documents, especially given the sophistication of many forging techniques and the wide availability of counterfeited documents. Secondly is the issue of the resources required to ensure effective implementation.

[41] *Ibid.*

[42] Boswell, 'Migration Control and Narratives of Steering' 13 *British Journal of Politics and International Relations* (2011) 12.

In order to provide an effective deterrent, enforcement agencies need to ensure there is a high enough chance of being detected and successfully prosecuted, and that penalties are sufficiently severe. This will require substantial resources for spot checks, court hearings, and so on.

For the firms involved, such regulations are even more problematic. Both employers and labour may see the regulations as unreasonable, and, aware of the impediments to enforcement, will try to circumvent regulation. Similarly, there is evidence that in many cases courts are reluctant to prosecute business, lacking the capacity to ascertain responsibility, or showing themselves to be sympathetic towards the (usually small) firms that are affected. Where low enforcement rates become the object of political and media attention, the political system is likely to step up efforts to enforce sanctions. As in the German case, this will typically involve more of the same: raising penalties, and increasing spot checks.

Such attempts at steering have also been known to produce a number of distortions. Where such measures are implemented, uncertainty about the status of potential employees may motivate discriminatory practices. If in doubt about the validity of documents, an employer may prefer to employ someone more 'obviously' British/German, etc. Another possibility is that smaller firms may go bankrupt, or that the intervention may lead to more substantial restructuring of the sector (not necessarily a negative externality).

These sorts of problems are not limited to interventions in the economic system. Parallel problems emerge where the political and legal systems have endeavoured to regulate inclusion of illegal immigrants into the health system. The public health system, like other social services in modern welfare states, operates according to an inclusive logic.[43] Its principle criterion of inclusion distinguishes between those who are sick and in need of treatment, who are relevant to the system; and those who are not in need of treatment, who are excluded from the system. Any attempts by the political system to impose other criteria of selection are experienced as an irritation, running against the grain of the function of the health system.

We have briefly looked at two rather different European countries, exploring how far illegal migration can be said to be a structural problem, and which of the three theories does the best job of explaining this. Interestingly, each case produced a rather different conclusion. In the case of Italy, immigration control appears to be impeded mainly by the business lobby, as well as the state's acute problems with steering. In Germany, the more important factors appeared to be the liberal constraint, and especially EU and Schengen commitments, as well as limitations to steering social systems. It should be noted that the Italian state faces far greater impediments to steering than does the German one. Yet as we saw, even in a state with a high degree of capacity to implement and enforce sanctions, there are nonetheless a range of limitations, distortions, and unintended effects produced by attempts to steer social systems through the law.

[43] N. Luhmann, *Political Theory in the Welfare State* (1981); Bommes, 'National Welfare State', *supra* n 28.

3. EU Cooperation on Irregular Migration

In the third and final section of this chapter, we shall discuss how EU cooperation fits into this picture. Can cooperation on illegal migration also be explained in terms of the three approaches set out above? I shall start by outlining how the three theories could be deployed to make sense of EU cooperation. I shall then offer a brief overview of some of the main areas of EU cooperation on irregular migration, and analyse how far these measures appear to endorse one or more of the theories.

A. Theories of European cooperation

Much has been written on the reasons why European states have pooled sovereignty to cooperate in the field of immigration and asylum policy. Illegal migration is one of the most developed areas of cooperation within this field, obviously begging the question as to why states should choose to join forces on this (while, for example, there has been much more limited cooperation in the area of the legal admission of labour migrants or immigrant integration).

One prominent explanation of the EU looks to neo-functionalist theory to explain cooperation. Indeed, a number of authors see cooperation as a paradigmatic case of 'functional spillover' from the Single Market project. On this account, cooperation on migration control was largely spurred on by the abolition of internal borders, which generated the need for 'flanking' measures to tighten external borders and regulate mobility between member states.[44] This account would fit well with the liberal constraint approach. As we saw, liberal constraint theorists locate impediments to migration control in domestic and international norms, which impede the state's capacity to introduce more stringent control measures. Thus it could be argued that it was precisely the EU's imposition of a liberal constraint on domestic policy-making that encouraged national governments to 'go European'. EU cooperation was seen as a way of compensating for a loss of control produced by the liberal constraint.

A number of other theorists have applied the liberal constraint thesis even more directly to EU cooperation. Given the various constraints on European governments from both domestic and international sources, so the argument runs, governments have tried to avoid such checks to their power by shifting decision-making up to the European level. Thus European cooperation could be understood as a way of trying to 'regain control'.[45] As Virginie Guiraudon has argued, officials in home affairs and justice ministries were keen to 'go European' in order to avoid domestic

[44] Koslowski, 'European Migration Regimes, Established and Emergent', in C. Joppke (ed.), *Challenge to the Nation-State* (1998) 153; Ucarer, 'Cooperation on Justice and Home Affairs Matters', in L. Cram, D. Dinan, and N. Nugent (eds), *Developments in the European Union* (1999); Jordan, Strath, and Triandafyllidou, 'Contextualising Immigration Policy Implementation in Europe' 29 *Journal of Ethnic and Migration Studies* (2003) 195.

[45] A. Geddes, *The Politics of Migration and Immigration in Europe* (2003).

constitutional constraints and scrutiny.[46] Again, the implication is that EU cooperation is a means of bypassing some of the structural impediments to controlling migration mentioned earlier in the chapter.

A more recent variant on this 'venue shopping' approach is offered by Sandra Lavenex, and her work on explaining the expansion of cooperation with external (non-EU) countries to try to control migration. In a 2006 article, Lavenex argued that the communitarization of immigration policy since the Treaty of Amsterdam has limited possibilities for states to avoid judicial and democratic scrutiny by 'going European'. Thus they seek to outsource forms of migration control to non-EU countries, through measures such as readmission agreements, pre-frontier checks, or supporting countries neighbouring the EU in controlling emigration or transit migration across their territory. Thus the preference for the external dimension represented an attempt to 'shift out' migration control functions to third countries as a means of evading such scrutiny.[47] So this is another example of how EU cooperation bypasses the liberal constraint, but this time it suggests that states have an interest in outsourcing policy to third countries, rather than simply shifting power up to Brussels.

How would the other two theories be applied to explain EU cooperation on immigration and asylum? The pluralist theory suggested that it was organized interests—and notably the business lobby—that exerted pressure on governments to tolerate irregular migration. If this is the case, it is not clear why such pressure would encourage EU cooperation, which would be likely to produce increased regulation of illegal migration. One possible explanation is that states can use EU cooperation as an essentially symbolic forum for policy-making. For example, European Councils typically produce quite forceful statements about EU cooperation, including on areas such as counterterrorism or the fight against illegal migration. Such rhetoric is low cost for governments, and can gain them credit with domestic electorates for acting with other countries to address shared problems. However, in practice, such measures may remain essentially symbolic, allowing governments to act tough while in practice continuing to tolerate illegal migration. Thus the measures may appease electorates, whilst meeting business interests.

There is a second, rather different, way in which pluralist theory could be applied to explain European cooperation. On this account, the focus would be not so much on explaining member states' cooperation, but on accounting for the policy preferences of the European institutions involved in decision-making—and notably the European Commission. If we see the European Commission as the EU's executive, we can analyse how far it is susceptible to lobbying from different interest groups. To be sure, the Commission has limited autonomy in decision-making

[46] Guiraudon, 'European Integration and Migration Policy: Vertical Policy-Making as Venue Shopping' 38 *Journal of Common Market Studies* (2000) 251; Guiraudon, 'The Constitution of a European Immigration Policy Domain: A Political Sociology Approach' 10 *Journal of European Public Policy* (2003) 263.

[47] Lavenex, 'Shifting Up and Out: The Foreign Policy of European Immigration Control' 29 *West European Politics* (2006) 329.

in this area. Nonetheless, it now has a significant role in drafting proposals and liaising between member states and different EU institutions. Thus it has become the target of interest group lobbying, including by business interests and groups defending the rights of migrants. Indeed, a number of authors have suggested that the emergence of EU cooperation on immigration and asylum, and especially changes since the mid-1990s, have opened up new opportunities for NGOs lobbying at EU level. Thus Guiraudon argues that the EU's relative insulation from electoral politics can enhance the possibilities for NGOs to exercise influence in an area which tends to be highly populist at national level.[48] Thus we might expect less populist (anti-immigrant) groups to exercise relatively more influence. Moreover, Adrian Favell and Andrew Geddes have pointed out how such lobbying at EU level tends to be elite-led rather than 'bottom-up' societal mobilization,[49] suggesting that it may be better at representing business interests than grass-roots anti-immigrant sentiment.

Finally, we should consider how systems theory might be applied to make sense of EU cooperation in this area. Systems theory sought to explain why illegal immigration was both appealing and feasible to migrants, and thus why it persisted. Moreover, it highlighted the inherent difficulties in government attempts to control illegal migration, through steering the social systems into which immigrants integrated. Given that all EU countries appear to face similar problems with illegal immigration and impediments to steering (although on different scales), we might expect that they would share an interest in cooperating to combat it. Thus the ubiquitous nature of the problem for all liberal welfare states might imply a common motivation to cooperate. At the same time, though, the structural limits to steering might imply the fundamental limitations of cooperation at EU level. If national governments find it difficult to steer migration processes on their own territory, how could one expect supranational measures emanating from Brussels to fare any better? On the contrary, one might seriously doubt the effectiveness of any measures adopted to cover 27 member states with very different state structures and practices of control, different labour markets, health systems, and education systems. Such EU level measures might be expected to produce even more problems of compliance, distortions, and unintended consequences than measures introduced at the national level.

Systems theory might, therefore, offer a theory to explain why EU cooperation to steer domestic systems might not be considered appropriate; and/or, insofar as such measures were adopted, it might help explain why they have limited success.

[48] Guiraudon, 'De-Nationalising Control', in V. Guiraudon and C. Joppke (eds), *Controlling a New Migration World* (2001) (see also Ireland, 'Facing the True "Fortress Europe": Immigrants and Politics in the EC' 29 *Journal of Common Market Studies* (1991) 246; Geddes, 'Lobbying for Migrant Inclusion in the European Union: New Opportunities for Transnational Advocacy?' 7 *Journal of European Public Policy* (2000) 632.

[49] Favell and Geddes, 'European Integration, Immigration and the Nation State: Institutionalising Transnational Political Action?' (1999) EUI Working Papers, RSC 99.

B. EU measures to combat irregular migration

How far do these different theories appear to be supported by the development of cooperation in this area? Initally, there was rather limited cooperation on illegal migration at European level. As we saw, many European countries were increasingly concerned about illegal immigration from the early 1980s onwards. But it was not until the Single European Act (SEA) in 1986 that states were galvanized into action. The SEA aimed to achieve an internal market by 1992, including the free movement of workers between EU states. Meanwhile, the Schengen Agreement of 1985, signed by a subset of EC countries (initially Germany, France, and Benelux), complemented and went further than the SEA, signing these states up to the gradual abolition of controls at internal borders. The SEA and Schengen are usually interpreted as classic examples of neo-functionalist spillover: the abolition of internal borders created the need for better migration control, especially in terms of better internal checks, and reinforced control of the EU's external borders.

So what form did cooperation on illegal immigration take? In terms of the formal expansion of competences through EU treaties, the Maastricht Treaty of 1992 established irregular migration as an 'area of common interest', but gave the Union no formal competence to make policy in this domain. The 1997 Amsterdam Treaty included much more extensive provisions on immigration and asylum. Article 63 of the Treaty Establishing the European Community (TEC) (now Articles 78 and 79 of the Treaty on the Functioning of the European Union (TFEU)) enabled the Council to adopt measures within the area of 'illegal immigration and illegal residence, including repatriation of illegal residents'.

In practice, most policies and programmes adopted since the 1990s have focused on measures to combat illegal migration through external border control, readmission, or cooperation with third countries, as outlined below.

i. Border control

Even before the EU was granted competence in the area of irregular migration, a series of developments from the early 1990s effectively gave the EU quite considerable influence in combating irregular migration. For a start, the Schengen countries had been steadily developing a range of common measures and approaches, including on external border controls, a common visa regime, and a database on third country nationals (TCNs) that should be refused entry into the Schengen area (the Schengen Information System).[50] Although Schengen included just a subset of EU states at the outset, in 1989 it was extended to include the Mediterranean countries, and the Treaty of Amsterdam formally incorporated it into the TEC. Already in the early 1990s, however, conformity to Schengen rules was one of the conditions for EU accession. Thus future member states in Central and Eastern Europe were obliged to incorporate the Schengen *acquis* into their national legislation, implying

[50] Grabbe, 'The Sharp Edges of Europe: Extending Schengen Eastwards' 76 *International Affairs* (2000) 519.

the introduction of stricter border and entry controls. The PHARE programme financed assistance to these countries for capacity building of border control infrastructure and training.

EU states have also cooperated to control entry through pre-frontier controls, and joint naval patrols of sea borders. More recently, in 2005 they established FRONTEX, the European external borders agency. The remit of FRONTEX is to strengthen external border control through better coordination between border officials. It conducts training and risk analysis, and provides technical and operational assistance to member states. Regulation 863/2007 of 11 July 2007[51] established Rapid Border Intervention Teams (RABITs) composed of national border guards having the right to act on the territory of other member states. By 2008 FRONTEX had around 130 personnel and a budget of €70m.

ii. Return and readmission

Another key area of cooperation has been on the return of third country nationals who are illegally present in the EU. The 2008 Return Directive standardized procedures for the return of illegal migrants to their countries of origin. It was agreed after three years of negotiations and following 70 amendments by the European Parliament. The objective of the Directive is to standardize the procedures regulating the expulsion of irregular migrants, by setting out minimum standards.

The Return Directive focuses on member states' actions in relation to return. Readmission agreements, meanwhile, set out the obligations of third countries regarding the readmission of their nationals or those who transited across their territory into the EU. Readmission agreements were initially developed by Germany from 1991 onwards, and subsequently began to be included in clauses in a number of EU association and cooperation agreements. The Treaty of Amsterdam granted the Council formal powers to enter such agreements, and from 2000 onwards, the European Commission began negotiating readmission agreements with Morocco, Sri Lanka, Russia, Pakistan, Hong Kong, Macau, Albania, Algeria, China, and Turkey. Under such agreements, countries of origin and transit are obliged to accept back illegal migrants or asylum seekers who originate from the respective country, or who entered the EU via their territory.

iii. The external dimension

Most of the measures outlined above involved some form of cooperation with third countries. The idea of combating illegal migration through external policy has been coined as the 'external dimension' of immigration and asylum. The policy was officially codified as a key EU goal in 1999, at the Tampere Special Council on Justice and Home Affairs. The Council's Conclusions stressed the need for a 'comprehensive approach to migration addressing political, human rights and

[51] [2007] OJ L299/30.

development issues in countries and regions of origin and transit'. It argued for 'a greater coherence of internal and external policies of the Union', so that 'all competences and instruments at the disposal of the Union, and in particular, in external relations must be used in an integrated and consistent way to build the area of freedom, security and justice. JHA concerns must be integrated in the definition and implementation of other Union policies and activities'.[52] This priority was reiterated by subsequent European Councils—in Feira (2000), Laeken (2001), Seville (2002), Thessaloniki (2003), and the Hague Programme (2004). More recently, in October 2005, the EU held a special meeting of heads of state at Hampton Court, which called for urgent action to develop the external dimension. The Hampton Court meeting produced a new 'Global Approach to Migration: Priority actions focusing on Africa and the Mediterranean', which was adopted by the European Council in December 2005.

Part of the external dimension involves the sorts of measures described above: readmission agreements, reinforced external border controls through naval patrols, FRONTEX, and pre-frontier checks. However, another aspect of this has involved cooperation with third countries to try to address the causes of migration. For example, it was argued that a share of development cooperation funding should be targeted to alleviate the conditions leading to emigration in major sending countries. Indeed, the Commission has attempted to integrate such considerations into its development cooperation, through its (seven-year) Country Strategy Papers and National Indicative Programmes for a number of third countries. Moreover, the Directorate General Development has earmarked a budget of €90 million to be spent on migration issues.[53]

In short, EU cooperation on illegal migration has focused predominantly on the external dimension: controlling external borders, providing resources and training to assist migration management in third countries, concluding readmission agreements, and channelling funds to relieve migration pressures in countries of origin. What is noticably missing from this repertoire of measures is the type of internal control approach characteristic of domestic policies. As we saw, most EU member states focus much of their efforts on either internal checks and controls, or on trying to prevent illegal migrants from integrating into social systems such as the labour market, housing, health, or education.

In fact, the European Commission did propose a Sanctions Directive in 2007, which came into force in 2009.[54] The Directive aims to harmonize national provisions relating to employer sanctions, and consists of three main elements: employers will be subject to a number of new administrative obligations that would need to be fulfilled before recruiting any third country nationals; non-compliance will lead to punitive measures, financial sanctions, and criminal penalties with

[52] Presidency Conclusions of the Tampere European Council, available at <http://www.refworld.org/pdfid/3ef2d2264.pdf>.

[53] Boswell, 'Evasion, Reinterpretation and Decoupling: European Commission Responses to the "External Dimension" of Immigration and Asylum' 31 *West European Politics* (2008) 491.

[54] Directive 2009/52 of the EP and the Council, [2009] OJ L168/24.

harmonized procedures; and each member state will be required to inspect the employee records in ten per cent of its registered companies. Yet so far this Directive is a rather isolated and limited measure in comparison to the wide panoply of policies and programmes on external border control and the external dimension. It suggests that while EU member states are keen to support quite radical measures relating to the external dimension, they are more reluctant to sign up to requirements in more sensitive areas of domestic policy.

What explains this asymmetry in cooperation in the areas of internal and external approaches to illegal migration? As we saw, the liberal constraint approach and the 'venue-shopping' theory might predict that member states would be keen to 'go European' to avoid some of the constraints to migration control at the domestic level. Thus, for example, we might expect them to be keen to Europeanize policies in areas such as return, where domestic courts might constrain approaches considered to infringe the welfare of migrants. The adoption of the 2008 Return Directive arguably supports this view. Yet as we have seen, this Directive was extremely controversial, and is a fairly isolated example of an attempt to harmonize domestic approaches to migration control.

Far more favoured were common approaches to the external dimension. This prioritization appears to support the 'shifting out' thesis advanced by Sandra Lavenex. EU countries did engage in venue-shopping to avoid scrutiny, but preferred the venue to be outside the EU.[55] For example, readmission agreements, pre-frontier controls, and supporting migration management in third countries could further the goal of preventing illegal migration, but without confronting the range of human rights and judicial constraints that kicked in at both domestic and EU level. So the liberal constraint argument does help explain EU cooperation, but it supports the thesis about shifting out to third countries, rather than simply shifting up to the European level.

What of the pluralist theory of cooperation? As we saw, following this approach we might expect governments to have an interest in primarily symbolic cooperation at EU level. The idea was that member states would be keen to demonstrate to their electorates that they were taking action through high-profile actions and tough rhetoric; but in practice, they continued to tolerate extensive irregular migration at home. This appears to be borne out in the case of some member states, such as the UK and Italy, which have supported a number of quite prominent initiatives. Thus both countries have been engaged in naval patrols of the Mediterranean, and the UK has been at the forefront of high-profile measures to combat smuggling and trafficking via the western Balkans. Both governments have regularly highlighted such initiatives in press briefings, speeches, and parliamentary debates.[56] Yet these types of measures are likely to have a limited impact on levels of illegal migration, especially if they are not combined with rigorous policies on internal control and employer sanctions. Indeed, as we saw, Italy has accompanied such measures with successive regularization programmes, which almost certainly provide a 'pull

[55] Lavenex, *supra* n 47. [56] Boswell, *Flux*, *supra* n 36.

factor' for potential migrants. In this sense, EU cooperation on irregular migration may provide an opportunity for governments to meet the demands of business and other domestic lobbies for lenient policies on illegal migration, whilst at the same time reassuring the electorate that they are pulling out all the stops to control illegal migration through European cooperation.

The second way in which the pluralist theory might be applied to understanding EU cooperation concerned patterns of interest group lobbying of EU institutions. Might the European Commission, in particular, be susceptible to lobbying by employer or migrant groups in Brussels? There is little evidence of interest groups having a great influence over policy in the department responsible for immigration—the Directorate General (DG) for Home Affairs. To be sure, officials in this DG have regular interaction with NGOs at various conferences and workshops, but there is little to indicate they are subject to lobbying by business. What is more likely is that their sister department, the DG for Employment, Social Affairs, and Inclusion, is subject to such influence. This DG has a strong tradition of incorporating the interests of employers and trade unions. Insofar as the DG for Employment has a role in policy-making on illegal migration, then, it is possible that the business lobby might have an influence on policy. However, while the DG for Employment appears to have some influence on Commission proposals on labour migration and especially anti-discrimination, there is limited evidence it has had much impact on illegal migration, which remains the remit of Home Affairs (and increasingly External Relations and Development).

Finally, can systems theory help shed light on patterns of cooperation at the EU level? This theory suggested that illegal migration was a shared problem endemic to modern welfare states, thus possibly implying a common interest in cooperation. And this is indeed borne out by the level of cooperation at EU level. Yet it also suggested the likely ineffectiveness of EU level attempts to steer processes of illegal migration. If attempts to steer illegal migration are difficult or impossible at the domestic level, then they are likely to be that much less feasible at the supranational level. The challenges for national administrations adequately to understand or steer the internal dynamics of functionally differentiated social systems within their domestic jurisdiction are pronounced enough; it becomes even more challenging where the European Commission or Council are drafting measures to attempt to steer such systems across 27 quite diverse member states. This may partly explain why EU governments have been reluctant to introduce common measures that target domestic control, instead favouring measures under the rubric of the external dimension.

However, systems theory would be equally sceptical about the capacity of governments—or the EU as a collective—to steer behaviour in third countries. International migration processes are immensely complex, and attempts to control irregular movement have, as we have seen, produced various unintended consequences: a rise in dangerous smuggling and trafficking practices, increasingly sophisticated techniques for forging travel documents, and an increasing incidence of overstay. At the same time, attempts to influence the behaviour of governments in third countries are also challenging. While in some cases—notably the

EU accession process—states have been willing to implement EU rules, in many others formal agreements have yielded limited cooperation in practice. Thus, for example, readmission agreements have been extremely difficult to negotiate and implement in practice.[57] Similarly, if EU governments find it difficult to reduce illegal migration in their own countries, how can they expect to be able to produce such effects in third countries through external relations?

Systems theory suggests that member states and EU institutions are likely to develop highly simplified narratives about the ways in which their interventions will effect the target of their policies. For example, Joergen Carling and Maria Hernandez-Carretero have shown how international actors tend to simplify the complexity of high-risk emigration from West Africa, basing policy interventions on misguided notions about the motivations of migrants, and about what sorts of sanctions might deter them from migrating.[58] These rather crude understandings of migration processes produce ineffective policy interventions that have a number of unintended and undesirable consequences. Yet as we saw earlier, such interventions may well have an important symbolic purpose for European governments. They are unlikely to have a serious impact in reducing the level of illegal migration—indeed they may well generate even more risk-taking, or nefarious forms of smuggling and trafficking. Yet they may perform an important role in reassuring European governments and the public that action is being taken to combat the problem. So while they may not deliver reduced levels of illegal migration, they demonstrate that governments and the EU are committed to protecting their citizens from the negative effects of unwanted migration.

4. Conclusion

This chapter explored the notion that illegal immigration is a structural problem for European states. It set out three different theories as to why this might be the case. The structuralist/liberal constraint theory argued that illegal immigration reflected a basic tension between liberal states' commitment to restricting immigration to mollify public opinion, while meeting various liberal and human rights norms. These latter emanated from both domestic and international sources. The pluralist account emphasized the role of organized interests in shaping policy. On this account, states act as brokers between different lobby groups, and are likely to be especially influenced by the powerful business lobby on immigration, which has a strong interest in more lenient policies. Indeed, many sectors are profoundly dependent on illegal labour to sustain their businesses. Finally, systems theory explained the scale and persistence of illegal migration as a product of the

[57] Schieffer, 'Community Readmission Agreements with Third Countries—Objectives, Substance, and Current State of Negotations' 5 *European Journal of Migration and Law* (2003) 343.

[58] Carling and Hernández-Carreto, 'Protecting Europe and Protecting Migrants? Strategies for Managing Unauthorised Migration from Africa' 13 *British Journal of Politics and International Relations* (2011) 42.

inclusive tendencies of social systems such as the economy, education, health, and welfare. According to this account, it is extremely difficult for the political and legal systems to regulate these systems, which continued to provide possibilities for the participation of illegal migrants, effectively undermining attempts to control the problem.

These theories were then applied to help make sense of policies on illegal immigration in Germany, Italy, and at EU level. The chapter found that the liberal constraint theory helped explain impediments to migration control in Germany, especially the existence of EU rules on free movement and the abolition of internal borders, as well as common visa policies. The pluralist theory appeared to be more applicable in the Italian case, with governments showing themselves highly susceptible to influence from the business lobby. In both cases, there was evidence of quite considerable constraints to controlling illegal immigration through steering social systems, especially in the Italian case.

EU cooperation, meanwhile, has focused a large part of its policies and resources on the external dimension, and on external border control. This may partially be explained by the attractiveness of 'shifting out' migration control to third countries, in order to avoid the liberal constraint in operation at domestic and EU level.[59] Thus the liberal constraint argument may partially explain the direction of EU cooperation towards the external dimension. Pluralist theory may also help explain the penchant of many member states for high-profile but largely symbolic action on the external dimension, which helps mollify public opinion while meeting business interests. However, as systems theory would predict, attempts to steer migration processes through the external dimension are likely to meet huge impediments. If it is already difficult to steer social systems at the domestic level, it is likely to be far more challenging for the EU to attempt to steer similar processes in third countries. Indeed, recent literature suggests that the EU has adopted highly simplistic approaches to combating illegal migration from third countries, relying on quite crude ideas about the motives and dynamics of emigrants. This reinforces the notion that a large part of EU policy on the external dimension remains largely symbolic: it is designed to allay public expectations about migration control, but remains very limited in its effects on migration flows, and may well be having a range of unintended effects.

[59] Lavenex, *supra* n 47.

4

Migration Policy and EU External Relations

*Bernd Martenczuk**

The European Union constitutes an area of freedom, security, and justice. This area is characterized by an absence of internal border controls on the movement of persons. The absence of internal borders benefits not only EU citizens, but also third country nationals (TCNs). As a consequence, it has become indispensable to develop a common policy on the crossing of the EU's external borders by TCNs. Since the entry into force of the Treaty of Amsterdam, the EU has, therefore, built an impressive body of law governing visa policy, border controls, and immigration policy.

However, building a common external EU policy on migration issues is, and remains, a complex task. Migration policy is sensitive since it is linked to the issues of long-term and economic migration, which raise complex economic and social questions hotly debated in many member states. It is thus not surprising that the process of supranationalization of migration policy at the level of the EU has been gradual, and is still far from complete. At the same time, migration policy is also an important tool for promoting tourism, trade, and international mobility in general, and has also become an important subject for EU foreign policy.

Against this background, the present chapter will consider the EU's external activities in the field of migration policy, and will try to assess to what extent there is a common EU external migration policy. Migration policy in this context shall be understood as all policies affecting the movement of TCNs across the EU's external borders; it therefore considers both short-term and long-term migration. By contrast, because of the specificities of the subject, the chapter does not address the EU's policies on asylum and refugee protection.[1] Moreover, the chapter only deals with the EU's external relations with third countries not associated with the Schengen *acquis*. It does not deal with the variable geometry of EU migration

* This chapter is partially based on an earlier publication (Martenczuk, 'Visa Policy and EU External Relations', in B. Martenczuk and S. van Thiel, *Justice, Liberty, Security: New Challenges for EU External Relations* (2008) 221), but has been significantly updated, revised, and expanded. The chapter expresses the personal view of the author only.

[1] On this see Garlick and Kumin, 'Seeking Asylum in the EU: Disentangling Refugee Protection from Migration Control', in B. Martenczuk and S. van Thiel, *Justice, Liberty, Security: New Challenges for EU External Relations* (2008) 111.

policy, including the non-participation of certain members in EU migration policy, nor with the association of certain third countries with EU migration policy.[2]

The chapter will begin by providing an overview of the historical development of EU migration policy (section 1). It will then present the current legal bases of EU migration policy (section 2). It will subsequently recall certain basic principles concerning the extent and nature of the EU's external competences in the field of migration policy (section 3). On this basis, it will analyse the EU's external activities in the fields of visa and border controls (section 4), long-term migration (section 5), and the fight against illegal immigration (section 6). Finally, the chapter will consider the links between certain other EU external policies and migration policy (section 7).

1. The Evolution of EU Migration Policy

The EU's competences in the field of migration policy have developed gradually, and the current state of EU law still bears some traces of this development. For this reason, this section will provide a brief overview of the historical development of EU migration policy.

A. The Treaty of Maastricht

The first provisions of EU law to deal explicitly with migration policy were introduced by the Treaty of Maastricht. First of all, the Maastricht Treaty inserted Article 100(c) of the Treaty Establishing the European Community (ECT). Until the Treaty of Amsterdam, this provision was the only element of migration policy subject to the first pillar and thus to the 'Community method'.

Article 100(c) of the ECT, which was contained in the chapter of the Treaty dealing with the harmonization of laws in the common market, covered two matters: (a) the list of third countries whose nationals must be in possession of a visa; and (b) a uniform format for visas. The Community legislated on both matters. The first Community measure on visas was Regulation 1683/95 laying down a uniform format for visas.[3] The second measure on the list of TCNs which must be in possession of a visa took considerably more time and was adopted only shortly before the entry into force of the Amsterdam Treaty with Regulation 549/1999.[4]

[2] On this see Martenczuk, 'Variable Geometry and the External Relations of the EU: The Experience of Justice and Home Affairs', in B. Martenczuk and S. van Thiel, *Justice, Liberty, Security: New Challenges for EU External Relations* (2008) 493; Fabrice and Filliez, 'Schengen/Dublin: the Association Agreements with Iceland, Norway and Switzerland', in B. Martenczuk and S. van Thiel, *Justice, Liberty, Security: New Challenges for EU External Relations* (2008) 145.

[3] Council Regulation (EC) 1683/95, [1995] OJ L164/1.

[4] Council Regulation (EC) 574/1999 determining the third countries whose nationals must be in possession of visas when crossing the external borders of the Member States [1999] OJ L72/2. On the difficult negotiations leading up to this measure, see Martenczuk, 'Visa Policy and EU External Relations', in B. Martenczuk and S. van Thiel, *Justice, Liberty, Security: New Challenges for EU External Relations* (2008) 21, at 23f.

As regards other aspects of migration policy, these were made subject to the third pillar of the European Union. In particular, according to Article K.1 of the EU Treaty, the member states were to regard as matters of common interest 'rules governing the crossing by persons of the external border of the Member States and the exercise of controls thereon' as well as 'immigration policy and policy regarding nationals of third countries'. However, these policies remained fully subject to the intergovernmental working methods applicable under the third pillar at the time, and little progress was made under the third pillar in terms of the adoption of relevant acts, which remained generally limited to non-binding guidelines and recommendations.[5]

B. The Schengen Cooperation

In June 1985, five member states[6] had signed an agreement in the Luxembourg village of Schengen 'on the gradual abolition of checks at their common borders'. The delicate balance of the agreement was encapsulated in Article 17 thereof, which foresaw the creation of an area of free movement to be made possible by the adoption of compensatory or flanking measures to safeguard internal security and prevent illegal immigration. Crystallizing the objectives of the Schengen agreement, and particularly the compensatory measures, was left to the Schengen Implementing Convention ('the Schengen Convention'), signed on 19 June 1990, also in Schengen, which became operational on 26 March 1995.[7]

The harmonization of visa policies had always been envisaged by the Schengen Agreement[8] and so, the Schengen Convention devoted a chapter to the matter, setting out the broad outlines of a visa policy. In terms of broad outlines, the visa policy as conceived by the Convention was based on three essential elements—common arrangements relating to third states whose nationals were subject to a visa requirement, the notion of a uniform visa valid for the entire territory of the contracting parties, and uniform criteria for issuing the uniform visa. It was left to the Schengen Executive Committee[9] to fill in the details of those essential elements, particularly as regards common rules for the examination of visas, their form, content, and validity and the fees to be charged for their issue. By 1999, and the entry into force of the Treaty of Amsterdam, the 'filling in of the details' represented a rather impressive body of work. Essentially, almost all aspects of visa policy had been harmonized. In particular, Schengen also harmonized the procedures and conditions which would govern the issuing of visas and, in doing so, it dealt with such matters as how to complete the application form, the accompanying

[5] See Degen in H. v.d. Groeben, J. Thiesing, and C.-D. Ehlermann, *Kommentar zum EU-/EG-Vertrag* (5th edn, 1997), Art. K.1, pt. 10.; S. Peers, *EU Justice and Home Affairs Law* (3rd edn, 2010), at 383 *et seq*.

[6] The Benelux States, Germany, and France.

[7] By that time, the original five had been joined by Italy, Spain, Portugal, and Greece. By 1999, 13 of the 15 member states were 'Schengen' states.

[8] See Art. 20 thereof.

[9] See Arts. 12(3) and 17.

documentation, the examination procedure, the fees, and the matter of consular organization and cooperation. The results of this activity were consolidated in the Common Consular Instructions (the CCI),[10] which constituted essentially a guidebook for the benefit of consular agents for the daily treatment of applications for visas.

By contrast, the Schengen cooperation did not in any significant way address the issue of long-term migration. On the contrary, Article 18 of the Schengen Convention clearly stated that visas for stays exceeding three months shall be national visas issued by one of the contracting parties in accordance with national law. The only explicit right granted to TCNs in this context was the right to transit to the territories of other contracting parties in order to reach the territory of the contracting state which issued the visa.

C. The Amsterdam Treaty

At the time of the entry into force of the Treaty of Amsterdam, EU migration policy was thus mostly focused on short-term migration, and derived from two sources: Community acts and the Schengen Convention. By virtue of the Protocol integrating the Schengen *acquis* into the framework of the European Union (hereinafter referred to as the 'Schengen protocol'), the Schengen Convention and all rules adopted thereunder were incorporated into the Union framework and thereby essentially became instruments of secondary Community law, or of Union law for those matters that remained with the 'third pillar'. On 20 May 1999, the Council, acting on the basis of the Schengen protocol, adopted Decision 1999/436/EC[11] which determined, in conformity with the provisions of the Treaty establishing the European Community and the Treaty on European Union (TEU), the legal bases for each of the provisions or decisions which constitute the Schengen *acquis*.[12]

This integration of the Schengen *acquis* into the framework of the European Community also had significant implications for the external relations of the member states in the field of visa policy. The Schengen cooperation had been intergovernmental in character and had, therefore, left the foreign relations powers of the Schengen member states relatively unaffected.[13] In contrast, with the communitarization of the Schengen *acquis*, the principles of the case-law of the Court of Justice on the exclusive competence of the Community would become applicable, with the potential consequence that the member states might lose some of their competences in this area. Conscious of this fact, the member states therefore

[10] The operative version in 1999 had been adopted by a Decision of the Executive Committee of 28 April—Sch/Com-Ex (99) 13 and was later published in [2000] OJ L239/317. Until that publication, the CCI were secret and unpublished outside the Schengen circle.

[11] [1999] OJ L176/17.

[12] See Kuijper, 'Some Legal Problems Associated with the Communitarization of Policy on Visas, Asylum, and Immigration under the Amsterdam Treaty and Incorporation of the Schengen acquis' 37 *CMLR* (2000) 345.

[13] However, Art. 136 of the Schengen Implementing Convention had already provided that agreements on border checks should be negotiated in consultation with other Schengen member states, and that agreements simplifying or abolishing border checks should be concluded with the agreement of the other Schengen member states.

concluded, with the Treaty of Amsterdam, a 'Protocol on external relations of the Member States with regard to the crossing of external borders'. This Protocol, which was annexed to the EC Treaty, provides that '[t]he provisions on the measures on the crossing of external borders included in Article 62 (2) (a) of Title IV of the Treaty shall be without prejudice to the competence of Member States to negotiate or conclude agreements with third countries as long as they respect Community law and other relevant international agreements'.[14]

With the Treaty of Amsterdam, Article 62 of the ECT became the legal basis for measures in the field of border controls and short-term visas. According to Article 62(2) of the ECT, the Council had to, within a period of five years after the entry into force of the Treaty of Amsterdam, adopt measures on the crossing of the external borders of the member states, including comprehensive rules concerning short-term visas, which were defined as visas for intended stays of no more than three months. In terms of procedure, those measures which already fell under Community competence prior to the Treaty of Amsterdam (namely the visa list and the uniform format for visas), were adopted by the Council acting by qualified majority and after consultation of the European Parliament.[15] By contrast, the measures falling under Article 62(2)(b)(ii) and (iv), which were originally subjects of the Schengen cooperation, were for the first five years adopted by the Council acting unanimously on a proposal from the Commission or on the initiative of a member state and after consulting the European Parliament, but since the end of the transitional period of five years from the Treaty of Amsterdam, adopted according to the co-decision procedure.[16]

On the basis of Article 62, the EC subsequently adopted major instruments in the area of border controls and visa policy. Council Regulation 539/2001,[17] which replaced the earlier Regulation 549/1999 still adopted on the basis of the Maastricht Treaty, contains the common lists both of the countries whose nationals must be in possession of a visa in order to cross the external borders, and the countries whose nationals are exempted from that requirement. In 2006, the European Parliament and the Council adopted the Schengen Borders Code,[18] which contains all relevant rules on the abolition of border checks at internal borders, and on controls at the EU's external borders, and to this extent replaces the provisions of the Schengen Convention. In 2009, finally, the EU Visa Code[19] entered into force, which contains all rules on the procedures and conditions for issuing short-term visas, thus replacing the provisions on short-term visas of the Schengen Convention and the former Common Consular Instructions. With the entry into force of these two

[14] Since the Treaty of Lisbon, this Protocol has become Protocol No 23. The Intergovernmental Conference of the Amsterdam Treaty equally adopted Declaration No 18, which stated that 'Member States may negotiate and conclude agreements with third countries in the domains covered by Article 63(3)(a) of the Treaty establishing the European Community as long as such agreements respect Community law'. This declaration has not been repeated at the time of conclusion of the Lisbon Treaty.

[15] Art. 67(3) ECT. [16] Art. 67(1) and (4) ECT. [17] [2001] OJ L81/1.

[18] Council Regulation 562/2006, [2006] OJ L105/1.

[19] Regulation (EC) 810/2009, [2009] OJ L243/1.

Codes, the provisions of the Schengen Convention on migration policy have by now almost fully been replaced by secondary Union law.

As regards long-term stays, the ECT equally contained a relevant legal basis in Article 63(3)(a), which allowed the adoption of measures on immigration policy in the area of 'conditions of entry and residence, and standards on procedures for the issue by Member States of long-term visas and residence permits, including those for the purpose of family reunion'. However, the procedural conditions for the exercise of this competence reflected a far more hesitant approach to harmonization with respect to long-term stays. Measures under Article 63(3)(a) were still decided by the Council with unanimity, and after mere consultation of the European Parliament. When the Council, at the end of the transitional period, decided to render the co-decision procedure applicable to most remaining matters under Articles 62 and 63, it consciously excluded Article 63(3)(a) of the ECT from these improvements.[20] This clearly reflects the political sensitivity of long-term migration, including economic migration, which makes member states reluctant to relinquish control over this policy area.

Another important difference between long-term and short-term visa policy resulted from the last paragraph of Article 63, which provided that measures in the field of long-term migration were not subject to the five-year transitional period. Reflecting this difference, it is not surprising that the progress of harmonization in the area of long-term visas and migration policy has been far slower than it has been in the area of short-term visas.[21]

Measures concerning illegal immigration were covered by Article 63(3)(b) of the ECT, which gave the Community the power to adopt measures on 'illegal immigration and illegal residence, including repatriation of illegal residents'. Until the end of the transitional period, such measures were adopted by the Council by unanimity and after consultation of the European Parliament; after the end of the transitional period, the co-decision procedure became applicable.[22]

2. The Current Legal Bases of EU Migration Policy

This section will present the current legal bases of EU migration following the entry into force of the Lisbon Treaty, distinguishing between visa policy and border controls, long-term migration and the fight against illegal migration.

A. Visa policy and border controls

The Treaty of Lisbon has not fundamentally changed the powers of the EU in the field of visa policy and border controls. According to Article 77(1) of the Treaty on the Functioning of the European Union (TFEU), the Union shall develop a policy

[20] See Art. 1(2) Council Decision 2004/927/EC, [2004] OJ L396/45.
[21] See section 2(B) below for more details.
[22] Art. 1(2) Council Decision 2004/927/EC, [2004] OJ L396/45.

with a view to (a) ensuring the absence of any controls on persons, whatever their nationality, when crossing internal borders; (b) carrying out checks on persons and efficient monitoring of the crossing of external borders; and (c) the gradual introduction of an integrated management system for external borders. Noteworthy in this regard is the explicit stipulation 'whatever their nationality' in Article 77(1)(a), which makes clear that the absence of internal borders also benefits TCNs. This absence of internal borders at the same time contributes to making migration policy a matter of common interest for all member states.

According to Article 77(2) of the TFEU, the European Parliament and the Council, acting in accordance with the ordinary legislative procedure, shall adopt measures concerning:

(a) the common policy on visas and other short-stay residence permits;
(b) the checks to which persons crossing external borders are subject;
(c) the conditions under which nationals of third countries shall have the freedom to travel within the Union for a short period;
(d) any measure necessary for the gradual establishment of an integrated management system for external borders;
(e) the absence of any controls on persons, whatever their nationality, when crossing internal borders.

The scope of these measures corresponds in essence to the scope of the previous Article 62 of the ECT. A procedural difference lies in the fact that all relevant measures shall now be adopted following the ordinary legislative procedure by the European Parliament and the Council. This ends the historical oddity resulting from Article 67(3) of the ECT according to which the European Parliament was merely consulted on the measures concerning the uniform visa format and the visa list.

All issues mentioned in Article 77(2) of the TFEU are by now covered by common rules. As regards visa policy, the first question is which individuals must be in possession of a visa for crossing the external borders of the Union. This question is regulated by Council Regulation 539/2001.[23] Regulation 539/2001 contains the common lists both of the countries whose nationals must be in possession of a visa in order to cross the external borders, and the countries whose nationals are exempted from that requirement.[24] The visa regulation is based on the principle of reciprocity, which gives it a strong relevance for EU external relations.[25]

According to Article 20(1) of the Schengen Convention, one of the few provisions of the Schengen Convention[26] on visa policy which still remains in force,

[23] *Supra* n 17. In 2011, the Commission made a proposal for the revision of this regulation, which provides, inter alia, for a safeguard mechanism allowing the emergency reintroduction of visa requirements by member states in case of sudden migratory fluxes, COM (2011) 290 final/2.

[24] On this Regulation, see Meloni, 'The Development of a Common Visa Policy under the Treaty of Amsterdam' 42 *CMLR* (2005) 1357, at 1365 *et seq*.

[25] For the details of the reciprocity mechanism and its external implications, see section 4(A) below.

[26] Published in [2000] OJ L239/19.

nationals who are exempted from the visa requirement may move freely within the territories of the member states for a period of maximum three months during the sixth months following the date of their first entry. The purpose of the stay is not regulated. However, according to Article 4(3) of Regulation 539/2001, member states may provide for exceptions from the visa exemptions for persons carrying out a paid activity during their stay.

Pursuant to Article 1(2) of Regulation 539/2001, certain further categories of persons are exempted from the visa requirement. This includes in particular the holders of a local border traffic card issued by member states pursuant to the provisions of Regulation 1931/2006 on local border traffic.[27] However, the local border traffic card must be limited to the border area of the member state, and thus does not give full freedom to travel in the territory of all member states.

A further specific regime is the Facilitated Transit Document and Facilitated Rail Transit Document established by Council Regulation (EC) 693/2003.[28] These documents, which replace the visa and are issued according to facilitated procedures, are intended to facilitate transit by land for TCNs who must necessarily pass through the territory of EC member states in order to travel between two parts of their country which are not geographically contiguous. This scheme was put into place to address the difficulties of transit between the Russian region of Kaliningrad and the rest of Russia following the 2004 enlargement of the EC, which led to Kaliningrad being separated from the rest of Russia by EU member states.

The conditions and procedures for issuing short-term visas are now regulated in the Visa Code.[29] According to its Article 1(1), the Visa Code establishes the procedures and conditions for issuing visas for transit through or intended stays in the territory of the member states not exceeding three months in any six-month period. It contains detailed rules governing the issuance of short-term visas, including the type of visa, the member state responsible for the issuance, the forms to be used for visa applications, documentation to be provided by the applicant, conditions regarding the return and means of subsistence, the possibility of personal interviews, criteria for the examination of applications, etc.[30] Equally harmonized is the fee payable for a Schengen visa, which currently stands at €60.[31] According to Article 19 of the Schengen Convention, which is another of the few surviving provisions of the Schengen Convention on visa policy, TCNs who hold a Schengen visa may move freely through the territory of all Schengen states.[32] Interestingly, there are no limitations on the purpose of the stay. The format of short-term visas is harmonized by Regulation 1683/1995.[33] Moreover, the EU has also established a Visa Information System (VIS) which enables member states' authorities to enter and update visa data and to consult these data electronically.[34]

[27] [2007] OJ L29/3. On the external implications of this Regulation see section 4(E) below.

[28] [2003] OJ L99/8.

[29] See *supra* n 19.

[30] For more details see Peers, *supra* n 5, at 261 *et seq*.

[31] Art. 16(1) Visa Code.

[32] On the variable geometry of the Schengen area, see Martenczuk, *supra* n 2.

[33] [1995] OJ L164/1.

[34] Council Decision 2004/512/EC, [2004] OJ L213/5.

The rules governing the movements of persons across borders are now covered by the Schengen Borders Code.[35] The Borders Code establishes the rules on the crossing of both the internal and the external borders of the EU. As regards the external borders, the code establishes the conditions for the crossing of the borders by TCNs, which include inter alia the possession of a valid visa for those persons who must be in possession of a visa according to Regulation 539/2001, except where such persons have a residence permit.[36] In addition, the Borders Code contains detailed rules as regards the way in which controls at the external borders must be carried out. As regards internal borders, the Borders Code reaffirms the principle of the abolition of checks on persons at the internal borders regardless of nationality[37] and regulates the conditions for the temporary reintroduction of controls at the internal borders in exceptional cases. In order to coordinate the management of the EU's external borders, the EU has also set up a European Agency for the Management of Operational Cooperation at the External Borders (Frontex).[38]

B. Long-term migration

Long-term migration policy is now addressed in Article 79 of the TFEU. According to Article 79(1) of the TFEU, the Union shall develop a common immigration policy aimed at ensuring, at all stages, the efficient management of migration flows, fair treatment of TCNs residing legally in member states, and the prevention of, and enhanced measures to combat, illegal immigration and trafficking in human beings. According to Article 79(2), the European Parliament and the Council, acting in accordance with the ordinary legislative procedure, shall adopt measures in the following areas:

(a) the conditions of entry and residence, and standards on the issue by Member States of long-term visas and residence permits, including those for the purpose of family reunification;
(b) the definition of the rights of third-country nationals residing legally in a Member State, including the conditions governing freedom of movement and of residence in other Member States.

A major positive development in this respect is that measures regarding long-term migration, which until the Treaty of Lisbon were subject to unanimity in the Council, may now also be adopted according to the ordinary legislative procedure, which implies qualified majority voting in the Council. However, reflecting the sensitivity of long-term migration policy for certain member states, in exchange a new provision was added in Article 79(5) of the TFEU, according to which '[t]his Article shall not affect the right of Member States to determine volumes of admission of TCNs coming from third countries to their territory in order to seek work,

[35] *Supra* n 18. [36] Art. 5(1)(b) Borders Code. [37] Art. 20 Borders Code.
[38] Council Regulation (EC) 2007/2004, [2004] OJ L349/1.

whether employed or self-employed'.[39] In terms of competence, this provision constitutes a setback compared to the situation prior to the Treaty of Lisbon, where no similar limitation existed. The implications of this provision for a common external migration policy shall be considered later.

Reflecting the sensitivity of long-term migration, the progress in the establishment of common rules on long-term migration has been far slower than on visa policy.[40] Under the Treaty of Amsterdam, under which long-term migration remained subject to unanimity voting in the Council, the Community had initially succeeded in adopting only a rather limited number of acts on long-term migration, namely regarding the admission of TCNs for the purposes of research,[41] and for the purposes of studies, pupil exchanges, unremunerated training, or voluntary service.[42] An important measure adopted on the basis of Article 63(3)(a) of the ECT was also Directive 2003/86/EC regarding the right to family reunification.[43]

By contrast, progress on measures concerning economic migration has been very slow. An early proposal from the Commission for a directive on the conditions of entry and residence of TCNs for the purpose of paid employment and self-employed economic activities[44] did not find support in the Council, and was subsequently withdrawn.[45] However, a first important measure was finally adopted with Council Directive 2009/50/EC on the conditions of entry and residence of TCNs for the purposes of highly qualified employment.[46] This Directive is supposed to harmonize the conditions of entry and residence of highly skilled workers and their families. It introduces an 'EU Blue Card', which is intended to compete with the US 'Green Card'. The Directive harmonizes the criteria for admission and defines who is to be regarded as 'highly skilled'; this includes in particular that the blue card applicant must have a binding offer for a work contract with a salary of at least 1.5 times the average gross annual salary in the member state concerned.[47] Anticipating the entry into force of Article 79 (5) of the TFEU, the Directive also provides that it shall not affect the right of member states to determine volumes of admission of TCNs entering its territory for the purposes of highly qualified employment.[48] This is a serious limitation of the level of harmonization, since in principle, it seems to leave the possibility to member states even to set the level of admission to zero. Moreover, the Directive also allows member states to continue applying the 'more favourable provisions' contained in 'bilateral or multilateral agreements between one or more Member States and one or more third countries'.[49]

Since the entry into force of the Lisbon Treaty, a Directive has been adopted providing for a single application procedure for a single permit for TCNs to reside

[39] Similarly already Art. III-267(5) European Constitution.

[40] On the state of harmonization in this area, see in more detail, the contribution of Peers, *supra* n 5, at 433 *et seq*.

[41] Council Directive 2005/71/EC, [2005] OJ L289/15.

[42] Council Directive 2004/114/EC, [2004] OJ L375/12.

[43] [2003] OJ L251/12.

[44] COM (2001) 386 final.

[45] [2006] OJ C64/3. See also Peers, *supra* n 5, at 222 *et seq*.

[46] [2009] OJ L155/17. On this, see also Peers, *supra* n 5, at 437 *et seq*.

[47] Art. 5(3) Directive 2009/50/EC.

[48] Art. 6 Directive 2009/50/EC.

[49] Art. 4(1)(b).

and work in the territory of a member state.[50] Moreover, the Commission has made a number of further proposals. In particular, it has proposed to establish common rules regulating the conditions of entry and residence of TCNs for the purposes of seasonal employment[51] and in the framework of intra-corporate transfers.[52] Both proposals contain the same provisions concerning the right of member states to reject applications on the basis of the establishment of admission volumes and to apply more favourable provisions in international agreements as already contained in the Blue Card Directive.

C. Illegal migration

The legal bases for measures against illegal migration are now contained in Article 79(2)(c) and (d) of the TFEU, according to which the Parliament and Council shall, according to the ordinary legislative procedure, adopt measures concerning:

(c) illegal immigration and unauthorised residence, including removal and repatriation of persons residing without authorisation;

(d) combating trafficking in persons, in particular women and children.

Article 79(2)(c) of the TFEU corresponds in essence to the former Article 62(3)(b) of the ECT, but the explicit reference to combating trafficking is new. However, certain measures against trafficking were already based on Article 62(3)(b) of the ECT and criminal law aspects of trafficking continue to be covered by Article 83(1) of the TFEU. Therefore, the new letter (d) should not lead to major practical changes.

A further significant change is the new Article 79(3) of the TFEU, according to which the 'Union may conclude agreements with third countries for the readmission to their countries of origin or provenance of TCNs who do not or who no longer fulfil the conditions for entry, presence or residence in the territory of one of the Member States'. However, prior to the Lisbon Treaty, the Community had already adopted numerous readmission agreements based on its implicit external powers.[53] Therefore, the new Article 79(3) of the TFEU merely renders a previously implicit external competence explicit. The new provision, therefore, does not constitute an enlargement of the EU's external competences.

Prior to the entry in force of the Lisbon Treaty, the EU had already adopted a host of measures on the basis of the provisions above.[54] A number of measures aim at the prevention of illegal immigration. A first such measure was Directive 2001/51/EC,[55] which further elaborated the obligations of air carriers in the return of illegal immigrants already contained in Article 26 of the Schengen Convention. In 2002, the Council adopted, acting under the first and third pillar, two parallel measures concerning the definition and penalization of the facilitation of

[50] Directive 2011/98/EU, [2011] OJ L343/1. [51] COM (2010) 379 final.
[52] COM (2010) 378 final. [53] See section 6 below.
[54] For more detail see Peers, *supra* n 5, at 530 *et seq.* [55] [2001] OJ L187/45.

unauthorized entry, transit, and residence.[56] A further measure intended to assist in the prevention of illegal immigration was the Directive on the obligation of air carriers to communicate passenger data.[57] In 2009, Parliament and Council adopted a Directive providing for minimum standards on sanctions and measures against employers of illegally staying TCNs.[58]

Further measures aim at facilitating and coordinating the return of illegal immigrants by member states. A Council Directive of 2001 provides for the mutual recognition of expulsion decisions between member states;[59] a Directive of 2003 deals with assistance between member states in cases of transit for the purposes of removal by air;[60] another Directive of 2004 concerns the organization of joint return flights;[61] and a Directive of 2008 of the European Parliament and the Council sets out the common standards and procedures in member states for returning illegally staying TCNs.[62]

3. The Extent and Nature of EU External Competence in the Field of Migration Policy: General Considerations

Until the entry into force of the Treaty of Lisbon, the EU Treaties contained no specific provisions concerning the general principles on the extent and nature of the external competences of the European Community. Rather, these principles had to be derived from the case-law of the European Court of Justice (ECJ). The Treaty of Lisbon has, through the insertion of Articles 3 and 216(1) of the TFEU, attempted to codify the general principles resulting from the case-law of the Court.[63]

Article 216(1) of the TFEU deals with the existence and extent of the EU's external competence. According to this provision, the EU 'may conclude an agreement with one or more third countries or international organisations where the Treaties so provide or where the conclusion of an agreement is necessary in order to achieve, within the framework of the Union's policies, one of the objectives referred to in the Treaties, or is provided for in a legally binding Union act or is likely to affect common rules or alter their scope'. In the context of migration policy, the only explicitly provided external competence is the competence to conclude readmission agreements according to Article 79(3) of the TFEU. However,

[56] Council Directive 2002/90/EC, [2002] OJ L328/17; Council Framework Decision 2002/946/JHA, [2002] OJ L328/1.

[57] Directive 2004/82/EC, [2004] OJ L261/24.

[58] Directive 2009/52/EC, [2009] OJ L168/24.

[59] Directive 2001/40/EC, [2001] OJ L149/34.

[60] Council Directive 2003/110/EC, [2003] OJ L321/26.

[61] Council Directive 2004/573/EC, [2004] OJ L261/28.

[62] Directive 2008/115/EC, [2008] OJ L348/98.

[63] On this, see generally Cremona, 'Defining Competence in EU External Relations: Lessons from the Treaty Reform Process', in A. Dashwood and M. Maresceau (eds), *Law and Practice of EU External Relations* (2008) 34; on the situation prior to the entry into force of the Lisbon Treaty, see O'Keeffe, 'Exclusive, Concurrent and Shared Competence', in A. and C. Hillion (eds), *The General Law of E.C. External Relations* (2000) 179.

it is uncontested that the conclusion of international agreements may also be necessary to fulfil the objectives of the Union in other fields of migration policy. Whether and to which extent such necessity exists is largely a question for the political judgment of the competent institutions involved with the treaty-making process of the Union. In any event, the implicit external competence in this area has been exercised in numerous cases and is not contested.

Far more important and difficult to answer is the question whether, and to what extent, the external competences of the EU in the field of migration policy are exclusive in nature, or shared with the member states. This question is governed by Article 3 of the TFEU. The relevance of these provisions for migration policy shall be examined in the following sections.

A. Exclusive competence 'by nature'?

According to Article 3(1) of the TFEU, the Union shall have an exclusive competence for the following areas:

(a) customs union;
(b) the establishing of the competition rules necessary for the functioning of the internal market;
(c) monetary policy for the Member States whose currency is the euro;
(d) the conservation of marine biological resources under the common fisheries policy;
(e) common commercial policy.

It is immediately obvious that migration policy is not among the areas which are listed as falling under the exclusive competence of the Union in this provision. The provision is also clearly intended as enumerative. This notwithstanding, it appears useful to briefly compare the features of migration policy with those of the other policies included in Article 3(1), and notably the common commercial policy (CCP), and to reflect on the reasons for the non-inclusion of migration policy among the list of exclusive policies.

In this context, it should be recalled that the exclusive character of the policies mentioned in Article 3(1) of the TFEU was originally not explictly stated in the Treaties, but developed by the Court of Justice taking into account the objectives and the nature of the policy area as established by the Treaty. In its Opinion on the OECD's Local Cost Standard, the ECJ referred to the need to avoid differences in conditions of competition for the undertakings of member states in export markets.[64] In *Donckerwolcke*, the ECJ focused more sharply on the internal working of the EC customs union. The ECJ began by noting that according to Article 24 of the ECT, goods originating in third countries which have cleared customs may circulate freely throughout the customs union just like EC goods.[65]

[64] Opinion 1/75, *OECD Local Cost Standard*, [1975] ECR 1355, pt. 2.
[65] Case C-41/76, *Donckerwolcke*, [1976] ECR 1921, Rec. 17.

The Court continued by noting that this assimilation of third country goods to EC goods could only take full effect if goods are subject to the same conditions of importation regardless of the state in which they were put in free circulation.[66] Moreover, the Court also noted the existence of a transitional period, by the end of which all necessary measures should have been adopted, and concluded that after the end of the transitional period, member states could no longer take measures in the field without authorization from the EC.[67]

There are some striking similarities between the characteristics of the CCP referred to in this case-law, and the characteristics of migration policy in the Schengen area.[68] As in the customs union, TCNs are to some extent—although not completely—assimilated to EU nationals in the sense that they are dispensed from internal border controls, and have the right—within certain limits—to travel throughout the Schengen area. This means that the visa and migration policy of each member state can have an immediate impact on all other member states. This is most obvious for the risk of illegal immigration: a TCN who decides to overstay his or her visa may very well do so not in the member state which has issued the visa, but in any other member state. Similarly, if a member state issues a visa to a person who presents a security risk, this risk is borne not just by the issuing member state, but by all member states part of the Schengen area. Finally, recognizing this need for uniformity, there was also a transitional period of five years from the entry into force of the Treaty of Amsterdam within which the measures foreseen in Article 62 had to be adopted.

However, the parallels end there. Contrary to trade in goods, not all cross-border movements of persons have been made subject to EU discipline. This is most obvious for all persons entering the EU for the purpose of long-term stays. Even though in an area without internal borders, long-term migration can equally have an impact on all member states, and not just on the member state which authorizes the entry, the member states have not drawn the same consequence as for short-term visas, namely that the issuance of long-term visas and residence permits should be made subject to uniform principles. This was made clear by the explicit exclusion of the matters from the original five-year transitional period. An even clearer indication of the national reservations in this respect is constituted by the explicit reservation of the right of member states to determine volumes of admission of TCNs seeking work in Article 79(5) of the TFEU as introduced by the Treaty of Lisbon.

Overall, it is clear that neither in Amsterdam nor Lisbon, member states had the will to accept that the conferral of competences to the EU in the field of migration policy would automatically deprive them of all external competences in the area.

66 *Ibid.*, Rec. 25. 67 *Ibid.*, Recs. 26 and 32.

68 On this comparison, see also Peers, 'EU Borders and Globalisation', in K. Groenendijk, E. Guild, and P. Minderhoud (eds), *In Search of Europe's Borders* (2003) 45.

B. Other grounds for exclusive competence in the area of migration policy

Since migration is not an *a priori* exclusive competence, it is a shared competence. This is also made clear by Article 4(2)(j) of the TFEU, which lists the 'area of freedom, security and justice', of which migration policy is part, as an area of shared competence.

However, even in an area of shared competence, the EU's competence may become exclusive under certain conditions. These conditions are now codified in Article 3(2) of the TFEU, according to which the EU 'shall also have exclusive competence for the conclusion of an international agreement when its conclusion is provided for in a legislative act of the Union or is necessary to enable the Union to exercise its internal competence, or in so far as its conclusion may affect common rules or alter their scope'.

i. Exclusive competence 'by necessity'

A first question could be whether the conclusion of international agreements could be regarded as 'necessary to enable the EU to exercise its internal competence'. This ground of exclusive competence has its origins in Opinion 1/76, in which the Court of Justice held that the EC had an external competence when the conclusion of an international agreement was necessary for the attainment of the objectives of the ECT.[69] The concrete agreement at issue in Opinion 1/76 was aimed at reducing overcapacity in shipping on the Rhine through the creation of a laying-up fund. The ECJ considered that the conclusion of an international agreement, as opposed to autonomous measures, was necessary for the attainment of the EC's objectives in the field of transport because Swiss vessels were also navigating on the Rhine and, therefore, had to be brought into the mechanism.[70] In the later case-law of the Court, Opinion 1/76 has frequently been referred to as authority for the proposition that EC external competence will be exclusive when the Community's internal competence can be exercised only at the same time as its external competence.[71]

However, as is made clear in Article 3(2) of the TFEU, there must not only be an internal competence, but the internal and external competence must be linked in such a way that the former cannot be exercised without the latter. It is not clear that such a statement can be made for EU migration policy in general.[72] In this context, it is also noteworthy that the Court of Justice has never, since Opinion

[69] Opinion 1/76, *Laying-up Fund for Inland Waterway Vessels*, [1977] ECR 741, Rec. 3.

[70] *Ibid.*, Rec. 2.

[71] Opinion 1/94, *Accession to the WTO*, [1994] ECR I-5267, Rec. 85; Case C-467/98, *Commission/Denmark (Open Skies)*, [2002] ECR I-9519, Rec. 57; Opinion 1/2003, *Lugano Convention*, [2006] ECR I-1145, Rec. 115. Even though in Opinion 1/76 the Court had not explicitly referred to exclusive competence, this interpretation appears to be based on Opinion 1/76, Rec. 7 in which the Court had found that the participation of certain member states in the Agreement was justified exclusively for the purpose of making amendments to certain pre-existing conventions to which the member states were parties.

[72] The more specific issue of readmission agreements shall be considered below in section 6.

1/76, found EU competence to be exclusive on account of the necessity to attain an EU objective. For instance, in the *Open Skies* judgments, the Court found that the conclusion of an international air transport agreement was not necessary to achieve the objectives of the Community in the field of air transport. In particular, the Court found that the conclusion of a Community agreement was not necessary to avoid distortions in the common market resulting from bilateral air transport agreements, arguing that the Community institutions could prescribe a uniform approach to be followed through autonomous measures.[73] Accordingly, it is not likely that migration policy would generally be considered as an area where internal and external competences are so inextricably linked that EU competence must be regarded as exclusive.

ii. Exclusive competence by virtue of internal exercise

An arguably much more important ground for exclusive external competence is the case that the conclusion of an international agreement 'may affect common rules or alter their scope'. This ground of Article 3(2) of the TFEU codifies the judgment of the Court of Justice in the *ERTA* case, in which the Court held that, to the extent that the Community has adopted common rules, the member states may no longer accept international obligations which might affect those rules or alter their scope.[74] Given the highly developed character of EU rules in the field of visa policy and border controls, it is clear that affectation of common rules is a potential ground for exclusive EU competence in this area. But even in the area of long-term migration, where harmonization is still far from complete, *ERTA* exclusivity may come into play.

However, the application of the *ERTA* doctrine to migration policy raises a number of complex questions, which shall be examined hereunder. A first question originates from Protocol No. 23 on the external relations of the member states with regard to the crossing of external borders, according to which the provisions of the measures on the crossing of external borders included in Article 77(2)(b) of the TFEU 'shall be without prejudice to the competence of Member States to negotiate or conclude agreements with third countries as long as they respect Union law and other relevant international agreements'. First of all, this provision only covers border controls, but not visa policy or other measures of migration policy. Moreover, the Protocol allows member states only to negotiate international agreements to the extent that they 'respect Union law'. It appears that this must also include Article 3(2) of the TFEU, which lays down the conditions for the exclusivity of the Union's competence, as well as Article 2(1) of the TFEU, which provides that in an area of exclusive competence, member states may act only with the authorization of the Union.[75] This means that to the extent that the Union has legislated on a matter of migration policy, including border controls, member states may no longer act unless explictly authorized to do so by the Union.

[73] Case C-467/98, *Commission/Denmark (Open Skies)*, [2002] ECR I-9519, Rec. 59.

[74] Case C-22/70, *ERTA*, [1971] ECR 263, Rec. 22.

[75] See Peers, *supra* n 5, at 222 *et seq.*

Another interesting question arises from the case-law of the Court according to which, where a policy area is covered 'to a large extent' by common rules, any agreement falling within this policy area will fall under exclusive competence, without it being necessary for the subject matter of the agreement and the internal rules to coincide in every respect.[76] Given the rather complete state of common rules at least for the area of visa policy and border controls, the question could arise whether the internal rules have already reached a stage of completeness at which it may be said that visa policy is harmonized 'to a large extent', even if isolated matters are not specifically addressed in EU legislation. In fact, in the area of short-term visas, the Union has regulated essentially all relevant questions including the definition of the nationals who need to be in possession of a visa, the procedure and conditions for obtaining a visa, and the format and legal effect of the visa. Even where a specific condition or procedural requirement for the obtention of a short-term visa is not specifically addressed in Community legislation, it is doubtful that member states may negotiate and conclude international agreements on such a matter, since any such agreement would most likely also have an effect on other aspects of EU visa rules.

However, of relevance in this context is also the new Protocol No. 25 'on the exercise of shared competence', which has been introduced by the Treaty of Lisbon. According to this Protocol, '[w]ith reference to Article 2(2) of the Treaty on the Functioning of the European Union on shared competence, when the Union has taken action in a certain area, the scope of this exercise of competence only covers those elements governed by the Union act in question and therefore does not cover the whole area'. The question arises whether this Protocol could limit the application of the case-law referred to above. Given the reference to Article 2(2) in Protocol No. 25, and not Article 3(2) of the TFEU, it is not fully clear whether this Protocol is even meant to clarify the meaning of the latter provision. However, if yes, the Protocol could be read as also applying to the conditions of *ERTA* exclusivity. Even if this is the case, a second question arises, namely what is meant by the 'whole area' in Protocol No. 25. It appears that the area in question is the one covered by the shared competence of the Union, not the area covered by the act in question. Therefore, it is still possible that a particular act may be regarded as a 'complete harmonization' of the matters which fall within its scope. However, Protocol No. 25 may make it difficult to argue that the various acts adopted in the field of visa policy and border control constitute a 'complete harmonization' of the specific policy. Rather, the demonstration that the issue in question has in fact been covered in a relevant EU act will remain crucial.

A related question finally arises with respect to the numerous provisions of the Schengen *acquis*, which provide a certain discretion to member states in the application of visa rules. It is clear that the fact that member states implement the common rules as such does not affect the exclusivity of the EU's external competence, which depends merely on the extent of EU legislation. In this context,

[76] See Opinion 2/91, *ILO Convention No. 170*, [1993] ECR I-1064, Recs. 25–6; Opinion 1/2003, *Lugano Convention*, [2006] ECR I-1145, Rec. 126.

therefore, the fact that the common visa rules allow the administrative authorities to exercise a certain level of discretion does not mean that the question is not harmonized by EU rules. Otherwise, member states could bind themselves through international agreements to exercise the discretion conferred upon them in a particular way. Such an approach would not be conducive to the uniform application of EU rules and must, therefore, be regarded as incompatible with the *ERTA* case-law.

4. The External Dimension of Visa Policy

The Union has developed extensive external activities in the field of visa policy. In this section, a number of important cases and issues will be discussed. Some of these examples will provide further illustrations for the difficult division of competences between the EU and its member states in this field.

A. Visa waiver and reciprocity

A first significant issue for EU external relations in the field of visa policy has been ensuring visa reciprocity as regards the granting of visa-free status under Regulation 539/2001.

i. The reciprocity mechanism of Regulation 539/2001

The fifth recital of Regulation 539/2001 explains that the determination of the countries subject to the visa requirement and those exempt from it is to be made on a case-by-case basis, taking into account factors such as illegal immigration, public policy and security, the EC's external relations with third countries, and regional coherence and reciprocity.

Under the Regulation as originally adopted in 2001, the introduction of a visa requirement by an exempted third country for the nationals of any member states would automatically have led to the reintroduction of a visa requirement for the nationals of the third country within a period of 30 days. This provision was likely to cause considerable difficulties following the enlargement of the EU by ten new member states in May 2004. Since a number of third countries still required visas for most of the new member states, a strict application of the reciprocity mechanism would have meant the reintroduction of visa requirements for a number of important third countries, including the US, Canada, and Australia. This reintroduction might then in turn have triggered the reintroduction of visa requirements for all EU citizens.

In order to avoid this consequence, Regulation 539/2001 was amended[77] to render the reciprocity mechanism more flexible and allow more time for

[77] See Regulation 851/2005, [2005] OJ L141/3.

negotiations. Under the new mechanism, as set out in Article 1(4) of Regulation 539/2001, if a visa-exempted third country introduces a visa requirement for nationals of a member state, the member state concerned shall notify this to the Council and the Commission. The Commission shall then make the necessary contacts with the third countries in order to seek the re-establishment of reciprocity, and shall report on the outcome of its efforts to the Council. If reciprocity has not been re-established, the Commission may also propose the temporary or definitive reintroduction of the visa requirement for the third country concerned. However, contrary to the old system, there is no automaticity towards the re-establishment of the visa requirement, since the Commission is not obliged to propose the reintroduction of the visa requirement at any given point.[78]

ii. The application of the reciprocity mechanism

On the basis of these provisions, member states have notified a lack of reciprocity in a number of cases. Most of the member states concerned are from the 12 new member states which acceded in 2004 and 2007, but some older member states are also concerned. In each of these cases, the Commission initiated contact with the third countries concerned with a view to the re-establishment of visa reciprocity. The Commission prepares an annual report on application of the reciprocity mechanism, which explains the progress made and the problems remaining.[79] In no case has there been a reintroduction of the visa requirement by the EU, although the threat has been uttered in certain instances. In many cases, reciprocity has subsequently been re-established, although sometimes difficult negotiations and transition periods were necessary. Only in one case has there been a step backwards in terms of reciprocity when Canada reintroduced a visa requirement for Czech citizens in 2009 following a sudden increase of asylum seekers from the Czech Republic.[80] This problem is currently the subject of discussions between the EU and Canada.

A particularly important and instructive example of the benefits and limits of the reciprocity mechanism is the case of the US. The US initially maintained a visa requirement on all the new member states except Slovenia, plus Greece from among the old member states. This led the Commission in 2006 to consider the reimposition of visa requirements on US nationals holding diplomatic or official passports.[81] A particular problem arose, however, from the fact that the US, in

[78] A limited revision of the mechanism was proposed by the Commission in 2011; see COM (2011) 290 final. However, wider discussions on a reform of the reciprocity mechanism are still ongoing in the course of the legislative procedure.

[79] As the most recent examples, see Sixth Report on certain third countries' maintenance of visa requirements in breach of the principle of reciprocity, COM (2010) 620 final; Seventh Report, COM (2012) 681 final.

[80] See Special Report from the Commission, COM (2009) 562 final.

[81] See COM (2006) 568 final. See also Faull and Soreca, 'EU-US Relations in Justice and Home Affairs', in B. Martenczuk and S. van Thiel, *Justice, Liberty, Security; New Challenges for EU External Relations* (2008) 393, at 402 *et seq.*

order for third countries to qualify for the US Visa Waiver Program, also required cooperation on certain issues of law enforcement cooperation, which as such at the time fell outside the competence of the European Community. As a consequence, in 2008, a twin track approach was agreed according to which the Commission would continue discussion with the US regarding visa reciprocity on issues falling under Community competence, and the member states would engage in discussions with the US on law enforcement issues. Under the bilateral track, numerous member states have concluded with the US bilateral memoranda of understanding on cooperation in the field of antiterrorism and information sharing. As a consequence, currently only four member states (Bulgaria, Cyprus, Romania, and Poland) remain excluded from visa reciprocity.[82]

It must be acknowledged that the twin track approach has permitted progress in EU–US visa relations. Notwithstanding this, the division of competences between the EU and member states can be regarded as somewhat problematic. Already prior to the entry into force of the Lisbon Treaty, an argument could have been made that all preconditions for visa reciprocity must be regarded as affecting Regulation 539/2001 and, therefore, should be regarded as falling under exclusive competence. Following the entry into force of the Lisbon Treaty, it is now clear that matters falling under the twin track can equally fall under Union competence and, to the extent that they affect any EU common rules, under exclusive competence. In this respect, the European Commission has already announced that the twin track approach may require a reconsideration.[83]

At the same time, new difficulties have arisen as regards visa reciprocity with the US. First, the US introduced an Electronic System for Travel Authorization (ESTA), which requires an electronic registration via the internet prior to departure for passengers travelling under the visa waiver programme. The Commission considered initially that this system as such could not be regarded as tantamount to a visa requirement.[84] However, the US has now also added a fee to be paid on the occasion of the registration. The Commission has expressed concerns about this new element, but has not yet taken a definitive position as to whether the ESTA system or fee can be regarded as equivalent to a visa requirement.[85]

Overall, despite its limitations, the visa reciprocity mechanism must be regarded as a success. It has led to the reintroduction of visa-free status for numerous member states in many third countries. It is clear that for many member states, in particular the smaller ones, the difficulties of obtaining visa-free status would have been considerably larger. In this sense, the reciprocity mechanism offers a clear added value to member states. At the same, it also has its limits. First, certain conditions for obtaining visa-free status in third countries depend on actions of the member states in the field of law enforcement cooperation or document security. Secondly, the only sanction foreseen is the reintroduction of the visa requirement for the third country. However, such a reintroduction might in turn entail the reintroduction of visa requirements on all member states, which is a consequence

[82] COM (2010) 620 final, at 12f.
[83] COM (2010) 620 final, at 11.
[84] COM (2009) 560 final, at 7.
[85] COM (2010) 620 final, at 12.

which may seem equally undesirable. It is, therefore, not surprising that the institutions have so far shied away from the reintroduction of visa requirements.

iii. Visa waiver agreements

A new phenomenon that has developed concerning visa-free status are visa waiver agreements. Regulation 539/2001 does not necessarily require the conclusion of international agreements in order to ensure visa reciprocity. However, the conclusion of such agreements can sometimes be necessary by virtue of the requirements of the third country.

Moreover, visa waiver agreements have the advantage to the EU that the third country can normally no longer unilaterally revoke the visa-free status of the EU, or of any EU member state in particular. Politically the EU can, therefore, make the conclusion of such agreements a condition for the granting of visa-free status. This was done in 2006 with respect to the placing on the visa-free list of a number of small island nations in the Caribbean and the Indian Ocean (Antigua and Barbuda, Barbados, Mauritius, the Bahamas, the Seychelles, and St Kitts and Nevis). The corresponding visa waiver agreements were concluded in 2009.[86]

A particularly complex case arose in connection with Brazil. Brazil still continued to require visas for the nationals of a number of member states. When approached by the Commission pursuant to the reciprocity mechanism of Regulation 539/2001, Brazil indicated its willingness to lift these visa requirements, but subject to two conditions.[87] First, for reasons linked to its internal constitutional requirements, Brazil insisted on the conclusion of an international agreement on this matter. Secondly, Brazil also wished to maintain in force bilateral visa exemption requirements concluded with a number of member states prior to the entry into force of the Amsterdam Treaty. These agreements had the advantage of allowing a stay of up to six months, compared to only three months under Schengen rules. Moreover, according to Article 20(2) of the Schengen Convention, these agreements are not affected by the Schengen Rules and can, therefore, continue to be applied. For this reason, Brazil proposed to negotiate with the Community an international agreement covering only those EU member states with which it does not have a bilateral agreement. However, since such an approach would have been incompatible with the uniform application of EU law throughout the Union, this approach was rightly rejected by the Commission.[88]

In 2010, the Commission was finally able to conclude the negotiations for a visa waiver agreement covering the whole of the EU.[89] The agreement in principle authorizes only stays for a maximum period of three months during a six-month period and to this extent is in conformity with the internal EU *acquis*.[90] However,

[86] The Agreements are published along with the decisions on signature in [2009] OJ L169. The conclusion decisions are published on [2009] OJ L321, at 38–43. On this see also Peers, *supra* n 5, at 289.

[87] On this and the following, see the Commission reports under Art. 1(5)Regulation 539/2001, COM (2006) 568 final, at 5, and COM (2006) 3 final, at 7.

[88] See COM (2006) 568 final, at 5.

[89] For the text of the agreement, see [2012] OJ L255/4.

[90] Art. 5 of the Agreement.

the agreement covers only stays for the purposes of tourism and business.[91] To the extent that existing bilateral agreements grant visa exemptions for other purposes, these agreements may continue to apply.[92] This compromise partially also preserves the possibility to stay longer than three months within a six-month period, but at the same time will finally allow visa-travel for most categories of visitors from all member states. In parallel, a second visa exemption agreement was negotiated for holders of diplomatic, service, or official passports.[93] The reason for this separate agreement was that unlike the first, it need not be approved by the Brazilian Congress and can thus be concluded more quickly. Both agreements have in the meantime been concluded.[94]

B. The ADS Agreement with China

The first specific agreement negotiated and concluded by the EC in the field of visa facilitation was the ADS (Authorized Destination Status) Agreement with China.[95] The full title of the agreement is 'Memorandum of Understanding on visa and related issues concerning tourist groups from the People's Republic of China'. However, despite its denomination as a Memorandum of Understanding (MoU), the ADS Agreement is in fact a full-fledged international agreement. This is made clear in Article 8(6) of the Agreement, which explains that the agreement shall be legally binding on both parties.

The ADS Agreement is essentially an agreement facilitating the entry of Chinese tourist groups into the EU. For this purpose, Article 4 of the Agreement establishes a simplified procedure for the granting of tourist visas, under which designated Chinese travel agencies obtain, under certain conditions, the right to lodge visa applications on behalf of Chinese group travellers. The main facilitation compared to the normal rules was that the applicant is not called upon to appear in person to explain the reasons for the application.[96] The visa to be issued will be a Schengen visa limited to a period of validity of 30 days, and marked 'ADS'. Article 5 deals with issues relating to the illegal overstay of tourists who have entered with an ADS visa; it also contains a readmission clause obliging the Chinese authorities to readmit any Chinese national who has overstayed illegally. Article 6 of the Agreement establishes an ADS Committee composed of representatives of both sides, who will monitor the implementation of the agreement and decide on implementing arrangements. Some further issues regarding the selection of travel agencies, tour

[91] Art. 1 of the Agreement. These terms are defined further in Art. 3.

[92] Art. 7 of the Agreement.

[93] For the text of the Agreement, see [2011] OJ L66/2.

[94] See the Council decisions approving the conclusion in [2011] OJ L66/1 and [2012] OJ L255/3.

[95] [2004] OJ L83/12. The term 'Approved Destination Status' refers to the requirements of Chinese law, according to which Chinese tourists are generally granted exit permission only for travel through 'approved destinations', with which China has previously concluded an agreement regulating the modalities of such travel. On the complex variable geometry of this agreement, see Martenczuk, *supra* n 2, at 510 *et seq.*

[96] Point III.4 of the CCI as in force at the time of the conclusion of the agreement required personal interviews as the general rule, which could, however, be waived. According to Art. 21(8) Visa Code, personal interviews are only required in 'justified cases'.

leaders, and tour guides are dealt with in a non-binding declaration attached to the Agreement.[97]

The Agreement was concluded by the Council on the basis of Articles 62(2)(b)(ii) and (iv) and Article 63(3)(b) of the ECT (now Articles 77(2)(a) and 79(2)(c) of the TFEU). In accordance with Article 216(2) of the TFEU, the Agreement is binding on the institutions and the member states, and thus constitutes an integral part of EU law. Its provisions concerning the granting of Schengen visas therefore prevail over the provisions of the Visa Code, and must be directly applied by the consular authorities of the member states. In order to ensure uniform application of the agreement by the member states' consular authorities, the Commission issued a recommendation setting out further details.[98] This recommendation foresees, inter alia, that the withdrawal of accreditation of a Chinese travel agency by one member state shall have immediate effect for all other member states. Both the Agreement and the recommendation are unique in setting out a complex scheme for the granting of Schengen visas, which requires a high degree of consular cooperation between the member states in the third country concerned.

It is also worth noting that the conclusion of the ADS agreement was preceded by important disagreements as to the nature of Community competence.[99] Before China had started negotiating with the Community, it had already concluded a bilateral ADS MoU with Germany. This bilateral MoU was similar to the later EC agreement in most respects, in particular as regards the issuance of Schengen visas by the German authorities. However, unlike the later EC agreement, it did not contain a readmission clause for Chinese overstayers. When apprised of the German agreement, the Commission took the position that this agreement violated the exclusive competence of the Community over visa matters since it dealt with issues regulated in Community rules. This applied in particular to the possibility of requiring a personal interview, which was waived in the MoU. The fact that the EU rules left member states the possibility of deciding not to require a personal interview in concrete cases did not mean that member states have an external competence to waive such a requirement through the conclusion of an international agreement.

Moreover, it was clear that the bilateral agreement could lead to serious distortions within the Schengen area and the common market. As a result of the agreement, all Chinese group travellers would enter the Schengen area through Germany and typically use German airlines and travel operators. However, since the visas were Schengen visas, the tour groups would then travel throughout the Schengen area. And so, whereas the economic benefits of the agreement would be reaped largely by German operators, the risks in terms of illegal immigration and security would be borne by all member states. It was, therefore, clear that the bilateral agreement was incompatible with the uniform application of the Schengen *acquis*, as well as with the necessary solidarity required in an area without internal borders.

97 This solution was chosen since it was not certain that these matters fell under EC competence.

98 [2004] OJ L296/23.

99 See Kuijper, 'The Evolution of the Third Pillar from Maastricht to the European Constitution: Institutional Aspects' 41 *CMLR* (2004) 609, at 619.

Since the EC finally succeeded in negotiating a Schengen-wide agreement which superseded the German agreement,[100] the question of the compatibility of the bilateral agreement did not have to be decided by the ECJ. However, the case of the German ADS MoU illustrates the risks and costs of bilateralism in the area of visa policy in general, and short-term visas in particular. A strict application of the *ERTA* case-law is therefore necessary in order to protect the uniform application of the harmonized rules in the field of short-term visas.

C. Visa facilitation agreements

More recently, the EU has begun negotiating and concluding full-fledged visa facilitation agreements with a number of third countries. From the point of view of the EU, such agreements are frequently a *quid pro quo* for the conclusion of readmission agreements by third countries. At the same time, to the extent that EU nationals are also subject to a visa requirement by the third country, visa facilitation agreements also aim at ensuring reciprocal visa facilitation for EU nationals.

The first visa facilitation agreement to have been concluded by the EU is the agreement with Russia, which entered into force on 1 June 2007. This agreement contains reciprocal commitments in the field of visa facilitation on issues such as documentary evidence regarding the purpose of the journey, the issuance of multiple entry visas, fees for processing visas, length of application procedures, and the like. The agreement also contains an exemption from visa requirements for the holders of diplomatic passports.[101] The entry into force of the visa facilitation agreement was linked to the entry into force of the readmission agreement, thus reflecting the close link between the two agreements.[102]

In the meantime, the EU has concluded further visa facilitation agreements with Albania,[103] Bosnia and Herzegovina,[104] Georgia,[105] Macedonia,[106] Montenegro,[107] Moldova,[108] Serbia,[109] and Ukraine.[110] The countries of the Western Balkans (Albania, Bosnia, Macedonia, Montenegro, and Serbia) have, since the conclusion of the agreements, been moved to the visa-free list.[111] However, the visa facilitation agreements remain applicable for persons to whom the visa requirement still applies (notably those who still do not have biometric passports).[112] More recently, the EU has also signed visa facilitation agreements with Armenia[113] and with Cape Verde,[114] which would be the first non-European country with which such an agreement is concluded.

To the extent that EU nationals are exempted from visa requirements by these countries, the objective of the agreement is primarily to facilitate the issuance of

[100] Art. 7 of the EC–China ADS Agreement provides that any similar MoU or Agreement shall no longer be applied.
[101] Art. 11 of the Agreement. [102] Art. 15(2) of the Agreement.
[103] [2007] OJ L334/84. [104] [2007] OJ L334/96. [105] [2011] OJ L52/33.
[106] [2007] OJ L334/120. [107] [2007] OJ L334/108. [108] [2007] OJ L334/168.
[109] [2007] OJ L334/136. [110] [2007] OJ L332/66.
[111] Regulation 1244/2009, [2009] OJ L336/1; Regulation 1091/2010, [2010] OJ L329/1.
[112] See Peers, *supra* n 5, 291. [113] [2012] OJ L288/1. [114] [2013] OJ L3/1.

visas to the nationals of the third country. However, the agreements also contain a clause which renders the visa facilitation applicable to EU nationals in the event of the reintroduction of visa requirements by the third country.[115]

D. Seafarers' Identity Document Convention

A question of visa policy also arose in connection with ILO Convention No. 185 on the Seafarers' Identity Document. This Convention, which was adopted in 2003, establishes a Seafarer's Identity Document. According to Article 6 of the Convention, the contracting parties shall allow seafarers who hold the document to go on shore for the purposes of shore leave and transit and transfer to other vessels. In other words, the holder of the Seafarer's Identity Document is exempted from any visa requirement which might otherwise apply.

The EC was not involved with the negotiation of the Convention and, like all ILO Conventions, the Seafarers' Identity Document Convention did not contain a clause allowing the Community to become a party. However, the question arose whether the Convention did not partially fall under exclusive EC competence, given that the requirement to be in possession of a visa for crossing the external EU borders is harmonized through Regulation 539/2001. As the same time, however, Article 4 of that Regulation allows member states to exempt from the visa requirement the civilian crew of ships navigating in international waters. Accordingly, the question was whether this authorization contained in Regulation 539/2001 also implicated the power of member states to conclude international agreements.

In the final result, the EU institutions opted for a cautious approach and concluded that the member states needed to be authorized to conclude ILO Convention No. 185.[116] This authorization was granted to all member states through a Council decision based on Articles 62(2)(b)(i) in conjunction with Article 300 of the ECT (now Articles 77(2)(a) and 218 TFEU).[117] Through this authorization, member states were enabled to act whilst at the same time safeguarding the exclusive competence of the EU. This approach is in line with Article 2(1) of the TFEU according to which, in an area of exclusive competence, member states may only act if they are empowered to do so by the Union.

[115] See for instance Art. 1(2) of the Visa Facilitation Agreement between the EC and Ukraine. More recently, the EU has negotiated a number of technical amendments to the first generation of visa facilitation agreements. See for instance the decision on the signature of an agreement amending the visa facilitation agreement with Ukraine, [2012] OJ L199/1; text of the agreement in COM (2012) 265 final.

[116] This approach can be seen as having been subsequently confirmed by the Opinion of the Court of Justice on the similar constellation in the case of the Lugano Convention; Opinion 1/2003, *Lugano Convention*, [2006] ECR I-1145, Recs. 148–9.

[117] Council Decision 2005/367/EC, [2005] OJ L136/1. On similar authorizations in the field of private international law, see Hix, 'Mixed Agreements in the Field of Judicial Cooperation in Civil Matters: Treaty-Making and Legal Effects', in B. Martenczuk and S. van Thiel, *Justice, Liberty, Security: New Challenges for EU External Relations*, (2008) 211, at 236 *et seq.*

E. Local border traffic

External relations issues have also arisen in relation to the local border traffic rules set out under Regulation 1931/2006.[118] Frequently, the establishment of local border traffic requires the conclusion of appropriate arrangements or agreements between the neighbouring states. The conclusion of such agreements by member states alone would affect the EU's common rules on visa policy and border controls. However, at the same time, such agreements are frequently only of local interest and it might therefore not be efficient for the European Union to start negotiating all local border agreements.

For this reason, Article 13 of Regulation 1931/2006 authorizes member states to conclude or maintain international agreements with third countries concerning local border traffic.[119] These agreements must comply with the substantive requirements set out in the Regulation. Article 14 of the Regulation also foresees that agreements with third countries must ensure comparable rights to those granted to the border residents of the third country to any of the border residents of the member states, including EU nationals and TCNs legally resident in the border area. Moreover, before concluding or amending any such agreement, the member states concerned must consult with the Commission as to the compatibility of the agreement with the Regulation. If the Commission considers the agreement to be incompatible with the Regulation, it shall notify the member state, who shall take all appropriate steps to amend the agreement to remove the incompatibilities established.

With this approach, the principle of EU exclusive competence is upheld; however, member states are authorized to negotiate local border traffic agreements subject to detailed substantive and procedural conditions. This appears to be a sensible approach given the primarily local interest of the agreements concerned, which nonetheless ensures that common rules are respected and a common approach is followed.

F. Conclusion

Overall, it can be concluded that due to the complete internal harmonization of the field, EU external competence in the field of visa policy and border controls can today be regarded as exclusive.[120] The EU has also fully assumed the external dimension of this competence and concluded numerous international agreements. Member states have lost practically all external competences in the area. The only cases in which member states can still conclude international agreements on visa policy and border controls are those where there is an explicit authorization from the EU.

[118] [2007] OJ L29/3.

[119] For a first evaluation of this mechanism, see the Report from the Commission, COM (2009) 383 final.

[120] See also Peers, *supra* n 5, at 288.

5. The External Dimension of Long-term Migration

Reflecting the limited progress in internal legislation on long-term migration, the external dimension of EU long-term migration policy is still relatively underdeveloped.

In fact, the only agreements which so far contain provisions on migration policy are association agreements concluded by the EU based on Article 217 of the TFEU (former Article 310 of the ECT).[121] The most important example in this regard is the EEA Agreement, which extends the EU rules on free movement of workers to the citizens of Norway, Iceland, and Liechtenstein. An agreement on the free movement of workers was also concluded as part of a package of seven agreements with Switzerland.[122] Important rules governing the access of Turkish nationals to the labour market in the EU are also contained in Decision 1/80 of the EC-Turkey Association Council. These rules do not give Turkish workers a right of entry and residence into the EU; however, once a Turkish worker has been admitted and worked legally for certain periods of time, he gains a right to also apply for other jobs in the same member state.[123] The family members of Turkish nationals are equally granted rights to apply for jobs under certain conditions.[124] For the rest, association agreements generally do not contain rights of entry for foreign workers, but frequently contain provisions governing the treatment of foreign workers once they have been admitted, notably by prohibiting any discrimination as regards working conditions, remuneration, and dismissal,[125] or in the area of social security.[126]

An interesting legal question concerns the substantive legal basis in EU law underlying these commitments in EU association agreements. There is no doubt that in substance, such provisions on free movement of workers affect migration policy. However, most of the association agreements in question were concluded at a time when the EU did not yet have any competences in the field of migration policy. Therefore, the Court of Justice justified the inclusion of such provisions into EU association agreements as constituting an association with the EU's policy on free movement of workers.[127] However, now that the EU has explicit competences in the field of migration policy, the question arises whether such commitments still constitute an external dimension of the free movement of workers, or rather

[121] For more detail on this, see Peers, 'EU Migration Law and Association Agreements', in B. Martenczuk and S. van Thiel (eds), *Justice, Liberty, Security: New Challenges for EU External Relations* (2008) 53.

[122] 2002] OJ L114/6.

[123] Art. 6(1) Decision 1/80. According to settled case-law, this provision has direct effect in the EU legal order; see Case C-192/89, *Sevince*, [1990] ECR I-3461.

[124] See Art. 7, Decision 1/80. On the direct effect of this provision, see for instance Case C-351/95, *Kadiman*, [1997] ECR I-2133.

[125] On such a provision in the EU-Russia Partnership Agreement, see Case C-265/03, *Simutenkov*, [2005] ECR I-2579. As the Court held in Case C-97/05, *Gattoussi*, [2006] ECR I-11917, such provisions may in certain cases also limit the right of member states to refuse a residence permit.

[126] On the cooperation agreement with Morocco, see Case C-18/90, *Kziber*, [1991] ECR I-199.

[127] Case 12/86, *Demirel*, [1987] ECR 175, Rec. 9.

of migration policy. Since the ordinary legislative procedure applies to both areas, the practical relevance of this question is mainly whether the opt-outs from migration policy of the UK, Ireland, and Denmark apply to such commitments in association and partnership agreements. So far, the question could be left open since the agreements are usually in any event concluded as mixed agreements to which the three member states concerned also are parties.[128] However, the question may have to be resolved in cases where the agreement is not mixed, or where only the provisions on migration policy of an association agreement are to be amended, since in that event, it is necessary to know which member states participate in the internal decision-making in the Council.

Apart from the case of association and partnership agreements, the EU has so far not concluded any other agreements in the field of long-term migration policy. However, it is likely that the conclusion of such agreements will also become necessary in the future. In particular, where international agreements affect the slowly growing EU *acquis* on long-term migration, it will be for the EU to negotiate and conclude such agreements. Of course, the likelihood of this happening depends very much on the speed of growth of the EU *acquis* in this area. Moreover, there are some limitations not found in the area of short-term migration. In particular, Article 79(5) of the TFEU, which reserves for member states the right to determine the volume of admission of TCNs entering in order to seek work, also limits the external competence of the Union. This means that if the Union were to conclude agreements on long-term migration of workers, it would either have to reserve the right of member states to set admission volumes, or else participation by member states in the agreement would become necessary.

Moreover, many recent directives and proposals on long-term migration allow member states to continue to apply the 'more favourable provisions' of 'agreements concluded between one or more Member States and one or more third countries'.[129] It is not entirely clear whether this provision is supposed to apply only to agreements already in force at the time of the adoption of the agreement, or also to agreements concluded thereafter. However, if the provisions in question are to be interpreted as also applying to future agreements, then they effectively limit the *ERTA* effect of the internal harmonization. The directives in this case become essentially minimum rules, and member states retain an external competence to conclude international agreements exceeding those rules.[130]

Overall, it can be concluded that the external dimension of long-term migration policy is still largely undeveloped, and it remains to be seen what the future development will be given the political and legal constraints described.

[128] On this, see Martenczuk, *supra* n 2, at 518 *et seq*.

[129] For the Blue Card Directive, see *supra* n 46.

[130] On the point that minimum standards do not create an exclusive external competence see Opinion 2/91, *ILO Convention No 170*, [1993] ECR I-1061, Rec. 18.

6. The External Dimension of the Fight against Illegal Migration

The external dimension of the EU policy concerning the fight against illegal migration has primarily centred on the issue of readmission of illegal immigrants by their countries of origin or transit. The significance of this issue is illustrated by the fact that this has now become an explicit external competence of the EU through the inclusion of Article 79(3) of the TFEU.

The return of illegal immigrants to the third countries of origin or transit naturally requires cooperation of the third countries concerned. In this context, even though every country is obliged to admit its own nationals, difficult situations can still occur. In particular, a frequent problem is that illegal immigrants destroy their identification documents. In this case, the nationality may have to be established in cooperation with the third country of origin. Specific difficulties also arise if return is sought to a country of transit rather than the country of origin, in which case a readmission obligation may not exist under general international law.

The Union's external activities in the field of readmission predate the entry into force of the Treaty of Amsterdam. Already in 1995, the Council had agreed on a standard 'readmission clause' which was to be inserted into association and cooperation agreements to be concluded by the Union and its member states.[131] This clause was initially to be inserted under sole member states' competence. However, with the entry into force of the Amsterdam Treaty, the Community became competent. Thereafter, disagreements soon arose as to under whose competence such 'readmission clauses' would be concluded. This issue became particularly controversial with respect to the readmission article contained in the Cotonou Agreement with the countries of Africa, the Caribbean, and the Pacific (ACP) signed in June 2000.[132] This Agreement contained, in Article 13(5)(c), a readmission obligation and a commitment on the part of the parties to conclude more detailed readmission agreements on request. However, the Commission and the member states could not agree on whether such future agreements should be concluded by the Community or the member states. In the end, this question was deliberately left open, and a Declaration of the Council and Commission declared that Article 13(5) should be 'without prejudice to the internal division of powers between the Community and its Member States for the conclusion of readmission agreements'.[133]

Notwithstanding this disagreement, the Community soon began to actively exercise its external competences for readmission policy.[134] It has by now concluded

[131] See Peers, *supra* n 5, at 586. [132] [2000] OJ L317/1.

[133] Declaration II to the Cotonou Agreement, [2000] OJ L317/316.

[134] On the following, see also Schieffer, 'Readmission and Repatriation of Illegal Residents', in B. Martenczuk and S. van Thiel, *Justice, Liberty, Security: New Challenges for EU External Relations* (2008) 89; Peers, *supra* n 5, at 586 *et seq.*

readmission agreements with 13 third countries or territories: [135] Hong Kong,[136] Macao,[137] Sri Lanka,[138] Albania,[139] Russia,[140] Ukraine,[141] the former Yugoslav Republic of Macedonia,[142] Bosnia and Herzegovina,[143] Montenegro,[144] Serbia,[145] Moldova,[146] Pakistan,[147] and Georgia.[148] Agreements with Armenia,[149] Cape Verde,[150] and Turkey[151] are in the process of conclusion, as negotiations with a number of other countries are still ongoing (Algeria, Belarus, China, and Morocco). All concluded agreements are similar in content. They establish the basic readmission obligation for the parties' own nationals, and also for illegal immigrants for whom it can be proven that they have entered illegally, coming directly from the territory of the other contracting party, or holding a residence permit or visa from that party. The agreements apply only to individuals who no longer fulfil the conditions for residence in the contracting party and are without prejudice to the obligations of the parties to grant refugee protection or asylum. The agreements then set out the readmission procedure to be respected as well as means of evidence concerning nationality. A Joint Committee supervises the execution of the Agreement.

Despite the considerable number of readmission agreements concluded by the EU, the negotiation of such agreements has proved difficult and time-consuming. This is due to the fact that the conclusion of readmission agreements is primarily in the interest of the Union, and not of the third countries which are countries of origin or transit of illegal immigrants. As a consequence, additional incentives are frequently needed to bring the negotiations to a conclusion.[152] In some cases (Hong Kong and Macao), the readmission agreement was a quid pro quo for the granting of visa-free status; in other cases (Ukraine, Russia, the Western Balkan countries, Moldova, and Georgia), the readmission agreement was concluded simultaneously with a visa facilitation agreement, and was a precondition for the entry into force of the latter.[153] Additional difficulties arise from the EU's insistence on the inclusion of a readmission obligation for TCNs, which has been met with resistance from some third countries. On the basis of this experience, the Commission has announced that it will propose the inclusion of TCNs only in cases where there is a specific need given the geographical position and the migration flows.[154]

An open legal question regarding readmission agreements is the nature of the EU's competence for the conclusion of such agreements. In fact, despite the EU's extensive activities in the field, numerous member states have concluded bilateral

[135] For an overview, see Evaluation of EU Readmission Agreements, COM (2011) 76 final. A readmission clause was also contained in the ADS agreement with China (see section 4(B) above).
[136] [2004] OJ L17/23. [137] [2004] OJ L97/97. [138] [2005] OJ L124/41.
[139] [2005] OJ L304/14. [140] [2007] OJ L129/38. [141] [2007] OJ L332/46.
[142] [2007] OJ L334/1. [143] [2007] OJ L334/65. [144] [2007] OJ L334/25.
[145] [2007] OJ L334/45. [146] [2007] OJ L334/148. [147] [2010] OJ L287/50.
[148] [2011] OJ L52/45.
[149] Commission Proposal for the conclusion of the agreement, COM (2012) 704 final.
[150] Commission Proposal for the conclusion of the agreement, COM (2012) 557 final.
[151] Commission Proposal for the conclusion of the agreement, COM (2012) 239 final; Council Decision approving signature of the agreement, [2012] OJ L244/4.
[152] See 'Evaluation of EU Readmission Agreements', COM (2011) 76 final, at 6 *et seq*.
[153] For instance, see Art. 14(2) Readmission Agreement with Ukraine (*supra* n 110).
[154] 'Evaluation of EU Readmission Agreements', COM (2011) 76 final, at 9.

readmission agreements with third countries and continue to negotiate and conclude such agreements. It is clear that where the EU has already concluded an agreement, this agreement will supersede bilateral agreements of the member state covering the same matter.[155] Similarly, where the Commission has received a mandate to negotiate a readmission agreement with a particular third country, it would no longer be compatible with the duty of cooperation resulting from Article 4(3) of the TEU for a member state to negotiate or conclude a bilateral agreement on the same matter with the same country.

However, the question is whether EU competence for readmission agreements should not in general be regarded as exclusive in nature. Of course, such exclusivity cannot follow from the principles of the *ERTA* case-law, since readmission agreements typically do not affect common rules or alter their scope. By contrast, a possible ground of exclusive competence could be the second alternative of Article 3(2) of the TFEU, according to which EU competence is exclusive if the conclusion of the international agreement 'is necessary to enable the Union to exercise its internal competence'. It could be argued that given the need for cooperation of third countries for a successful return of illegal immigrants, the conclusion of readmission agreements is indeed indispensable for the EU to attain its objectives.[156] This argument receives further support from the inclusion of an explicit competence for readmission agreements in Article 79(3) of the TFEU. However, in the absence of clear guidance from the case-law of the Court on this ground, it is impossible to predict whether such reasoning would succeed in Court. However, it is clear that the current division of competences—where the EU negotiates with some third countries on readmission and member states negotiate with others—is highly unusual and not compatible with the objective of a coherent and unified external policy on readmission. Sooner or later, EU competence in the field of readmission will, therefore, have to be recognized as exclusive in nature.

For the remainder, EU external activities in the area of illegal immigration have been limited to the conclusion of two Protocols—the Protocol Against the Smuggling of Migrants and the Protocol Against the Trafficking in Persons, which both supplement the United Nations Convention against Organized Crime.[157] Both Protocols affected certain EU common rules, including the Directive on the Facilitation of Unauthorized Entry, and therefore fell partially under exclusive EU competence. Any future agreement that affects the slowly growing internal *acquis* on illegal migration will of course also have to be concluded by the European Union.

[155] This is confirmed by a clause on the relation to bilateral readmission agreements contained in all of the agreements referred to above (see for instance Art. 19 of the Agreement with Sri Lanka and Art. 18(2) of the Agreement with Russia).

[156] On this see Schieffer, *supra* n 134, at 102 *et seq.* and Kuijper, *supra* n 99, at 617–18.

[157] See [2006] OJ L262/34 (Smuggling Protocol) and [2006] OJ L262/51 (Trafficking Protocol).

7. Visa Policy and Other EU External Policies

This section will examine the relationship between migration policy and certain other external relations policies, namely the common foreign and security policy (CFSP), the common commercial policy, and development cooperation with third countries.

A. Migration policy and CFSP

In recent years, migration-related measures have become a foreign policy tool commonly used in the context of the CFSP. Most importantly, the EU has in a number of cases imposed travel bans on the leaders of third countries or organizations which the EU intends to sanction.[158] Such travel bans oblige member states to prevent the entry into, or transit through, their territory of the persons concerned. The bans prevent the granting of both visas, and of long-term residence permits, and thus have a direct link to migration policy. Still, such travel bans are adopted purely through CFSP measures and implemented by the member states individually.[159] This contrasts with trade sanctions or measures affecting capital movements and payments, which are implemented through regulations based on the specific legal bases of Article 215 of the TFEU.

In some cases, it may also be the granting of a visa or residence permit which becomes a foreign policy instrument. In 2002, the EU adopted a common position concerning the temporary reception of 12 Palestinians who had to be evacuated from the Bethlehem Church of Nativity.[160] The common position stated that the Palestinians concerned shall obtain national permits to enter the territory of the member states and stay for a period of up to 12 months.[161]

This practice of regulating migration issues in CFSP actions is doubtful from a legal point of view. According to Article 40 of the TEU, the implementation of the CFSP may not affect other competences of the EU, and vice versa. The Court of Justice has clarified that there is an affectation whenever a measure adopted on the basis of CFSP could have been adopted on the basis of non-CFSP competences.[162] However, precisely this seems to be the case for both travel bans and reception measures. Regardless whether the intended stay is short-term or long-term, the

[158] See Common Position 2004/293/CFSP on measures in support of the effective implementation of the mandate of the International Criminal Tribunal for the former Yugoslavia, [2004] OJ L94/65; Common Position 2004/661/CFSP concerning restrictive measures against certain officials of Belarus, [2004] OJ L301/67; Common Position 2006/318/CFSP on restrictive measures against Burma/Myanmar, [2006] OJ L116/77; most recently, see Art. 5 Council Decision 2011/137 concerning restrictive measures in view of the situation in Libya, [2011] OJ L58/53.

[159] Each member state may also issue an alert through the Schengen Information System in accordance with Art. 96 of the Schengen Convention.

[160] Common Position 2002/400/CFSP, at 33.

[161] *Ibid.*, Art. 3.

[162] Case C-176/03, *Commission v. Council*, [2005] ECR I-7879, Rec. 40; Case C-170/96, *Commission v. Council*, [1998] ECR I-2763, Rec. 17.

Union clearly has competence, on the basis of Articles 77(2)(a) and 79(2)(a) of the TFEU, to establish the conditions under which visas or residence permits shall be granted or refused. The fact that such measures may be politically motivated does not exclude them from falling within the scope of migration policy. In fact, in its settled case-law, the Court has held that a trade ban does not cease to be a commercial policy measure merely because it is also motivated by foreign policy considerations.[163] It is not clear why a different approach should apply to migration policy.[164]

Prior to the entry into force of the Lisbon Treaty, the fact that travel bans had no legal basis in Community law meant that the Court of Justice did not have jurisdiction to review the legality of such measures.[165] These consequences in terms of availability of judicial review have been mitigated by the Lisbon Treaty. According to Article 275(2) of the TFEU, the Court now has jurisdiction 'to rule on proceedings, brought in accordance with the conditions laid down in the fourth paragraph of Article 263 of this Treaty, reviewing the legality of decisions providing for restrictive measures against natural or legal persons adopted by the Council on the basis of Chapter 2 of Title V of the Treaty on European Union'. Unlike in Article 215(1) of the TFEU, restrictive measures in Article 275(2) are not limited to economic and financial matters and, therefore, also include travel bans. However, other differences remain. In particular, Article 275(2) only covers annulment action. This means for instance that requests for preliminary rulings based on Article 267 of the TFEU on the validity or interpretation of CFSP decisions ordering travel bans still remain excluded.

B. Migration policy and the common commercial policy

Points of contact between the migration policy and the common commercial policy exist in particular with respect to trade in services.[166] Classical trade policy concerns trade in goods and as such does not directly concern cross-border movements of persons. However, migration policy and trade policy may come into contact when it comes to trade in services. As the Court of Justice explained in Opinion 1/94, all modes of service provision other than GATS mode 1 (cross-border provision of services) are characterized by the movement of persons, be it the consumer or the provider of the service. This close link with the movement of persons was the reason the Court considered in Opinion 1/94 that all

[163] Case C-70/94, *Werner*, [1995] ECR I-3139; Case C-83/94, *Leifer*, [1995] ECR I-3231.

[164] This view also finds support in Declaration No. 16 to the Treaty of Amsterdam, which provided that 'foreign policy considerations of the Union and the Member States shall be taken into account in the application of Art. 62(2)(b) of the Treaty' (now Art. 77(2)(a) TFEU).

[165] See the former Art. 46 TEU.

[166] Similar issues may also arise with respect to investment protection, which since the Treaty of Lisbon is also within the scope of the CCP, to the extent that investment protection treaties increasingly also address issues concerning the cross-border movement of staff or personnel of investors (on this see UNCTAD, *Bilateral Investment Treaties 1995-2006, Trends in Investment Rulemaking*, at 69 *et seq.*).

modes of service provision other than cross-border provision of services could not be assimilated to trade in goods and, therefore, did not fall under the CCP.[167]

This situation already changed with the entry into force of the Treaty of Nice, which conferred on the Community a shared competence for trade in services.[168] Further changes were made by the Treaty of Lisbon, which fully integrated trade in services into the scope of the CCP.[169] As a consequence, the EU now has exclusive competence over all matters regarding trade in services, regardless of whether they involve cross-border movements of persons or not.

Wherever the service providers or service consumers of the parties are crossing a frontier, be it for short- or long-term stays, the question arises how such agreements relate to migration policy. On the one hand, it is clear that trade agreements should not normally prevent the application of general visa rules, for instance the right to refuse a visa to an individual who presents a security risk or a risk of illegal immigration. On the other hand, neither should visa rules be used in such a way as to frustrate the free flow of services in accordance with the commitments of the agreement. This is in essence also what paragraph 4 of the Annex on Movement of Natural Persons Supplying Services under the WTO Agreement on Trade in Services (GATS) provides, which specifies that the GATS 'shall not prevent a Member from applying measures to regulate the entry of natural persons into, or their temporary stay in, its territory . . . provided that such measures are not applied in such a manner as to nullify or impair the benefits accruing to any Member under the terms of a specific commitment'.[170]

However, if no specific provisions are included, international agreements in the field of trade in services may have a direct impact on migration policy. A useful example is provided by the judgment of the Court of Justice in the *Soysal* case.[171] This judgment resulted from a case brought by Turkish lorry drivers against the requirement to obtain visas in order to provide services in the form of the international transportation of goods by road. According to Regulation 539/2001, Turkish nationals must in principle be in possession of a visa to cross the external borders of the European Union. However, on 1 January 1973, when the additional protocol entered into force, Turkish nationals who were engaged in the international transportation of goods by road for a period of no more than two months did not have to obtain a visa for entering Germany.

The applicants argued that the introduction of the visa requirement, which had already been introduced in Germany in the 1980s but was not based on Regulation

[167] Opinion 1/94, *Accession to the WTO*, [1994] ECR I-5267, Recs. 44–7.

[168] Former Art. 133(5) ECT. For a detailed analysis of this provision, see Herrmann, 'Common Commercial Policy after Nice: Sisyphus Would Have Done a Better Job' 39 *CMLR* (2002) 7.

[169] Art. 207(1) TFEU. See Müller-Graff, 'The Common Commercial Policy Enhanced by the Reform Treaty of Lisbon?', in A. Dashwood and M. Maresceau, *Law and Practice of EU External Relations* (2008), at 188.

[170] More generally on this J. Trachtman, *The International Law of Economic Migration* (2009), at 241 *et seq.*; Hilpold, 'Migration und Internationales Wirtschaftsrecht', in P. Hilpold and C. Perathoner, *Immigration und Integration* (2010) 13, at 20 *et seq.*; Grynberg and Qalo, 'Migration and the World Trade Organisation' 41 *Journal of World Trade Law* (2007) 751.

[171] Case C-228/06, *Soysal*, [2009] ECR I-1031.

539/2001, constituted a violation of the standstill clause contained in Article 41(1) of the Additional Protocol of 1973 to the EC-Turkey Association Agreement, according to which the 'Contracting Parties shall refrain from introducing between themselves any new restrictions on the freedom of establishment and the freedom to provide services'. In its judgment, the Court first of all confirmed its earlier case-law according to which Article 41(1) of the Additional Protocol precludes generally the introduction of any new measures having the object or effect of making the exercise by a Turkish national of the economic freedoms on the territory of a member state subject to stricter conditions than those which applied to him at the time when the Additional Protocol entered into force with regard to the member state concerned.[172] It then went on to confirm that the visa requirement had to be regarded as a new restriction on the freedom to provide services, and was, therefore, incompatible with Article 41(1) of the Additional Protocol.[173] The Court explicitly noted that the visa requirement resulted from an EU measure, namely Regulation 539/2001. However, in this regard, the Court held that 'it is sufficient to recall that the primacy of international agreements concluded by the Community over provisions of secondary Community legislation means that such provisions must, so far as is possible, be interpreted in a manner that is consistent with those agreements'.[174] Given the fact that the provisions of Regulation 539/2001 were rather clear, the Court of Justice in reality thus held that the Regulation had to be set aside to the extent that it conflicted with Article 41(1) of the Additional Protocol.

The practical consequence of the judgment is that the visa requirement resulting from Regulation 539/2001 cannot be applied to Turkish nationals who provide services and were not subject to a visa requirement in the member state concerned at the time of entry into force of the Additional Protocol. The Commission has issued practical guidelines for the application of the *Soysal* judgment, according to which visa-free entry is possible in Germany and Denmark, these being the only member states where no visa requirement existed at the time.[175] For transit through other member states a visa is still required. Whereas the practical impact of the judgment is thus likely to be limited, it is nonetheless of great legal interest, since it shows that commitments on trade contained in international agreements may limit the applicability of EU migration rules.

C. Development cooperation and cooperation with other third countries on migration issues

Migration policy may also become an issue in relation to development cooperation and cooperation with other third countries pursuant to Articles 208 and 212 of the TFEU. In fact, according to the case-law of the Court of Justice, development

[172] *Ibid.*, Recs. 47–8, referring to Case C-37/98, *Savas*, [2000] ECR I-2927, Recs. 69 and 71; Joined Cases C-317/01 and C-369/01, *Abatay and ors*, [2003] ECR I-12301, Recs. 66 and 117.

[173] *Soysal*, *supra* n 171, Rec. 55.

[174] *Soysal*, *supra* n 171, Rec. 59.

[175] COM (2009) 7376 final. These guidelines take the form of an amendment to the *Practical Handbook for Border Guards* (Schengen Handbook).

cooperation and other cooperation policies may also address issues which are root causes of underdevelopment.[176] Moreover, the Court has confirmed that cooperation policies can also address areas of cooperation which internally would fall under different policy areas of the EU, or even outside EU competence, provided that the obligations in this area do not take on such a weight as to constitute objectives distinct from development cooperation.[177]

An efficient migration policy, and in particular efficient control of the external borders, may be a necessary element for sustainable development in third countries. For this reason, most of the cooperation agreements concluded by the Union have provisions on cooperation on migration policy.[178] Moreover, the main development and cooperation finance instruments of the European Union allow the financing of cooperation measures in the area of migration and asylum.[179] Of course, it is clear that such measures must be primarily in the interest of the third country concerned. Measures which directly affect the way migration policy is conducted within the EU have to be based on the appropriate legal basis of Articles 77, *et seq.* of the TFEU.

9. Conclusion

The European Union is increasingly asserting itself as an international actor in the field of migration policy. This development is the logical consequence of the increased harmonization in this area of EU law. It also reflects the increased importance of issues linked to legal immigration in international relations.

However, the division of competences between the EU and its member states in this area still remains uneasy. Migration policy is not yet an area which could be regarded as falling in its entirety under the exclusive competence of the EC. Rather, the EU has exclusive competence only to the extent that it has achieved internal harmonization. Whereas the state of internal harmonization for visa policy and border controls must be regarded by now as more or less complete, with the consequence that member states can no longer negotiate international agreements in this area, this is not so for the rules governing long-term stays. Accordingly, with

[176] Case C-91/05, *Commission v. Council*, [2008] ECR I-3651, Recs. 98–9 (on Small Arms collection project); C-403/05, *European Parliament v. Commission*, Case C-403/05, [2007] ECR I-9045, Recs. 57–8 (Philippines Border Management Project). It should be noted that the annulment by the latter judgment of the Commission's financing decision for lack of legal basis was due to the fact that the basic regulation applicable at the time did not contain a provision covering the objectives pursued. However, the Court did not exclude that in secondary legislation, Parliament and Council could enable the Commission to finance similar projects.

[177] Case C-268/94, *Portugal v. Council*, [1996] ECR I-6177, Rec. 39.

[178] See for instance Art. 13 of the Cotonou Agreement with the ACP Countries.

[179] See Regulation 1905/2006 establishing a development cooperation instrument, [2006] OJ L378/41 (Art. 16); Regulation 1638/2006 establishing a neighbourhood and partnership programme, [2006] OJ L310 (Art. 2(r)). Originally, this matter was covered by Regulation 491/2004 establishing a programme for financial and technical assistance to third countries in the areas of migration and asylum (AENEAS), [2004] OJ L80/1, which was based on Arts. 179 and 181 ECT.

respect to long-term visas and residence permits, the Union and its member states still share competences. Moreover, the explicit reservation of the member states' right to determine admission volumes of TCNs seeking work has made the effective regulation of economic migration at EU level more difficult, and introduces an area of member state exclusive competence. Even more awkward is the division of competences in the area of illegal migration, where the EU and member states both negotiate readmission agreements with third countries.

It is to be hoped that the current division between Union and national competence will only be of a transitional nature. For trade in goods, it has been recognized for decades that rules governing the external customs regime of the Community must be uniform, and must be applied in a uniform manner. The same development should also unfold for the external borders of the area of justice, liberty, and security, in which not only EU nationals, but also TCNs are able to move freely and unimpeded by internal borders. Since a chain can only be as strong as its weakest link, the goal of EU migration policy must, therefore, be the full harmonization of all rules governing entry into the Union by TCNs. Time will tell whether there is sufficient political will to achieve such full harmonization, in particular in the area of economic migration.

5

Which Borders for the EU Immigration Policy? Yardsticks of International Protection for EU Joint Borders Management

Seline Trevisanut

The external borders of the European Union (EU) are both its own borders and those of its member states. Their legal regime is the product of competition between the domestic and supranational spheres of governance. While EU institutions strive for integrated border management (IBM), member states tend to resist such ambitions and seek to stay in charge of decision-making processes. At the same time they need mechanisms at the European level for a whole range of reasons, among others to remedy the repercussions of open internal borders as well as to shift and share the burdens of external border control. This tension pervades the politics, law, and legal practice on the EU's external borders. Notably, it has the potential to undermine full compliance with obligations stemming from human rights law and international protection.

Member states' particular self-understanding, their relationship with neighbouring countries, and their powers in controlling their external borders have so far stood in the way of a level of European integration that would allow for a coherent and much needed management of external borders. The initial difficulties were mainly related to the member states' reluctance to delegate powers in such a traditional field of governance and to the resulting lack of sufficient competences for the Community to achieve an integrated and coherent policy. But the events of 11 September 2001 as well as the following security imperatives boosted political momentum, moving the integration process forward in this field.[1]

In November 2001, the European Commission's communication 'On a Common Policy on Illegal Immigration'[2] highlighted the need for a 'coherent strategy' on European border management. The following Laeken European Council Conclusions of

[1] Carrera, 'Towards a Common European Border Service?', CEPS Working Document No. 331, June 2010, at 2. Boswell affirms that 'the received wisdom is that 9/11 provided an opportunity for the securization of migration'; see Boswell, 'Migration Control in Europe after 9/11: Explaining the Absence of Securization' 45 *Journal of Common Market Studies* (2007) 589, at 589.

[2] COM (2001) 672 final, at 9.

December 2001 reiterated the necessity of more effective and integrated management of the EU external borders.[3] The link between border management and control over criminal activities, including irregular migration, has progressively gained importance after the terrorist attacks in Madrid (2004) and London (2005).[4] In the Declaration on the occasion of the 50th anniversary of the signature of the Treaty of Rome, the Presidency of the Council declared: 'We will fight terrorism, organized crime and illegal immigration *together*'.[5] As one scholar has pointed out, the movement of people has since become 'a suspicious activity potentially linked with criminality and organised crime' and this approach has placed the immigrants 'at the heart of insecurity discourses and practices'.[6]

The European Agency for the Management of the Operative Cooperation at the External Borders of the Member States of European Union (Frontex) was established by Council Regulation 2007/2004[7] (hereafter 'Frontex Regulation') in precisely this context. The Frontex Regulation creates a set of mechanisms for cooperation between member states and for assistance to member states with regard to technical and operational issues concerning the management of the EU external borders. These mechanisms aim at preventing as well as managing arrivals at the external borders of irregular migrants, in particular by sea, whatever their status.[8] Notably, the Frontex Regulation, in its original drafting,[9] did not contain any mention of either the terms 'asylum', 'refugee', or 'international protection'. Paragraph 22 of the Preamble laconically stated that the Regulation 'respects the fundamental rights and observes the principles recognized by Article 6(2) of the Treaty on European Union (TEU)[10] and reflected in the Charter of Fundamental Rights of the European Union' (hereinafter 'the Charter'[11]).

The Frontex activities started on an operational level in 2006 and raised several criticisms concerning their compliance with international and EU law obligations as well as with standards of international protection. Joint operations (JOs) at

[3] European Council, Presidency Conclusions of the Laeken European Council of 14 and 15 December 2001, SN 300/1/01, para. 12.

[4] Puntscher Rieckmann, 'Security, Freedom and Accountability: Europol and Frontex', in E. Guild and F. Geyer, *Security versus Justice* (2008) 19, at 20. See also Bigo, 'EU Police Cooperation: National Sovereignty Framed by European Security', in *ibid.*, 91, at 93; in which the author affirms that the new god of the European Union is 'security' which has become the 'first and foremost fundamental human right'.

[5] Declaration on the occasion of the 50th anniversary of the signature of the Treaty of Rome, 25 March 2007, available at <http://www.eu2007.de> (emphasis added).

[6] Carrera, *supra* n 1, at 10.

[7] Council Regulation 2007/2004, [2004] OJ L349/1. See also <http://www.frontex.europa.eu>.

[8] Flows of irregular migrants by sea are mixed flows, ie they are composed of migrants who fall within different categories (economic migrants, refugees, asylum seekers, displaced persons, etc).

[9] Subsequent amendments have introduced in the Regulation text references to fundamental rights and asylum; see section 2(B) below.

[10] Art. 6(2) TEU: 'The Union shall respect fundamental rights, as guaranteed by the European Convention for the Protection of Human Rights and Fundamental Freedoms signed in Rome on 4 November 1950 and as they result from the constitutional traditions common to the Member States, as general principles of Community law.'

[11] Adopted in Nice on 7 December 2000, adapted in Strasbourg on 12 December 2007, [2007] OJ C303/2.

sea carried out under the seal of Frontex have above all stirred debates because of their *modus operandi*. Alleged violations of human rights have been brought to the attention of international supervisory mechanisms, judicial and non-judicial, in order to remedy instances in which the prohibition of torture, for instance, or inhuman and degrading treatment were not respected. Breaches of the principle of *non-refoulement* have also been at issue.[12]

This chapter analyses and comments on the legal framework regulating Frontex activities and relevant practice in order to assess their compliance with international protection obligations. In section 1, EU policy for the management of the external borders is briefly described from a historical and normative perspective in order to then focus on Frontex in section 2. The analysis of its composition and functions highlights how member states still control the decision-making process and the operative activities. The focus is then on Frontex JOs, which are the epiphenomenon of the EU external border policy. Frontex JOs have been strongly criticized both for the ambiguities of the applicable legal framework and their *modus operandi*. Commentators and practitioners have pointed out how states participating in these JOs violate or may violate obligations deriving from human rights and asylum law (section 3). The entry into force of the Lisbon Treaty,[13] the subsequent amendments to the Frontex Regulation, and the Stockholm Programme[14] might be conducive to an IBM in compliance with international protection imperatives. Present times could show the political, and legal, momentum to direct EU policy in the fields of irregular immigration and of external borders towards enhanced respect and enforcement of international protection obligations, towards better governance of EU external borders (section 4).

[12] See the case-law: Committee Against Torture, *J.H.A. v. Spain*, 41st session (3–21 November 2008), UN Doc CAT/C/41/D/323/2007, 21 November 2008, 22 *International Refugee Law Journal* (2010) 104; *Hirsi and ors v. Italy*, ECHR (2012) Appl. No. 27765/09, 23 February 2012. The first case concerns the JO at sea carried out under Spanish control along the coasts of North-Western Africa; for a comment, see Wouters and Den Heijer, 'The *Marine I* Case: a Comment' 22 *International Journal of Refugee Law* (2009) 1. The second case regards the JO at sea carried out by Italian authorities in collaboration with Libya on the Central Mediterranean. The latter were performed on the basis of a bilateral agreement between the two countries; Frontex was not formally involved in this programme. However, the *modus operandi* of the operation raised similar problems to those of Frontex. For comments on the *Hirsi* case, see, inter alia, Giuffrè, 'Watered-Down Rights on the High Seas: *Hirsi Jamaa and Others v. Italy* (2012)' 61 *International and Comparative Law Quarterly* (2012) 728; Giuffrè, 'State Responsibility beyond Borders: What Legal Basis for Italy's Push-backs to Libya?' 24 *International Journal for Refugee* Law (2012) 692; Tondini, 'The Legality of Intercepting Boat People under Search and Rescue and Border Control Operations: With Reference to Recent Italian Interventions in the Mediterranean Sea and the ECtHR Decision in the *Hirsi* Case' 18 *Journal of International Maritime Law* (2012) 59.

[13] Treaty of Lisbon amending the Treaty on European Union and the Treaty establishing the European Community, signed at Lisbon, 13 December 2007, entered into force on 1 December 2009, [2007] OJ C306/1.

[14] European Council, The Stockholm Programme—An Open and Secure Europe Serving and Protecting Citizens, [2010] OJ C115/1.

1. EU Policy for the Management of EU External Borders: Legal Basis and Content

A. Between Amsterdam and Lisbon

The issue of the management of the Community's external borders has grown in importance with the progressive elimination of the controls at the internal frontiers deriving from the Schengen Conventions and the Schengen *acquis*.[15] The need to adopt a concerted approach concerning external borders arose from two main aims member states wanted to pursue: to secure the common space and to control immigration in the common space. However, if the police and judicial cooperation was already in progress between member states,[16] no such concerted approach existed in the field of immigration,[17] in particular with regard to the prevention of irregular migration. The lack of harmonized legislation in this field and the consequent differences in treatment directed migrants towards those states having legislation more favourable to them. Above all, asylum seekers and refugees chose the route of clandestinity in order to succeed in presenting their application in the destination country they preferred. Some member states thus suffered an increased and uneven burden. At the same time, the lack of internal borders allowed asylum seekers to multiply their demands. The 1990 Dublin Convention on the determination of the European state responsible for the examination of the asylum claim tried to respond to this phenomenon[18]—the first step towards a common asylum policy.[19]

[15] The 1985 Schengen Agreement was concluded among five founding European countries (Benelux (Belgium, Netherlands, Luxembourg), France, and Germany) in order to create an area without controls at their common borders for a better integration of the common market. This agreement has then been progressively extended with a series of conventions successively subscribed to by other European states, creating the so-called 'Schengen area'.

[16] The creation of a common market, with the 1957 Rome Treaty, already contained the seeds of cooperation in police and enforcement matters, in particular in the field of criminal legislation.

[17] The 1957 Treaty of Rome does not contain any mention of migration. However, with the international economic crisis of the 1970s and the protectionist approach adopted by some European states, the need emerged to open a dialogue in this field in order to achieve a common market. The attention focused on legal migration and subsequent to the Schengen Convention and Agreements, common standards in the field of visa and residence permits could be adopted. The Treaty of Maastricht realized the first step towards a harmonization in this field thanks to the integration of the Schengen *acquis*. However, immigration issues (legal and irregular) have globally been comprehended only in the last decades.

[18] [1997] OJ C254/1. 'The prevailing policy in Europe, elaborated in both the Schengen Agreements and Dublin Convention, takes no account of these critical variations. It is rather assumed that the treatment a refugee claimant receives in one contracting state can reasonably be taken as discharging the duty of all other participating governments. This position is in direct conflict with the international legal duty of each state independently to implement its obligations under the Refugee Convention.' See Hathaway, 'Harmonizing for Whom? The Devaluation of Refugee Protection in the Era of European Economic Integration' 26 *Cornell International Law Journal* (1993) 719, at 726. In relation to the other critical points of the Dublin system, see Commission Staff Working Paper, 'Evaluation of the Dublin Convention', SEC (2001) 756.

[19] The EU asylum policy is further discussed below, see section 3(B)(i).

The different policies concerning direct or indirect immigration and border control developed on parallel tracks. Pursuant to the institutional structure created by the TEU in 1992, and until 2009, the management of European external borders was a cross-pillar issue involving migratory and asylum aspects related to the first pillar, as well as the relationship with third states and security issues within the field of the second and the third pillars. Article 11(1) of the TEU, the first article of Title V on Common Foreign and Security Policy (CFSP), ie the second pillar, stated that:

> The Union shall define and implement a common foreign and security policy covering all areas of foreign and security policy, the objectives of which shall be: ... to strengthen the security of the Union in all ways, to preserve peace and strengthen international security, in accordance with the principles of the United Nations Charter, as well as the principles of the Helsinki Final Act and the objectives of the Paris Charter, including those on *external borders*. (emphasis added)

Pursuant to this article, external borders management was also within the ambit of the European Security and Defence Policy, a field in which the Council could conclude treaties (on recommendation of the presidency) so as to realize the CFSP (Article 24 of the TEU). A combined reading of Article 11 of the TEU and Protocol No. 31 (on external relations of the member states with regard to the crossing of the external borders), showed that member states and the Community were exercising shared competences. Both were entitled to enter into agreements with third states in this field. Pursuant to Article 62(2) of the Treaty of Amsterdam (ECT),[20] however, the Community aimed to achieve uniform conditions and standards with regard to external borders controls within a period of five years after the entry into force of the ECT (1999). In so doing, the Community had to deal with competing demands, for instance arising from the conduct of international trade, the exchange of goods and services, the internal labour market, the control of migration flows, the challenges of unlawful trafficking, and the need to protect human rights.[21]

After the entry into force of the Schengen Conventions in 1995, several regulations concerning the management of external borders were adopted, mainly regulations concerning the granting of visa and the collection and exchange of data. To these acts have to be added all the agreements concluded by member states and the EU in their field of competence, between them and with third states. The legislative productivity and political activism of the Community intensified after 1999, resulting in some first attempts at coordination among member states in the field of immigration and border control. The 2001 Laeken European Council gave to the Council and the Commission the mandate to work out 'arrangements

[20] The Treaty of Amsterdam (adopted in 1997, entered into force in 1999) incorporated the Schengen *acquis* (ie the set of rules and practices created by the Schengen Agreement and Conventions) in EC law with a special protocol (Protocol (No. 2) integrating the Schengen *acquis* into the framework of the European Union (1997)).

[21] Peers, 'EU Border and Globalisation', in K. Groenendijk, E. Guild, and P. Minderhoud (eds), *In Search of Europe's Borders* (2003), 45.

for co-operation between services responsible for border control and to examine the conditions in which a mechanism or common services to control external borders could be created'.[22] The result was the institution of the ARGO Programme[23] on administrative cooperation in the field of visa, asylum, and immigration, and the AENEAS Programme,[24] which completed the ARGO programme providing technical and financial assistance for realizing the cooperation.[25]

Two important documents were adopted in 2002: the Commission Communication entitled 'Towards an integrated management of external borders'[26] and the Council's 'Plan for the management of the external borders'.[27] However, little progress was concretely made towards the achievement of integrated management of external borders and the time had come for a step forward, the adoption of the Frontex Regulation.[28]

The use of the term 'management' instead of 'control' merits emphasis. In the view of one scholar,[29] this terminology implies a shift from a security-related approach to a more global one; for others, it indicates an attempt at depoliticizing the issue in a way that helps to create a Community agency, ie the Frontex.[30] It can also be considered a careful legal wording, which reflected the existing Community's competences in the field, ie shared competences. Article 2(2) of the Frontex Regulation embeds this repartition:

> Without prejudice to the competencies of the Agency, Member States may continue cooperation at an operational level with other Member States and/or third countries at external borders, where such cooperation complements the action of the Agency. Member States shall refrain from any activity which could jeopardise the functioning of the Agency or the attainment of its objectives. Member States shall report to the Agency on these operational matters at the external borders outside the framework of the Agency.

The Frontex Regulation does not, however, contain any definition of IBM which appears in its Article 1. This notion was formally defined two years later, in the Conclusions of the Justice and Home Affairs Council meeting of December 2006.[31] The IBM accordingly consists of:

> [a] *common corpus of legislation*, in particular the Schengen Borders Code as well as the Regulation on local border traffic; *[o]perational cooperation* between Member States,

[22] See *supra* n 3, at para. 42. [23] Council Decision 2002/463, [2002] OJ L161/11.

[24] Parliament and Council Regulation 491/2004, [2004] OJ L80/1.

[25] Both programmes are now part of Frontex's mission.

[26] COM (2002) 233 final.

[27] JHA Council on 13 June 2002, text available at <http://ec.europa.eu/justice/funding/2004_2007/doc/plan_management_external_borders.pdf>.

[28] Neal, 'Securitization and Risk at the EU Border: The Origins of FRONTEX' 47 *Journal of Common Market Studies* (2009) 333, at 341–2.

[29] Corrado, 'Negotiating the EU External Borders', in S. Carrera and T. Balzacq (eds), *Security versus Freedom: A Challenge for Europe's Future* (2006) 183, at 183.

[30] Mitsilegas, 'Border Security in the European Union: Towards Centralised Controls and Maximum Surveillance', in A. Baldaccini, E. Guild, and H. Toner, *Whose Freedom, Security and Justice? EU Immigration and Asylum Law and Policy* (2007) 359, at 364.

[31] Conclusions of the Justice and Home Affairs Council meeting 4–5 December 2006, at 26.

including cooperation as coordinated by the European Agency for the Management of Operational Cooperation at the External Borders of the Member States of the European Union (FRONTEX); *[s]olidarity* between Member States and the Community through the establishment of an External Borders Fund.

This document provides furthermore a non-exhaustive list of elements and activities, which compose the IBM and thus create the conceptual and substantial framework of Frontex activities.[32] The listed elements and activities encompass border checks and surveillance, the four-tier access model, cross-border crime investigation, and inter-agency and international cooperation to ensure coordination and coherence of actions at the EU level. In practice it sets up risk filters from the third country and involves the so-called deterritorialization of EU borders by externalizing the controls.[33]

Similarly, the Frontex Regulation does not provide any definition of 'external borders' or 'internal borders'. These concepts were legally defined in the Schengen Borders Code[34] in 2006, when the Frontex had already begun its operational tasks. This text sets the common rules governing the movement of persons across borders and contains the following definitions:

Internal borders: (a) the common land borders, including river and lake borders of member states; (b) the airports of the member states for internal flights; (c) sea, river and lake ports of the member states for regular ferry connections.

External borders: member states' land borders, including river and lake borders, sea borders and their airports, river ports, sea ports, *provided that they are not internal borders*. (emphasis added)

This negative definition of the EU external borders reflects their non-stable nature, which results from later enlargements. It is important to note the inclusion of maritime borders in the definition. This element is particularly relevant in consideration of the application of international protection obligations and standards during JOs at sea.[35]

The legal framework concerning the management of external borders has been thickened with the creation of the Rapid Border Intervention Teams (RABITs) in 2007.[36] RABITs consist of specially trained experts from member states who can be deployed at short notice to deal with urgent and exceptional migratory pressure at the external borders. The deployment of RABITs has become an additional task of Frontex. This strengthens the authority of Frontex vis-à-vis member states given

[32] Baldaccini, 'Extraterritorial Border Controls in the EU: The Role of Frontex in Operations at Sea', in B. Ryan and V. Mitsilegas (eds), *Extraterritorial Immigration Control: Legal Challenges* (2010) 229, at 233.

[33] *Ibid.* See also Neal, *supra* n 28, at 333; Guild and Bigo, 'The Transformation of European Border Control', in Ryan and Mitsilegas, *ibid.*, at 258; where the authors refer to a policy of 'remote control'; Rijpma and Cremona, 'The Extra-Territorialisation of EU Migration Policies and the Rule of Law', EUI Law Working Paper No. 2007/01, 1–24.

[34] Council Regulation 562/2006, [2006] OJ L105/1.

[35] This issue will be further analysed below; see sections 2(C) and 3.

[36] Parliament and Council Regulation 863/2007, [2007] OJ L199/30.

that RABIT operations are based on the principle of 'compulsory solidarity'.[37] Member states must make border guards available for RABIT deployment at the request of Frontex 'unless they are faced with an exceptional situation substantially affecting the discharge of national tasks' (Article 4(3) of the Frontex Regulation). This new operational mechanism enhances the centrality of the Frontex role in the management of external borders and constitutes an important shift from the previous intergovernmental approach to a more supranational one. However, emergency mechanisms can be triggered only at the request of a member state and, then, the request has to be approved by a three-quarter majority of the Frontex Management Board, which is mainly composed of states' representatives.

Member states remain principally in charge, both politically and operationally, of the integrated management of the EU external borders. In so doing they rely on a diversified and complex institutional and normative framework. However, the Treaty of Lisbon has introduced some elements which strengthen the EU institutions' powers in this field in order to enhance the coherence of both political and operational actions.

B. After the Lisbon Treaty

With the entry into force of the Lisbon Treaty,[38] the integration of the EU Third Pillar, ie Police and Judicial Cooperation in Criminal Matters (Title VI of the TEU) into the 'EC Pillar' has widened EU competences in relation to external border management, including maritime surveillance.[39] Article 77 of the Treaty on the Functioning of the European Union (TFEU) (formerly Article 62 of the Treaty Establishing the European Community (TEC)) is the first article of Chapter 2 on 'Policies on Border Checks, Asylum and Immigration' and provides a legal basis for other activities not strictly related to border checks and surveillance. Article 77 of the TFEU reads:

1. The Union shall develop a policy with a view to: ... (c) the gradual introduction of an integrated management system for external borders.
2. For the purposes of paragraph 1, the European Parliament and the Council, acting in accordance with the ordinary legislative procedure, shall adopt measures concerning:

[37] Baldaccini, *supra* n 32, at 235. See also Caligiuri, 'Le Operazioni di Contrasto Dell'Immigrazione Clandestina Alle Frontiere Marittime Dell'Unione Europea e la Tutela dei Richiedenti Asilo', in A. Caligiuri, G. Cataldi, and N. Napolitano (eds), *La Tutela dei Diritti Umani in Europa: Tra Sovranità Statale e Ordinamenti Sovranazionali* (2010) 359, at 369; Papastavridis, '"Fortress Europe" and FRONTEX: Within or Without International Law?' 79 *Nordic Journal of International Law* (2010) 75, at 78.

[38] See *supra* n 13. With the Treaty of Lisbon, the Treaty establishing the European Community was renamed the Treaty on the Functioning of the European Union (TFEU). A consolidated version of the Treaty on the European Union (TEU) and the TFEU is available at [2010] OJ C83/47.

[39] Maritime surveillance is 'the effective understanding of all activities carried out at sea that could impact the security, the safety, economy, or environment of the European Union and its Member States', in 'Towards the Integration of Maritime Surveillance in the European Union: Questions and Answers', MEMO/09/454, 15 October 2009.

... (d) any measure necessary for the gradual establishment of an integrated management system for external borders...

4. This Article shall not affect the competence of the Member States concerning the geographical demarcation of their borders, in accordance with international law.

Article 77 of the TFEU predicts the drafting not only of common rules on standards and procedures for the control of external borders, but also the adoption of any other measure needed in order to achieve the IBM. Consequently, the Frontex role could be adapted to a variety of border management functions beyond those more closely related to the control of persons and surveillance of the EU external borders. However, this extension of competences goes beyond the legal basis on which the Agency was established. Any new initiative undertaken by Frontex pursuant to the now existing legal framework, and not perfectly matching the former one, could raise doubts concerning its legality. The 2011 amendments of the Frontex Regulation have, however, partially solved this problem.[40]

Moreover, with the Lisbon Treaty, the European Court of Justice (ECJ) is empowered to review the legality of acts of bodies, offices, and agencies of the Union intended to produce legal effects vis-à-vis third parties (Article 263 of the TFEU). For the time being, Frontex structure and powers do not imply any competence to adopt acts producing direct legal effects vis-à-vis third parties.[41] However, Article 263 of the TFEU does not specify if the legal effect has to be direct or indirect. According to certain commentators, this means that agencies like Frontex will not be exculpated from claims against their legal acts for or in the name of the EU.[42] But Article 276 of the TFEU restricts the jurisdiction of the Court of Justice 'to review[ing] the validity or proportionality of operations carried out by the police or other law-enforcement services of a Member State or the exercise of the responsibilities incumbent upon Member States with regard to the maintenance of law and order and the safeguarding of internal security'. Moreover, according to Article 10(1) of Protocol No. 36 on Transitional Provisions attached to the Lisbon Treaty, during a transitional period of five years from its entry into force, the competences of the European Commission and the Court of Justice shall remain the same as before concerning the enactment and interpretation of legal acts regarding police cooperation.[43] The combined reading of these provisions suggests that Frontex operations would not be subject to any judicial review for quite some time.

The Lisbon Treaty has also created the Standing Committee on Operational Cooperation on Internal Security (COSI) to ensure effective coordination and cooperation between law enforcement and border management authorities, including

[40] European Parliament and Council Regulation 1168/2004, [2011] OJ L304/1; the content of these amendments is further discussed below, see section 2(B)(iii).

[41] Frontex consists of a so-called regulatory agency with operational tasks. The notion of regulatory agency will be discussed below, see section 2(A).

[42] Baldaccini, *supra* n 32, at 237; Fischer-Lescano, Löhr, and Tohidipur, 'Border Control at Sea: Requirements under International Human Rights and Refugee Law' 21 *International Journal of Refugee Law* (2009) 256, at 295.

[43] For a comment, see Carrera, *supra* n 1, at 12.

the control and protection of external borders, and when appropriate judicial cooperation in criminal matters relevant to operational cooperation (Article 71 of the TFEU). The work of this Committee will be based, above all, on national and EU threat assessments and priorities. Stringent cooperation between EU agencies and bodies involved in EU internal security (Europol, Frontex, Eurojust, Cepol, and Sitcen) must also be ensured by COSI so as to encourage increasingly coordinated, integrated, and effective operations. It will presumably have an important role in supervising the implementation of the cooperation agreement concluded between Frontex and the European agency for fundamental rights (FRA) in May 2010.[44]

In February 2010, the Presidency of the Council submitted the Draft Internal Security Strategy for the European Union: 'Towards a European Security Model'.[45] According to this text, security is in itself a basic right for EU citizens. It proposes a global approach to the securitization of the EU Area of Freedom, Security, and Justice (AFSJ) to be achieved thanks to 'the potential synergies that exist in the areas of law-enforcement cooperation, integrated border management, and criminal-justice systems. Indeed, these fields of activity in the AJFS are inseparable: the Internal Security Strategy must ensure that they complement and reinforce one another'.[46] The Internal Security Strategy must be performed 'respecting fundamental rights, *international protection*, the rule of law and privacy' (emphasis added).[47]

The new legal framework and the new institutional arrangement do not jeopardize the right of member states to conclude agreements with third states in the field of the management of external borders. A more sophisticated machinery will permit increased efficiency and coherence at the internal level. At the external level, the EU and its bodies, primarily Frontex, have to share the scene with member states. This multitude of actors and the consequent multiplication of decision-making fora blur even more the legal framework in which Frontex JOs are carried out.

2. Frontex Joint Operations between Domestic Diplomacy and Foreign Policy

A. The role of EU agencies in the area of freedom, security, and justice and in EU foreign policy

Frontex consists of a so-called regulatory agency[48] in charge of operational activities. Like all EU agencies, it is supposed to contribute to the efficient and flexible implementation of EU legislation and policies, particularly in areas based on technical

[44] Text available on the FRA website at <http://www.fra.europa.eu>.

[45] Presidency of the Council of the European Union, JAI 90, 5842/2/10 REV 2, 23 February 2010.

[46] *Ibid.*, at 2. [47] *Ibid.*, at 9.

[48] A regulatory agency is set out on its own legal basis (its own sectoral regulation) and has a specific role assigned. Regulatory agencies are also called 'traditional agencies', because of their long-standing, or 'decentralized agencies', because they spread across Europe. See 'European Agencies—The Way Forward', COM (2008) 135 final, at 3–4, 7.

and scientific considerations,[49] while at the same time it has to encourage the harmonization of regulatory practices in the member states.[50]

The case-by-case establishment of EU agencies—on a proposal from the Commission, but with the decision taken by the European Parliament and/or the Council of Ministers—has not been accompanied by an overall vision of the place of agencies in the Union. The lack of such a global vision has made it more difficult for agencies to work effectively[51] and to perform coherently in the different sectors. For instance, when Frontex was created, only part of the existing legal and institutional context was actually taken into consideration. No real reflection on the consequences of Frontex operational activities for the fulfilment of human rights and asylum law obligations was engaged in; neither were considered the potential problems arising from Frontex JOs carried out outside EU external borders, ie on the high seas or on the territory of third states.[52]

The Commission first considered the issue of this lack of a global vision and the need for a coherent approach in its White Paper on 'European Governance' of 2001.[53] In 2005 it then proposed an inter-institutional agreement on the operating framework for the European regulatory agencies,[54] which still remains a draft now. The multiplicity and diversity of existing agencies, and the lack of interest shown until now by member states, indicate that a global approach to agencies might unfortunately have to wait. Recently, the Commission, however, called for the removal of 'all the obstacles in the way of effective law enforcement cooperation between Member States. EU agencies and bodies such as FRONTEX, Europol and Eurojust, as well as OLAF, have a crucial role to play. They must cooperate better and be *given the powers and resources necessary to achieve their goals within clearly defined roles*' (emphasis added).[55] This statement echoes the elements of novelty introduced by the Lisbon Treaty and recognizes the fundamental role of EU agencies, acting in the AFSJ, for the diffusion of regulatory practice.[56] It also

[49] Groenleer, Kaeding, and Versluis, 'Regulatory Governance through Agencies of the European Union? The Role of the European Agencies for Maritime and Aviation Safety in the Implementation of European Transport Legislation' 17 *Journal of European Public Policy* (2010) 1212, at 1213; Majone, 'The Agency Model: the Growth of Regulation and Regulatory Institutions in the European Union' 3 *Eipascope* (1997) 9, at 10.

[50] So far, evidence for EU agencies' contribution to improving implementation is lacking; see Groenleer, Kaeding, and Versluis, *supra* n 49, at 1213.

[51] 'European Agencies—The Way Forward', *supra* n 48, at 2. See Christensen and Nielsen, 'Administrative Capacity, Structural Choice and the Creation of EU Agencies' 17 *Journal of European Public Policy* (2010) 176–204; D. Curtin, *Executive Power of the European Union* (2009), at 146 ff; Wonka and Rittberger, 'Credibility, Complexity and Uncertainty: Explaining the Institutional Independence of 29 EU Agencies' 33 *West European Politics* (2010) 730, at 737.

[52] International law issues, specifically law of the sea matters, will be considered below; see sections 2(C) and 3.

[53] COM (2001) 428 final.

[54] COM (2005) 59 final.

[55] Commission Communication on 'Delivering an Area of Freedom, Security and Justice for Europe's Citizens, Action Plan Implementing the Stockholm Programme', COM (2010) 171 final, at 6.

[56] R. D. Keleman, *The Rules of Federalism: Institutions and Regulatory Politics in the EU and beyond* (2004), at 104. See also Rijpma, 'Hybrid Agentification in the Area of Freedom, Security and Justice and its Inherent Tensions: the Case of Frontex', in M. Busuioc, M. Groenleer, and J. Trondal (eds), *The Agency Phenomenon in the European Union: Emergence, Institutionalisation and Everyday Decison-making* (2012) 84, at 90 ff.

emphasizes the fact that each agency cannot work in isolation but must be well aware of its legal, institutional, and political framework and context.

B. Frontex institutional and political framework

i. Composition and functions

In light of its composition, Frontex can be considered an 'intergovernmental agency'. The Frontex Regulation indicates the main organs of the agency: the Management Board and the Executive Director. The Management Board consists of one representative of each member state and two representatives of the Commission (Article 21). The Management Board appoints the Executive Director with a decision adopted by a two-thirds majority among the candidates proposed by the Commission (Article 26). The Executive Director manages the Agency and should be 'completely independent in the performance of his/her duties' and should 'neither seek nor take instructions from any government or from any other body' (Article 25). But the Management Board is largely composed of representatives of the member states, which ultimately control the decision-making process as they make up the wide majority of the Board. Moreover, Frontex relies on the voluntary participation of member states (Article 3). The 2011 amendments, however, create an obligation for member states to 'contribute to the European Border Guard' and to 'make the border guards available for deployment at the request of the Agency' on the basis of annual bilateral agreements concluded between the Agency and member states (Article 3(b)(1)–(2)).

Frontex has been established with a view to improving the integrated management of the external borders of the EU member states (Article 1(1)). Consequently, its main functions consist of coordinating operational cooperation between member states in the field of management of external borders; assisting member states on training of national border guards, including the establishment of common training standards; carrying out risk analyses;[57] following up on the development of research relevant for the control and surveillance of external borders; assisting member states in circumstances requiring increased technical and operational assistance at external borders; and providing member states with the necessary support to organize joint return operations (Article 2(1)). Considering the fact that the IBM falls under shared competences, the exercise of those tasks does not jeopardize member states' right to cooperate and conclude agreements between them and/or with third countries (Article 2(2)).

Like all European agencies, in order to achieve its tasks Frontex has legal personality (Article 15). It can perform all acts legal persons are allowed to by member states and may cooperate with Europol and international organizations in the framework of working arrangements concluded with those bodies (Article 13).[58] Frontex can

[57] The 2011 amendments (*supra* n 40) state that carrying out risk analyses also includes 'the assessment of the capacity of Member States to face threats and pressures at the external borders' (Art. 1.3(a)(i)).

[58] A proposal has been presented on information exchange between Europol, Eurojust, and Frontex, to be realized in 2011; see COM (2010) 171 final, *supra* n 55, at 32.

also conclude working arrangements with authorities of third countries (Article 14).[59] These arrangements are considered 'administrative arrangements' in the sense that they are concluded between administrations, even of different states and at different levels of governance, and are mainly of a technical nature. However, these arrangements are the legal and technical basis for carrying out JOs under the Frontex umbrella. It is, therefore, regrettable that these arrangements are difficult, if not impossible, to find. It undermines the legitimacy of Frontex activities and supports the criticism often levelled against the Agency because of its lack of transparency.[60]

This criticism is also linked to the lack of available information concerning JOs, notwithstanding the efforts made to build a user-friendly website and to publish regular reports on the progress of its activities. Still, it is not always possible to determine who is doing what, where and when. This lack of traceability hampers the determination of responsibilities when violations of international law and EU law concerning the respect for human rights and refugee law are alleged.[61]

ii. Frontex joint operations: a brief description

Pursuant to Article 3(1) of the Frontex Regulation, Frontex 'shall evaluate, approve and coordinate proposals for joint operations and pilot projects made by Member States. The Frontex may itself, and in agreement with the Member State(s) concerned, launch initiatives for joint operations and pilot projects in cooperation with Member States'. Moreover, Frontex 'may itself, and in agreement with the Member State(s) concerned, launch initiatives for joint operations and pilot projects in cooperation with Member States' (Article 3(2)). The assistance of the agency may also be requested by 'one or more Member States confronted with circumstances requiring increased technical and operational assistance when implementing their obligations with regard to control and surveillance of external borders' (Article 8). Frontex has a staff of experts and technical equipment that are put at the disposal of member states in order to execute the different programmes (Article 3(3)). The patrols (ie the military/police staff), the vehicles, aircrafts, and vessels implied in the operational dimension of the programmes are made available by participating states on a voluntary basis. While involved in the operations, the staff, both of the Agency and of the participating member states, is subject to the national law of the member state on which territory the operation is taking place (Article 10).

[59] As of June 2012, Frontex had concluded working arrangements with the authorities of 17 countries: the Russian Federation, Ukraine, Croatia, Moldova, Georgia, the former Yugoslav Republic of Macedonia, Serbia, Albania, Bosnia and Herzegovina, the United States, Montenegro, Belarus, Canada, Cape Verde, Nigeria, Armenia, and Turkey, as well as with the CIS Border Troop Commanders Council and the MARRI Regional Centre in the Western Balkans; information is available on the Frontex website at <http://www.frontex.europa.eu>.

[60] Papastavridis, *supra* n 37, at 88.

[61] UNCHR, 'Border Management and Human Rights. A Study of EU Law and the Law of the Sea (10-Point Plan Expert Roundtable No. 1: Controlling Borders while Ensuring Protection)', 21 November 2008; UNHCR, 'UNHCR Urges EU and FRONTEX to Ensure Access to Asylum Procedures, amid Sharp Drop in Arrivals via the Mediterranean', 10 December 2010. Both available at <http://www.unhcr.org>.

Several operations have been launched since 2006, when Frontex became operational. They use the large majority of the Frontex budget—in 2011 around 74 per cent (ie €87 million of the €118 million total budget).[62] About 56 per cent of this 74 per cent is committed to JOs at sea; this approximately amounts to €49 million.[63] Currently six maritime JOs are conducted under Frontex auspices, focusing on the Southern borders of the EU, both in the Mediterranean Sea and in the Atlantic Ocean, in order to prevent and counter migratory flows coming mainly from the African Continent. These operations have reduced the number of irregular migrants attempting to reach Europe the maritime way and have increased the number of those rescued at sea. They also have had the vicious effect of changing the routes, pushing the flows towards longer and more risky maritime routes or diverting them to land.[64] JOs at sea are also the ones most subject to criticism both on humanitarian and legal grounds.[65]

The structure created in 2004 has been completed by the 2007 RABITs Regulation.[66] This regulation enhances the centrality of the Frontex role, but the initiative remains a prerogative of member states on the basis of Article 8 of the Frontex Regulation. Articles 7 and 8 of the RABITs Regulation articulate in detail the tasks, powers, and legal status of the members of the teams. Members of the teams remain 'national border guards of their home Member States and shall be paid by them' (Article 8) but they 'may perform tasks and exercise powers from and, as a general rule, in the presence of border guards of the host Member States' (Article 7(3)). They continue to wear their own uniform but must also bear a 'blue armband with the insignia of the European Union and the Agency ... identifying them as participating in a deployment of the teams' (Article 7(4)). While performing their tasks, they can use force with the consent of their home state and of the host state and in the presence of border guards and in accordance with the national law of the latter (Article 7(5)). Moreover, they have to perform their tasks and powers in accordance with the national law of the host state, but they are subject to the law of their national member state concerning disciplinary measures (Article 9). The first RABIT operation was launched in October 2010 along the land border between Greece and Turkey;[67] there is obviously very little practice which is therefore, for the time being, difficult to evaluate. It can, however, be noticed that the four levels of normative stratification (application of the legislation of the host member state, of the national member state, and of the relevant EU, and international law) created by the RABITs Regulation certainly mirrors the existing division of competences. But it creates a complex legal framework, which might be difficult to apply and enforce

[62] See Frontex General Report 2011, at 23–6, available at <http://www.frontex.europa.eu>.

[63] *Ibid.*

[64] The vast majority of irregular migration actually reaches Europe using land routes and not maritime ones. See the statistics available on the UNHCR website at <http://www.unhcr.org>.

[65] See sections 2 and 3 below.

[66] See *supra* n 36.

[67] For the time being, some training programmes and some moot operations have been organized; see the Frontex website at <http://www.frontex.europa.eu>.

iii. The 2011 amendments

In February 2010, the European Commission presented a Proposal for a regulation amending Council Regulation (EC) 2007/2004.[68] This proposal mainly aimed to clarify the legal framework in which Frontex operates and it specifically introduced an explicit reference to international law and international protection obligations. It also attributed new powers to the Agency. The final text was adopted on 25 October 2011.[69]

The legal basis of the amendments lies in two articles of the TFEU: Articles 74 and 77. Article 74 provides that the Council shall adopt measures to ensure administrative cooperation between the relevant departments of the member states in the areas covered by Title V (AFSJ), as well as between those departments and the Commission. Article 77(1)(b) and (c) empowers the Union to develop a policy in order to carry out checks on persons and efficient monitoring of the crossing of external borders, and the gradual introduction of an integrated management system for external borders. The amendments respect the shared competences set out in the TFEU in that member states remain responsible for controlling their external borders. They also take into account the shared powers and responsibilities among member states; ie Article 1(2) clearly states that 'the responsibility for the control and surveillance of external borders lies with the Member States' and, in the context of operations coordinated by Frontex, the 'home Member State shall provide for appropriate disciplinary or other measures in accordance with its national law in case of violations of fundamental rights or international protection obligations' (Article 3(1)(a)). The amendments aim, however, at giving wider powers to Frontex in the management of its activities. They aim to strengthen the independence of the Agency, even if they do not provide any change concerning the composition of the main organs of the Agency. Therefore, member states still monopolize the decision-making process.

The new Article 1(2) provides that:

> the Agency shall facilitate and render more effective the application of existing and future European Union measures relating to the management of external borders, in particular the Schengen Borders Code ... The Agency shall fulfil its tasks in full compliance with relevant Union law, including the Charter of Fundamental Rights of the European Union ... ; the relevant international *law,* including the [Geneva Convention]; obligations related to access to international protection, in particular the principle of non-refoulement; and fundamental rights, and taking into account the reports of the Consultative Forum referred to in Article 26a of this Regulation

The Consultative Forum will be the 'effective mechanism to monitor the respect for fundamental rights in all the activities of the Agency' (Article 26a(1)). It shall assist the Executive Director and the Management Board in fundamental rights matters and shall be consulted on the development and implementation of the 'Fundamental Rights Strategy' and of the 'Code of Conduct'.[70]

[68] COM (2010) 61 final. [69] See *supra* n 40.

[70] Code of Conduct for All Persons Participating in Frontex Activities, adopted by decision of the Executive Director on 21 March 2011, document available at <http://www.frontex.europa.eu>. The

A new paragraph 1a now complements Article 2 and states that:

[N]o person shall be disembarked in, or otherwise handed over to the authorities of, a country in contravention of the principle of *non-refoulement*, or from which there is a *risk of expulsion or return to another country in contravention of that principle*. The special needs of... persons *in need of international protection* and other vulnerable persons shall be addressed in accordance with Union and international law. (emphasis added)

Moreover, the 2011 amendments address the need to provide border guards with adequate training in the field of fundamental rights and international protection. The new Article 5(1) affirms that:

The Agency shall establish and further develop *common core curricula for the training of border guards* and provide training at European level for instructors of the national border guards of Member States, including with regard to *fundamental rights, access to international protection and relevant maritime law*. (emphasis added)

The 2011 amendments also widen the number of institutional partners with which Frontex may cooperate. New Article 13 suggests that Frontex may cooperate with the European Asylum Support Office and the FRA in addition to Europol, which was already listed in the original text of the Regulation. Again, this amendment indirectly recognizes the need to formalize the role Frontex is called to perform in the field of human rights and asylum law. In the Action Plan Implementing the Stockholm Programme,[71] the Commission commits to delegate to the European Asylum Support Office (EASO) the task of 'develop[ing] methods to better identify those who are in need of international protection in mixed flows, and [cooperating] with Frontex wherever possible'. This of course echoes the call made by the Council in the Stockholm Programme:

The strengthening of border controls should not prevent *access to protection systems* by those persons entitled to benefit from them, and especially people and groups that are in vulnerable situations. In this regard, priority will be given to those in need of international protection and to the reception of unaccompanied minors. *It is essential that the activities of Frontex and of the EASO* are coordinated when it comes to the reception of migrants at the Union's external borders.[72] (emphasis added)

The debates concerning Frontex reform also concentrated on the above-mentioned lack of transparency that characterizes Frontex operational activities and the working arrangements related thereto. In a document presented in February 2010,[73] the European Commission in particular noticed that '[t]he current [Frontex] Regulation contains no rules on how operations should be prepared and

Code of Conduct is 'applicable to all operations coordinated by the Agency' and it 'shall lay down procedures intended to guarantee the principles of the rule of law and respect for fundamental rights' (Art. 2a). The Fundamental Rights Strategy also calls for the appointment of a 'Fundamental Rights Officer' who, at the time of writing, has not yet been nominated.

[71] Proposal for a regulation amending Council Regulation (EC) No. 2007/2004, COM (2010) 61 final, at 45.

[72] See *supra* n 14, at 26.

[73] Commission Staff Working Paper, 'Impact Assessment Accompanying the Proposal for a Regulation of the European Parliament and of the Council Amending Council Regulation (EC) No.

concluded... depending on ad hoc arrangements'. In the same text, the Commission further highlights the lack of real supervising and enforcement powers. In particular, the Commission pointed out how the legal basis of the operations (ie the ad hoc working arrangements) did not specify what 'the Agency can or should do to ensure that the plan is actually agreed and properly implemented'. This was (and still is) particularly problematic because of the different backgrounds, both operational and technical, of the border guards involved in such operations. This particular problem is addressed in the 2011 amendments concerning the 'organisational aspects of joint operations and pilot projects' (Article 3a).

In the Stockholm Programme, the Council invited the Commission to propose as well 'clear common operational procedures containing clear rules of engagement for joint operations at sea, with due regard to ensuring protection for those in need who travel in mixed flows, in accordance with international law'.[74] Without entering into detail, it is worth recalling that rules of engagement (ROEs) are usually composed by the domestic military authorities or by some international military organizations, such as NATO. Considering that competences in military matters are issued in the European Security and Defence Policy (ESDP—Articles 42–3 of the TEU) and that the ESDP mainly aims at carrying out operations outside member states' territory (except when there is an attack against one of them), it is questionable whether the Commission is entitled to deal with ROEs to be applied by member states' military staff that participate in police activities such as the management of external borders. Consistent with this, the 2011 amendments do not mention the adoption of ROEs, even if Article 3a(1)(a) ambiguously provides that '[the operational plan shall include] a description of the situation, with *modus operandi and objectives* of the deployment, including the operation aim' (emphasis added). Moreover, the operational plan shall also include information concerning 'command and control provisions, including the names and ranks of the host Member State's border guards responsible for cooperating with the guest officers and the Agency' (Article 3(a)(1)(f)); and 'regarding sea operations, specific information on the application of the relevant jurisdiction and legislation in the geographical area where the joint operation or pilot project takes place, including references to international and Union law regarding interception, rescue at sea and disembarkation' (Article 3(a)(1)(j)). The same obligation also applies in the context of rapid interventions at sea (Article 8e(1)(b)(j)).

C. Frontex joint operations and international law

i. Frontex and the law of the sea

Since summer 2006, Frontex and member states have carried out several JOs at sea, mainly focused on preventing and countering irregular migration by sea, and

2007/2004 Establishing a European Agency for the Management of Operational Cooperation at the External Borders of the Member States of the European Union (FRONTEX)', SEC (2010) 149, at 13–14.

[74] See *supra* n 14, at 26.

exercised in cooperation with third states. These JOs entail the exercise of external competences of the European Union with the risk of overlapping with member states, in particular concerning the implementation and/or the enforcement of international obligations deriving from the law of the sea, a field of shared competences.

In the past years, in particular since the Green Paper on a Future EU Maritime Policy,[75] the activity of the European Union in maritime affairs has become frenetic. The European Commission has elaborated several documents from which the main features of the Integrated Maritime Policy (IMP) can be gathered. One of the central concepts of the IMP is the 'EU maritime domain', defined as follows:

> The *EU maritime domain* encompasses the EU Member States' Territorial waters, Exclusive Economic Zones and Continental Platforms [*sic!*] as defined by the 1982 United Nations Convention on Law of the Sea as well as all maritime-related activities carried out therein, on the seabed, subsurface, surface and above the sea such as installations, cargo, small boats and vessels flagged, owned, managed by or *bound to the EU*. Beyond the above, it also comprises any *Search and Rescue Area and any Area of Operations that has been designated for an EU Maritime Operation under civil or military authority.*[76] (emphasis added)

Another key notion for better clarifying the legal and political framework of Frontex JOs at sea is the so-called 'maritime surveillance' which is 'the effective understanding of all activities carried out at sea that could impact the security, the safety, economy, or environment of the European Union and its Member States'.[77] From these documents, the will of EU institutions clearly emerges to extend their range of maritime activities through monitoring sectors of activity, which previously derived only from member states competences. There also is a particular attention for Frontex JOs at sea both in the expression 'EU Maritime Operation under civil and military authority' and in recalling 'security' in maritime surveillance.

Member states and EU institutions shall perform these activities in accordance with the law of sea, mainly embedded in the text of the United Nations Convention on the Law of the Sea (UNCLOS).[78] The law of sea is the framework in which all maritime activities can be exercised in the different maritime zones. Each maritime zone is subject to specific rules determining who can do what, where, and how. All EU member states and the European Community (EC) in 1998 have ratified UNCLOS.[79] With the entry into force of the Lisbon Treaty, the EU substitutes and

[75] COM (2006) 275 final, available at <http://ec.europa.eu/maritimeaffairs>.

[76] 'Towards the Integration of Maritime Surveillance: A Common Information Sharing Environment for the EU Maritime Domain', COM (2009) 538 final, at 2. On the perplexities deriving from this definition, see Trevisanut, 'Search and Rescue Operations in the Mediterranean: Factor of Cooperation or Conflict?' 25 *International Journal of Marine and Coastal Law* (2010) 523, at 536.

[77] 'Towards the Integration of Maritime Surveillance in the European Union: Questions and Answers', *supra* n 39.

[78] Adopted 10 December 1982, entered into force the 16 November 1994; 21 ILM [1982] at 1261; the text of the Convention is also available at <http://www.un.org/Depts/los/index.htm>.

[79] The EC simultaneously deposited the ratification instrument and a declaration, according to which 'the Community has the honour of declaring its acceptance, *in respect of matters for which competence has been transferred to it by those of its Member States which are parties to the Convention*, of the rights and obligations laid down for States in the Convention and the Agreement' (emphasis added); text of the declaration is available at <http://www.un.org/Depts/los/convention_agreements/convention_declarations.htm>.

succeeds to the EC in international treaties (Article 1(3) of the TEU). Moreover, the 2011 amendments introduce a preambular paragraph, no. 30, which affirms that: 'The implementation of this Regulation should not affect the rights or obligations of Member States under the United Nations Convention on the Law of the Sea, the International Convention for the Safety of Life at Sea, the International Convention on Maritime Search and Rescue'.

Frontex JOs include the interception of vessels and their redirection to the state of origin, ie the state from where they have started their trip and which is participating in the JO pursuant to Article 14(2) of the Frontex Regulation. The operational cooperation has been taking place on the high seas along the coasts of the interested member states and, when agreed, also in the territorial waters of the participating third states. Member states units, however, operate outside European territorial waters, within the framework of international law.

a. Frontex joint operation on the high seas

Member states' units participating in Frontex JOs extend their control and surveillance beyond the EU external borders, carrying out pre-border operations on the high seas. The extraterritoriality of border control and the extraterritorial application of the Schengen Border Code is provided by the code itself with regard specifically to general checking procedures on maritime traffic in order to prevent unauthorized border crossing (Annex VI). In the exercise of such prerogatives, Frontex JOs have to be consistent with the rights and obligations deriving from the freedom of the high seas.

High seas are defined by Article 86 of the UNCLOS as 'all parts of the sea that are not included in the exclusive economic zone, in the territorial sea or in the internal waters of a state, or in the archipelagic waters of an archipelagic State'. High seas are characterized by the prohibition of appropriation (Article 89 of the UNCLOS). The freedom of the high seas does not imply the absence of rules but rather indicates that freedoms are granted equally to all states. Article 87 of the UNCLOS gives a non-exhaustive list[80] of freedoms,[81] among which is the freedom of navigation:

1. The high seas are open to all States, whether coastal or land-locked. Freedom of the high seas is exercised under the conditions laid down by this Convention and by other rules of international law. It comprises, *inter alia*, both for coastal and land-locked States: (a) freedom of navigation...
2. These freedoms shall be exercised by all States with due regard for the interests of other States in their exercise of the freedom of the high seas, and also with due regard for the rights under this Convention with respect to activities in the Area.

[80] 'There are high-seas activities alleged by some States to constitute freedoms, but denied this status by other States. The principle on which such disputes should be resolved is that any use compatible with the status of the high seas ... should be admitted as a freedom unless it is excluded by some specific rule of law', see R. R. Churchill and V. A. Lowe, *The Law of the Sea* (3rd edn, 1999), at 206.

[81] The other freedoms listed in Art. 87 are: freedom of overflight; freedom to lay submarine cables and pipelines; freedom to construct artificial islands and other installations permitted under international law; freedom of fishing; and freedom of scientific research.

The freedom of navigation encompasses two principles: the vessel sailing under the flag of any state has the right to navigate;[82] the navigation of a vessel sailing under the flag of one state should not be hampered by other states. A vessel can sail under the flag of only one state, which exercises its exclusive jurisdiction (Article 92(1)),[83] except in the cases explicitly provided by UNCLOS[84] or in accordance with another agreement stating expressly the exception. Article 110 of the UNCLOS on the right of visit allows states to mutually recognize the right of visit against their own ships in cases other than those listed in the same Article.[85] On the ground of this provision, states can organize what is known as naval interdiction programmes.

The practice of naval interdiction on the high seas consists of the action of one state or more, undertaken on the basis of an international agreement, aimed at exercising the right of visit in relation to criminal activities not listed in Article 110 of the UNCLOS, performed by ships without nationality or by vessels sailing the flag of a state or a group of states.[86] In the migratory field, several interdiction programmes have been established to prevent and obstruct irregular flows, for instance the agreement concluded between the US and Haiti in 1981[87] or the exchange of letters between Albania and Italy in 1997.[88] Frontex JO Hera, carried out in the Atlantic Ocean between the coasts of Mauritania and Senegal and the Spanish Canary Islands, was legally based on two cooperation agreements concluded by Spain with respectively the two mentioned third states.[89]

[82] Art. 90 UNCLOS, Right of Navigation: 'Every State, whether coastal or land-locked, has the right to sail ships flying its flag on the high seas'; this implies equal access to the high seas for any State. See Momtaz, 'The High Seas', in R.-J. Dupuy and D. Vignes (eds), *A Handbook on the Law of the Sea*, Vol. 1, (1991), at 396.

[83] The vessel sailing under the flag of more than one state is considered as a vessel without nationality (Art. 92(2)), consequently it does not enjoy the protection of any state and the freedom of navigation.

[84] Art. 100 (repression of piracy); Art. 110 (Right of visit); Art. 111 (Right of visit).

[85] Art. 110(1): '*Except where acts of interference derive from powers conferred by treaty*, a warship which encounters on the high seas a foreign ship ... is not justified in boarding it unless there is reasonable ground for suspecting that ... ' (emphasis added). See Churchill and Lowe, *supra* n 80, at 218; Syrigos, 'Developments on the Interdiction of Vessels on the High Seas', in A. Strati, M. Gavouneli, and N. Skourtos (eds), *Unresolved Issues and New Challenges to the Law of the Sea* (2006), at 166 ff.

[86] For a detailed analysis on the naval interdiction legal framework and practice, see D. Guilfoyle, *Shipping Interdiction and the Law of the Sea* (2009), in particular on irregular migration, at 180 ff. See also Papastavridis, 'The Right of Visit on the High Seas in a Theoretical Perspective: *Mare Liberum* versus *Mare Clausum* Revisited' 24 *Leiden Journal of International Law* (2011) 45.

[87] Pursuant to this agreement, the US and Haiti established 'a cooperative programme of *selective interdiction and return* to Haiti of certain Haitian migrants and vessels involved in illegal transport of persons coming from Haiti' (emphasis added); see Agreement to stop clandestine migration of residents of Haiti to the US, 20 ILM [1981], 1198.

[88] 'Scambio di Lettere Relativo alla Cooperazione per la Prevenzione Degli atti Illeciti che Ledono l'ordine Giuridico dei due Paesi e l'Immediato Aiuto Umanitario, Quando è Messa a Rischio la Vita di Coloro che Tentano di Lasciare l'Albania', *Gazzetta Ufficiale della Repubblica Italiana*, Suppl No. 163, 15 July 1997.

[89] 'Acuerdo entre el Reino de España y la Republica Islamica de Mauritania en Material de Inmigración', Madrid, 1 July 2003, *Boletín Oficial del Estado*, No. 185, 4 August 2003, 30050. The agreement with Senegal has not been made public by Frontex; neither was the present author able to find it anywhere else.

The action of one state or more may also be undertaken on the basis of the Protocol against Smuggling of Migrants by Land, Sea, and Air to the UN Convention against Transnational Organized Crime,[90] which created a multilateral cooperation mechanism. Article 7 of the Palermo Protocol provides a duty of cooperation in the field of migration by sea in order to 'prevent and suppress the smuggling of migrants by sea, *in accordance with the international law of the sea*' (emphasis added).

The expression 'in accordance with the international law of the sea' indicates that the Palermo Protocol aims at strengthening the existing legal framework;[91] however, it does not add much. Actually, the articles specifically addressing irregular migration by sea (Articles 7–9) reproduce the UNCLOS legal setting on the exclusivity of flag state jurisdiction and the need for specific authorization from the flag state to hamper the exercise of the freedom of navigation.[92] The Palermo Protocol thus creates a more specific institutional framework in which state parties can conclude cooperation agreements in order to facilitate or eventually exclude the need for an explicit authorization on a case-by-case basis. However, the narrow scope of application of the Protocol needs to be noted. It only applies to irregular migrants who participate in a 'smuggling' operation, in the framework of a transnational criminal organization. Those helped by friends or family in irregularly crossing borders are not encompassed by the Protocol.

Naval interdiction programmes in the field of migration consist of two main phases performed on the high seas: the interception of the vessel transporting migrants; the eventual redirection or diversion of the vessel. The law of the sea does not define what kind of actions can be considered as an interception. The UNHCR Executive Committee (ExCom) has defined interceptions 'as encompassing all measures applied by a State, outside its national territory, in order to prevent, interrupt or stop the movement of persons without the required documentation crossing international borders by land, air or sea, and making their way to the country of prospective destination'.[93] This broad definition includes a wide range of measures going from the right to approach[94] to the right of visit as provided by Article 110 of the UNCLOS. The right to approach is propaedeutic for exercising the right of visit either in order to ask the flag state for the necessary

[90] UNGA Res. 55/25, 15 November 2000. The Protocol entered into force on 28 January 2004. As of January 2011, 127 states are party to the Palermo Protocol, including the European Union.

[91] Obokata, 'The Legal Framework Concerning the Smuggling of Migrants at Sea under the UN Protocol on the Smuggling of Migrants by Land, Sea and Air', in Ryan and Mitsilegas, *supra* n 32, at 157.

[92] 'For the time being, insofar as the law of the sea is concerned, the Protocol cannot be considered a point of departure for creating new customary international law'; see Ronzitti, 'Coastal State Jurisdiction over Refugees and Migrants at Sea', in N. Ando, E. McWhinney, and R. Wolfrum (eds), *Liber Amicorum Judge Shigeru Oda* (2002) 1271, at 1286.

[93] UNHCR Executive Committee (ExCom), 'Interception of Asylum-seekers and Refugees: The International Framework and Recommendation for a Comprehensive Approach', UN Doc EC/50/CRP.17, 9 June 2000, para. 10.

[94] The right to approach (*le droit d'enquête du pavillon*) consists in the 'customary right of every warship to approach a vessel on the high seas in order to ascertain its identity and nationality, usually by requesting it to show its flag'; see Papastavridis, *supra* n 37, at 82.

authorization, or to directly conduct the visit if the suspected vessel is stateless (Article 110(1)(d)). The latter case is the most common one in the field of irregular migration, as vessels transporting migrants rarely have a flag.

Once the stateless vessel is apprehended and the suspicions confirmed, there are two options: either the warship escorts the vessel to one port of its national state in order to complete the investigation and eventually proceed with the arrest of the vessel and its crew; or it diverts it back to the state of origin. None of these actions are expressly provided by UNCLOS, which does not contain any provision on enforcement jurisdiction as far as migration is concerned.[95] International law does not provide for it, but it does not forbid it.[96] Arguably, states may exercise such enforcement jurisdiction on stateless vessels as far as they do not violate other international obligations, as for instance obligations deriving from human rights and asylum law.

b. Frontex joint operations in the territorial waters of third countries

Frontex JOs at sea are also conducted in the territorial waters of third countries on the basis of treaties concluded by the host member state, or the participating member states with these third countries. The agreements concluded by Spain with Mauritania and Senegal legally funded Frontex JO HERA. According to Frontex, these agreements allow not only Spanish patrols but also those of other member states to intervene in the territorial waters of these two countries.[97] According to international law, coastal states exercise their full sovereignty in their territorial sea (Article 2 of the UNCLOS)[98] with the only limit of the right of innocent passage (Article 17 of the UNCLOS)[99] and of treaty-based self-limitation. In contrast to the assertion by Frontex, the agreement with Mauritania[100] provides that the contracting parties, Mauritania and Spain, might intercept and divert in any place of their territory, including the territorial sea, any third state national who does not comply with the entry conditions in force in the two states (Articles I(1), VI(i)(ii), and IX(1)(a)); no permission to extend the patrolling prerogative to a state different from Spain can be found at any place in this agreement.

Moreover, according to Frontex, '[a] Mauritanian or Senegalese law enforcement officer is always present on board of deployed Member States' assets and is

[95] Concerning piracy, for example, Art. 110 provides the legal basis for exercising the right of visit and Art. 105 for the enforcement jurisdiction; similarly Arts. 109 and 110 regarding unauthorized broadcasting. See Churchill and Lowe, *supra* n 80, at 214; M. H. Nordquist (ed), *United Nations Convention on the Law of the Sea 1982: A Commentary, Volume III* (1993) at 127; Papastavridis, *supra* n 37, at 84.

[96] Trevisanut, 'La Collaborazione Italia—Libia in Materia di Contrasto all'immigrazione Clandestina via Mare: Profili di Diritto del Mare', 3 *Diritti Umani e Diritto Internazionale* (2009) 609, at 615.

[97] See *Frontex Annual Report 2006* available at <http://www.frontex.europea.eu>.

[98] 'The sovereignty of a coastal State extends, beyond its land territory and internal waters ... to an adjacent belt of sea, described as the territorial sea.'

[99] 'Subject to this Convention, ships of all States, whether coastal or land-locked, enjoy the right of innocent passage through the territorial sea.'

[100] See *supra* n 89.

always responsible for the diversion'.[101] This presence provides a legal basis for the operation carried out in the Mauritanian and Senegalese territorial waters and testifies to the acquiescence of Mauritania and Senegal. Doubt remains in cases of an incident occurring during operations which constitutes a wrongful act: can such an act be imputed to Mauritania and Senegal? Is the presence of a law enforcement officer on board of participating member states' vessels an adequate criterion for the attribution of international responsibility?[102] Furthermore, the presence of a Mauritanian or Senegalese officer has no effect with regard to the right of deployed member states' crafts to intervene on the high seas against any vessel coming from the coasts of these two states; neither does this provide a legal basis for the diversion.[103]

There are other problematic aspects concerning the nationality of the patrolling vessels and of the vessels that are intercepted. With regard to the nationality of the vessels that are intercepted and diverted, it is important to recall that according to Article 92(1) of the UNCLOS, vessels can sail under the flag of only one state and are under its exclusive jurisdiction. In territorial waters a vessel is subject to the coastal state's jurisdiction within the limits of Articles 17ff of the UNCLOS; the coastal state might delegate part of its powers in the territorial waters to a third state on the basis of a treaty. Pursuant to the above-mentioned agreement, Spain has been authorized to exercise its jurisdiction, even in relation to third states' vessels/nationals, but only in Mauritanian waters. Such a delegation of powers cannot extend to the high seas.

ii. Frontex and the duty to render assistance

The Frontex success story is, however, undermined by 'a significant obstacle to the effectiveness of [JOs] in the contrasting interpretations of the International Law of the Sea by Member States'.[104] Interpretative disagreements arise in particular with regard to the duty to render assistance.

The duty to render assistance at sea is set out by Article 98 of the UNCLOS:

> Every State shall require the master of a ship flying its flag, in so far as he can do so without serious danger to the ship, the crew or the passengers:
>
> (a) to render assistance to any person found at sea in danger of being lost;

[101] Frontex 'HERA 2008 and NAUTILUS 2008 Statistics', News Releases, 30 September 2008, available at <http://www.frontex.europa.eu/news/hera-2008-and-nautilus-2008-statistics-oP7kLN>.

[102] These situations are perfect hypotheses of shared responsibilty, ie the sharing of international responsibilities among multiple actors who contribute to the wrongful act. On this issue, see Nollkaemper and Jacobs, 'Shared Responsibility in International Law: A Conceptual Framework', SHARES Research Paper No. 3, 2011, available at: <http://www.sharesproject.nl/publication/shared-responsibility-in-international-law-a-concept-paper>. See also the case *Marine I*, analysed below with regard to the right to liberty and security; see section 3(A)(ii).

[103] Trevisanut, 'Maritime Border Control and the Protection of Asylum-Seekers in the European Union' 12 *Touro International Law Review* (2009) 157, at 159.

[104] Frontex 2009 General Report, at 43.

(b) to proceed with all possible speed to the rescue of persons in distress, if informed of their need of assistance, in so far as such action may reasonably be expected of him;
(c) after a collision, to render assistance to the other ship, its crew and its passengers and, where possible, to inform the other ship of the name of his own ship, its port of registry and the nearest port at which it will call.

Although this Article is placed in the UNCLOS section concerning the high seas, the duty to render assistance applies in all maritime zones.[105] This rule is closely connected with the principle of safety of life at sea, which is the only real limit to the freedom of navigation.[106] Consequently, and because of its repetition in treaty and domestic law and in state practice, the duty to render assistance is generally recognized as a principle of customary law, even if it has only fairly recently been recognized as such. In fact, during the Indochinese crisis in the 1970s,[107] the duty to rescue persons in danger at sea was still considered as a treaty obligation and thus binding only on states parties to the relevant instruments.[108] In the wake of instances of non-rescue at sea, as well as a number of humanitarian tragedies,[109] the need to identify the recipient of the duty to actually accomplish rescue operations and to clarify the consequences of this duty arose with new vigour. Under the impact of such events, the Search and Rescue (SAR) Convention was adopted in 1979.

The SAR Convention aims to create an international system for coordinating rescue operations that guarantees their efficiency and safety. States parties are thus invited to conclude SAR agreements with neighbouring states to regulate

[105] During the negotiation of the UNCLOS, the wording of this Article was debated (J. K. Gamble Jr (ed), *Law of the Sea: Neglected Issues* (1979), at 261) but pursuant to its literal interpretation ('any person found at sea' and not 'any person found on the high seas') in light of the object and purpose, as required by Art. 31 of the 1969 Vienna Convention on the Law of Treaties, 1155 UNTS 18232, it was noted that this duty could not disappear just because of the crossing of a maritime frontier. Nordquist, *supra* n 95, at 170.

[106] '[D]ans la plupart des cas, l'élément décisif qui détermine les priorités entre les activités en mer (...) est la sauvegarde de la vie humaine'; see Treves, 'La Navigation', in R.-J. Dupuy and D. Vignes (eds), *Traité du Nouveau Droit de la Mer* (1985) 688, at 717. See also Pallis, 'Obligations of States towards Asylum Seekers at Sea: Interactions and Conflicts between Legal Regimes' 14 *International Journal of Refugee Law* (2002) 329, at 335 where the author states: 'Explicit links have been drawn between the concept of distress and the preservation of human life'.

[107] We refer to the Indochinese crisis in relation to the movement of refugees coming from the former French Indochina as a consequence of armed conflict, as in Vietnam, and emergence of a dictatorial regime, as in Cambodia. Chetty, 'Resolution of the Problem of Boat People: The Case of a Global Initiative' 1 *ISIL Yearbook of International Humanitarian and Refugee Law* (2001) 144, at 145.

[108] In particular, two instruments applicable only in territorial waters were invoked: the 1910 Brussels International Convention for the Unification of Certain Rules of Law Relating to Assistance and Salvage at Sea, adopted 23 September 1910, in force 1 March 1913 (available at <http://www.unidroit.info>) and the 1974 Safety of Life at Sea (SOLAS) Convention, 1184 UNTS 1861, adopted 1 November 1974, in force 25 May 1980.

[109] As a result of the growing number of refugees coming from the former Indochina, the countries of the region which received the refugees decided to close their frontiers and did not accept any more disembarkation (see 'Opening Statement by Mr Poul Hartling, the United Nations High Commissioner for Refugees, at the Consultative Meeting with Interested Governments on Refugees and Displaced Persons in South East Asia', Geneva, HC Statements, 11 December 1978). Merchant ships consequently did not perform any further rescue operations as they did not know what to do afterwards. Many boat people were thus left to the mercy of the waves.

and coordinate SAR operations and services in the agreed maritime zone.[110] Such agreements technically and operatively implement the obligation set out in Article 98(2) of the UNCLOS, which provides that, where needed, neighbouring states shall cooperate through regional agreements to promote and maintain adequate and effective SAR services.[111] Such agreements also diminish the risks of non-rescue incidents.

At the EU level, maritime activities involving security and police activities still fall within the field of shared/parallel competences. In particular, the role of the EU in SAR activities is problematic, as it is not a member of the International Maritime Organization (IMO) and thus is not a party to the relevant conventions. Even if the SAR activities are meant to be included in the IMP[112] and, in a certain manner, to be coordinated at the EU level, the existing institutional framework does not allow such a development.[113] However, the EU is party to the UNCLOS and consequently would have to comply with the duty to render assistance set out in Article 98. Actually, this obligation falls on flag states and a unified 'EU flag' does not exist yet. But the EU has shared competences in the field of transport,[114] and has shown interest in safety of navigation. Aware that 'in most Mediterranean States, each sectoral policy is pursued by its own administration',[115] the EU has created and managed different fora where stakeholders can exchange information and organize cooperation; one of these is Frontex.

In the field of managing irregular migration by sea, disagreements between EU member states have emerged concerning the content of the duty to render assistance. In fact, carrying out rescue operations does not exhaust the duty to render assistance, which extends to the disembarkation of the rescued persons in a place of safety. The IMO Maritime Safety Committee (MSC) adopted two resolutions that amended the Safety of Life at Sea (SOLAS)[116] and SAR Conventions,[117] which entered into force 1 July 2006. In particular Article 3(1)(9) of the SAR Convention now provides:

> Parties shall co-ordinate and co-operate to *ensure that masters of ships providing assistance by embarking persons in* distress *at sea are released from their obligations* with minimum further deviation from the ships' intended voyage, provided that releasing the master of the ship from the obligations does not further endanger the safety of life at sea. The Party

[110] The Secretary-General of the International Maritime Organization (IMO) is the depositary of the SAR Convention and receives notification of the conclusion of any SAR agreement and of any modification to an existing SAR agreement. For an example of such a SAR Agreement, see IMO, 'Notification of an Arrangement on Search and Rescue Regions and co-ordination herewith the text of an Arrangement for the co-ordination of search and rescue services concluded between the Government of Australia and the Government of Indonesia and submitted in accordance with paragraph 2.1.4 of the Annex to the 1979 SAR Convention, as amended', SAR.6/Circ.22,13 April 2004.

[111] 'Every coastal State shall promote the establishment, operation and maintenance of an adequate and effective search and rescue service regarding safety on and over the sea and, where circumstances so require, by way of mutual regional arrangements cooperate with neighbouring States for this purpose.'

[112] See the definition of 'European maritime domain', *supra* n 76.

[113] See Trevisanut, *supra* n 76, at 535–6.

[114] Title VI TFEU.

[115] Commission (EC), 'Towards an Integrated Maritime Policy for a Better Governance of the Mediterranean', COM (2009) 466 final, at 3, available at <http://www.ec.europa.eu/maritimeaffairs>.

[116] MSC.153 (78), 20 May 2004.

[117] MSC.155 (78), 20 May 2004.

responsible for the search and rescue region in which such assistance is rendered shall exercise *primary responsibility* for ensuring such co-ordination and co-operation occurs, so that survivors assisted are disembarked from the assisting ship and *delivered to a place of safety*, taking into account the particular circumstances of the case and guidelines developed by the Organisation. In these cases, the relevant Parties *shall arrange for such disembarkation to be effective as soon as reasonably practicable.* (emphasis added)

According to the MSC Guidelines,[118] a 'place of safety' means a location where the rescue operations can be considered as completed. In accordance with Principle 6.14 of the Guidelines, even the rescue unit can be the place of safety, but only provisionally. In fact, the text insists on the role that the flag state and the coastal state should play in substituting for the master of the rescuing vessel. Principle 6.13 provides:

An assisting ship should not be considered a place of safety based solely on the fact that the survivors are no longer in immediate danger once aboard the ship. … Even if the ship is capable of safely accommodating the survivors and *may serve as a temporary place of safety*, it should be relieved of this responsibility as soon as alternative arrangements can be made. (emphasis added)

Moreover, the state in whose SAR zone the operation took place has the duty to provide or, at least, to secure a place of safety for the rescued persons (Principle 2.5). This Principle does not include either a right of entry into the territory of the interested state by the rescued persons or a right of access to the ports of the coastal state. It simply demands that the coastal state carries out the SAR operations and brings them effectively to an end, ie, to not leave the rescued persons (whatever their status) at sea. The coastal state has a 'residual' obligation to allow disembarkation on its own territory when it has not been possible to do so anywhere else. This has been clarified by the IMO Facilitation Committee (FAL), which adopted 'Principles relating to administrative procedures for disembarking persons rescued at sea'[119] in January 2009. Principle 3 establishes that:

If disembarkation from the rescuing ship *cannot be arranged swiftly elsewhere*, the Government responsible for the SAR area *should accept the disembarkation of the persons rescued* in accordance with immigration laws and regulations of each Member State into a place of safety under its control in which the persons rescued can have timely access to post rescue support. (emphasis added)

The fact that the FAL had to intervene indicates that the amendments of 2004 have been insufficient to enhance the safety of persons rescued at sea. State practice in the Mediterranean has given rise to interesting discussions in this regard. Some Mediterranean states engaged in a debate at the IMO that precisely centred on the application of the 2004 amendments. Spain and Italy submitted to the IMO Sub-Committee on Flag State Implementation (FSI) a joint statement[120] in

[118] MSC.167 (78), 20 May 2004. [119] FAL.3/Circ.194, 22 January 2009.

[120] IMO, 'Measures to Protect the Safety of Persons Rescued at Sea, Compulsory Guidelines for the Treatment of Persons Rescued at Sea' (submitted by Spain and Italy), FSI 17/15/1, 13 February 2009.

which they complained about the non-compliance of some coastal states with the implementation of their SAR obligations. They found that 'in the majority of the operations where Spanish- or Italian-flagged ships have been involved, the Governments responsible for the SAR regions, where persons have been rescued, have failed to provide a safe place for their disembarkation'.[121] They thus highlighted the resulting excessive burden of responsibility left on the shipmasters of the rescuing units and proposed further amendments to the SAR and SOLAS Conventions in order to strengthen the obligations of the state responsible of the SAR zone.

This proposal was contested by Malta,[122] which proposed a model in which the central concept is 'that disembarkation should occur in the nearest safe haven namely that port closest to the location of the rescue which may be deemed as a place of safety'. Moreover, Malta pointed out a weakness of the model created by the 2004 amendments (to which it is not a party) in that they 'have not tackled in sufficient depth that the land mass of the Contracting Party responsible for a given SAR may not provide the most appropriate option to ensure the timely disembarkation of rescued persons'. Malta suggests that rescued persons should be disembarked in the nearest port to the place of rescue, regardless of whose zone they are found in. Malta builds its model on the basis of its own particular situation: namely that of a small island with an enormous unilaterally declared SAR zone.[123] But the SAR Convention asks states to guarantee continuous and efficient SAR services in the area under their responsibility. A state should declare a SAR zone whose extension allows it to fulfil its international obligations.

These ongoing debates in the IMO framework between EU member states which all actively participate in Frontex JOs at sea confirm the existing difficulties in adopting a common interpretation of law of the sea obligations. This undermines the effectiveness of Frontex JOs, but also the effectiveness of the humanitarian principle of the safety of life at sea.

iii. Frontex and international human rights

As long as Frontex was perceived as a pure 'technical actor', humanitarian concerns were incidental.[124] Consistently, the 2004 Frontex Regulation was not prolix concerning human rights in general and international protection in particular.

[121] *Ibid.*

[122] IMO, 'Measures to Protect the Safety of Persons Rescued at Sea: Comments on Document FSI 17/15/1' (submitted by Malta), FSI 17/15/2, 27 February 2009.

[123] In 2008–09, an online petition was organized to request a referendum aimed at, inter alia, reducing the extension of the Maltese SAR zone in proportion to its land size. The petition pointed out that '[t]his area [Maltese SAR zone] is greater than Great Britain and is in urgent need of downsizing and updating with present day realities'. See <http://www.gopetition.com/petitions/malta-illegal-immigration-solution.html>.

[124] Baldaccini, *supra* n 32, at 243.

Subsequent EU legislation filled this gap. First, the RABITs Regulation introduced a specific provision, Article 2, which states:

> This Regulation shall apply without prejudice to the rights of refugees and persons requesting international protection, in particular as regards non-refoulement.

Moreover, the EU's commitment to respect for fundamental rights has been included in the Schengen Border Code. Recital 12 of the Preamble provides that the Code is compatible with fundamental rights and the principles recognized in the Charter.[125] The same Recital states that it 'should be applied in accordance with the Member States' obligations as regards international protection and *non-refoulement*'. Article 3(b) furthermore specifies that the legislation does not affect 'the rights of refugees and persons requesting international protection, in particular as regards *non-refoulement*'. Article 6(1) recalls that, while performing their duties, border guards must fully respect human dignity and their measures should be subject to the principle of proportionality and of non-discrimination on the basis of 'sex, racial or ethnic origin, religion or belief, disability, age or sexual orientation'.[126] According to the extraterritorial application of the Schengen Border Code (Annex VI), these safeguards clauses apply to all persons involved in Frontex operations, also on the high seas.

This interpretation is confirmed by Council Decision 2010/252/EU of April 2010 supplementing the Schengen Borders Code as regards the surveillance of the sea external borders in the context of Frontex JOs.[127] According to Article 1 of this document, the surveillance of the sea external borders in the context of Frontex JOs 'shall be governed by the rules laid down in Part I to the Annex'. Among the principles that should govern JOs, two are particularly relevant:

> 1.1. Measures taken for the purpose of the surveillance operation shall be conducted *in accordance with fundamental rights* and in a way that does not put at risk the safety of the persons intercepted or rescued as well as of the participating units.
> 1.4. Member States shall ensure that *border guards participating in the surveillance operation are trained with regard to relevant provisions of human rights and refugee law*, and are familiar with the international regime on search and rescue. (emphasis added)

The Lisbon Treaty has also completed the human rights legal framework in which Frontex operates. Article 6 of the TEU has conferred a legally binding nature on the Charter, which now has the same legal value as the Treaties. Article 41(1) of the Charter grants to everyone whose rights and freedoms under EU law have been violated the right to an effective remedy before a tribunal. Article 19(1) prohibits

[125] See *supra* n 11. [126] Baldaccini, *supra* n 32, at 246; Carrera, *supra* n 1, at 17.

[127] [2010] OJ L111/20. The European Court of Justice annulled this decision (GC, C-355/10, 5 September 2012), which, however, continues to apply pending the adoption by the competent EU institutions of new rules (para. 90).

collective expulsion and consequently recognizes the right to receive an individual examination of an application for asylum or other forms of protection.[128]

As mentioned above, the 2011 amendments introduced into the Frontex Regulation many references to the promotion of and respect for human rights and of the principle of non-refoulement.[129] They have also created the 'Fundamental Rights Strategy' of Frontex (new Article 26a), which led to the adoption of a 'Code of Conduct for All Persons Participating in Frontex Activities'.[130] The latter affirms that all participants in Frontex activities have the obligation to 'promote and respect human dignity and fundamental rights of every individual', and 'promote compliance with the relevant international and European instruments regarding fundamental rights protection' (Article 4). Concerning international protection, participants in Frontex activities shall 'promote, in full compliance with the principle of non-refoulement, that persons seeking international protection are recognised, receive adequate assistance, are informed, in an appropriate way, about their rights and relevant procedures and are referred to national authorities responsible for receiving their asylum requests' (Article 5).

Moreover, Article 6 of the TEU has also conferred on the EU the possibility to accede to the European Convention for the Protection of Human Rights and Fundamental Freedoms (ECHR)[131] to which all member states are party. In performing border control, EU member states are already bound by international obligations deriving from the ECHR, but also from other relevant international treaties, such as the 1966 International Covenant on Civil and Political Rights (ICCPR)[132] and the Convention against Torture and Other Cruel, Inhuman, or Degrading Treatment or Punishment (CAT).[133] These instruments presuppose for their application the exercise of jurisdiction by the contracting state. It is then important to determine whether, during Frontex JOs at sea, member states are extending their jurisdiction on the high seas and, eventually, in the territorial waters of the participating third state. The European Court of Human Rights (ECtHR) has developed substantial case-law concerning the application of the ECHR at sea[134] and recently ruled on the application of the principle of non-refoulement at sea. But first, it is useful to recall here the relevant case-law.

[128] Carrera, *supra* n 1, at 17. [129] See *supra* section 2(B)(iii). [130] See *supra* n 70.

[131] CETS 5; 213 UNTS 2886, at 222.

[132] UNGA Res. 2200(XXI), 16 December 1966.

[133] UNGA Res. 39/46, 10 December 1984.

[134] On this issue, see Cacciaguidi-Fahy, 'The Law of the Sea and Human Rights' 19 *Sri Lanka Journal of International Law* (2007) 85; Oxman, 'Human Rights and the United Nations Convention on the Law of the Sea' 36 *Columbia Journal of Transnational Law* (1997) 399; Papastavridis, 'European Convention on Human Rights and the Law of the Sea: The Strasbourg Court in Unchartered Waters?', in M. Fitzmaurice and P. Merkouris (eds), *The Interpretation and Application of the European Convention of Human Rights Rights: Legal and Practical Implications* (2012) 117; Tavernier, 'La Cour Européenne des Droits de l'Homme et la Mer', in *La Mer et son Droit, Mélanges Offerts à Laurent Lucchini et Jean-Pierre Quéneudec* (2003) 575; Treves, 'Human Rights and the Law of the Sea' 28 *Berkeley Journal of International Law* (2010) 1; Vukas, 'Droit de la Mer et Droits de l'homme', in G. Cataldi (ed.), *La Mediterranée et le Droit de la Mer à l'aube du 21e Siècle* (2002) 85.

In *Xhavara and ors v. Italy and Albania*,[135] the ECtHR considered that the Albanese vessel *Kater I Rades*—sunk because of a collision incident with the Italian warship *Sibilla* in the international waters of the Otranto Channel on 28 March 1997—was subject to Italian jurisdiction on the basis of the factual circumstances of the collision.[136] In order to attribute international responsibility to Italy, the Court recalled in particular that the collision happened in the framework of operations carried out on the basis of a bilateral cooperation agreement concluded by Italy and Albania on 25 March 1997.[137] The ECtHR did not provide more detail on this point. It is, however, arguable that the mere existence of an agreement conferring enforcement powers to a state is sufficient to prove the exercise of jurisdiction. It is for sure a relevant element of proof but it has then to be appreciated on a case-by-case basis with regard to the actual circumstances.[138]

In the *Medvedyev and ors v. France* case,[139] concerning the crew of a Cambodian vessel intercepted by a French warship on the high seas because of suspicions of drug trafficking, the ECtHR again examined in detail the factual background and maintained that French authorities exercised effective, continuous, and uninterrupted control on the vessel. Consequently, the persons on board were subject to French jurisdiction (para. 67). This case-law shows that ECHR contracting parties are subject to scrutiny under the ECtHR for actions exercised on the high seas[140] when carried out in the framework of an agreement which gives enforcement powers and/or when state authorities exercise effective control on vessels and their passengers. On the basis of the existing case-law, it is unclear, however, if these two conditions have to be applied cumulatively or not.

In *Hirsi Jamaa and ors v. Italy*,[141] the applicants (11 Somali nationals and 13 Eritrean nationals) were part of a group of about 200 individuals who left Libya aboard three vessels with the aim of reaching the Italian coast. On 6 May 2009, three ships of the Italian authorities intercepted them. The occupants of the intercepted vessels were transferred onto Italian military ships and returned to Tripoli

[135] *Xhavara and ors v. Italy and Albania* (Admissibility Decision), ECHR (2001) Appl. No. 39473/98, 11 January 2001.

[136] Lagrange, 'L'Application de la Convention de Rome à des Actes Accomplis par les Etats Parties en Dehors du Territoire National', 112 *Revue Générale de Droit International Public* (2008) 521, at 544–5.

[137] For a comment on this agreement, see Cannizzaro, 'Sui Rapporti fra Responsabilità Internazionale dello Stato e Responsabilità Penale dell'Agente per Incidenti Conseguenti ad Attività Protettive. Considerazioni sull'Incidente nel Canale di Otranto del 28 Marzo 1997 fra le Navi *Kades I Rades* e *Sibilla*', in A. De Guttry and F. Pagani (eds), *La Crisi Albanese del 1997* (1999) 258; Scovazzi, 'Le Norme di Diritto Internazionale sull'Immigrazione Illegale via Mare con Particolare Riferimento ai Rapporti tra Italia e Albania', *ibid.*, at 239.

[138] P. De Sena, *La Nozione di Giurisdizione Statale nei Trattati sui Diritti dell'Uomo* (2002) at 228–9.

[139] *Medvedyev and ors v. France*, Appl. No. 3394/03, 29 March 2010.

[140] The Court in particular pointed out that 'the special nature of the maritime environment cannot justify an area outside the law where individuals are covered by no legal system capable of affording them enjoyment of the rights and guarantees protected by the Convention which the States have undertaken to secure to everyone within their jurisidiction'; *ibid.*, para. 81.

[141] See *supra* n 12.

on the basis of the 2008 bilateral agreement between Italy and Libya.[142] The applicants alleged a violation of Article 3 of the ECHR (prohibition of torture), Article 4 of Protocol No. 4 (prohibition of collective expulsion), and Article 13 of the ECHR (right to an effective remedy). On whether the applicants were under Italian jurisdiction, the Grand Chamber held that:

> [T]he events took place entirely on board ships of the Italian armed forces, the crews of which were composed exclusively of Italian military personnel. In the Court's opinion, in the period between boarding the ships of the Italian armed forces and being handed over to the Libyan authorities, the applicants were under the continuous and exclusive de jure and de facto control of the Italian authorities. ... Accordingly, the events giving rise to the alleged violations fall within Italy's 'jurisdiction' within the meaning of Article 1 of the Convention.

This last case is particularly important in relation to Frontex activities. Even if Frontex was not formally involved in the specific events, the activities under scrutiny were carried out following a *modus operandi* similar to operations performed under Frontex coordination. Consequently, Frontex operations, which repeat the same pattern, might be deemed in violation of the ECHR.

3. The Need to Balance Security Imperatives and Human Rights Obligations

The control of borders presupposes a right to protect the territory framed by these borders, to guarantee security for the population of the territory. But this right is not absolute, and in its execution it certainly cannot brush aside any countervailing considerations and legal commitments. Obligations deriving from international and EU law and humanitarian considerations limit the exercise of this right. Any actor, be it a state or a supranational entity, needs to balance security imperatives and human rights obligations.

In order to achieve this balance in the framework of Frontex, two main issues have to be analysed. First, the human rights mainly challenged by Frontex JOs must be identified and examined in order to propose future improvements concerning

[142] 'Trattato di Amicizia, Partenariato e Cooperazione', *Gazzetta Ufficiale della Repubblica Italiana*, No. 40, 18 February 2009. For a comment, see De Vittor, 'Soccorso in Mare e Rimpatri in Libia: Tra Diritto del Mare e Tutela Internazionale dei Diritti dell'Uomo' 92 *Rivista di Diritto Internazionale* (2009) 806; Munari, 'Controllo dei Flussi Migratori tra Obblighi dell'Unione Europea e Rapporti Bilaterali dell'Italia', in E. Triggiani (ed.), *Europa e Mediterraneo* (2010) 267; Fioravanti, 'Scatole Cinesi. Quale Controllo Democratico Sulla Cooperazione "Italo-Libica-Europea" in Materia di Immigrazione?', in G. Brunelli, A. Pugiotto, and P. Veronesi (eds.), *Il Diritto Costituzionale come Regola e Limite al Potere, Scritti in Onore di Lorenza Carlassare*, vol. II (2009) 539; Ronzitti, 'Il Trattato Italia-Libia di Amicizia, Partenariato e Cooperazione', Istituto di Affari Internazionali (IAI), Contributi di Istituti di Ricerca Specializzati, No. 108, January 2009; Terrasi, 'I Respingimenti in Mare di Migranti alla Luce della Convenzione Europea dei Diritti Umani' 3 *Diritti Umani e Diritto Internazionale* (2009) 591; Trevisanut, 'La Collaborazione Italia—Libia in Materia di Contrasto all'Immigrazione Clandestina via Mare: Profili di Diritto del Mare' 3 *Diritti Umani e Diritto Internazionale* (2009) 609.

their implementation. Secondly, criticism against Frontex JOs mainly focuses on alleged violations of the principle of non-refoulement. This principle is at the core of asylum protection. It is thus necessary to analyse the effectiveness of asylum protection in the frame of Frontex JOs.

A. Human rights challenged by EU joint border management

i. The right to emigrate

Frontex JOs at sea challenge the effectiveness of the right to emigrate in forcibly redirecting intercepted migrants to the country from which they left. The right to emigrate was first recognized by the Universal Declaration of Human Rights (UDHR),[143] which states that '[e]veryone has the right to leave any country, including his own, and to return to his country' (Article 13(2)). This right was then affirmed in Article 12(2) of the ICCPR and Article 2(2) of Protocol No. 4 to the ECHR.[144] The European Parliament affirmed the fundamental nature of this right in Recommendation No. 1449 of 2000.[145] The right to emigrate has also been defined as an 'inconvenient right'[146] giving voice to the perception that developed countries have of it. Indeed, the right to emigrate jeopardizes one of the fundamental elements of state sovereignty: the control of borders.

In order to be exercised, the right to emigrate implies two consecutive conditions: the individual shall be allowed to leave his/her country of origin or of residence;[147] then, he/she has to have a place where to go.[148] The second condition of course is most critical because it would imply that a state does not have complete control over who can or cannot enter its territory. In a period in which security has become one of the core functions of modern states,[149] in which migration is commonly criminalized, the inconvenience of the right to emigrate has induced developed states—ie states of destination of the flows—to exercise pressure on developing states—ie states of origin or of transit of the flows—in order to control irregular movement of their citizens and/or aliens in transit on their territories. Consequently states of destination avoid having to deal with it.

[143] UNGA Res. 217(III), 10 December 1948. The UDHR is not formally binding, but most of the norms contained have progressively acquired the status of customary law and, consequently, bind the states members of the international community.

[144] Protocol No. 4 to the Convention for the Protection of Human Rights and Fundamental Freedoms, securing certain rights and freedoms other than those already included in the Convention and in the first Protocol thereto, adopted 16 September 1963, in force 2 May 1968, CETS 46.

[145] EP Rec. No. 1449(2000), 28 January 2000 on Clandestine migration from the south of the Mediterranean into Europe.

[146] Juss, 'Free Movement and the World Order' 16 *International Journal of Refugee Law* (2004) 289, at 291.

[147] The right to leave was often invoked against the closure of borders exercised by communist regimes during the Cold War. It is today systematically violated by authoritarian regimes which impede their own citizens from moving outside their borders.

[148] Because of this second condition, the expression 'right to emigrate' seems to better express the content of such right than the expression 'right to leave'.

[149] Harvey and Barnidge, 'Human Rights, Free Movement, and the Right to Leave in International Law' 19 *International Journal of Refugee Law* (2007) 1, at 2.

The right to emigrate is, however, not absolute. In its General Comment No. 27[150] the Human Rights Committee affirms the possibility for states to adopt exceptions and restrictions which 'must be based on clear legal grounds and meet the test of necessity and the requirements of proportionality'. Harvey and Barnidge illustratively commented that these exceptions and restrictions must not 'swallow the rule'.[151]

When exercised on the high seas, interception measures hamper migrants from reaching any country in the region. EU member states not only prevent the irregular crossing of their borders, but also impede migrants from going anywhere else. In the above-mentioned *Xhavara* case of the ECtHR, the Court rejected the applicability of the right to leave because Italian measures aimed at preventing Albanians from entering Italian territory and not from leaving Albania.[152] This statement of the Court invites several criticisms. First, the ECtHR itself recalls that these 'preventing entry' measures were taken on the basis of a bilateral agreement concluded with Albania authorizing Italian authorities to intercept vessels transporting migrants who irregularly left Albania. Italy was then assisting Albania in controlling its borders and preventing irregular movement of the Albanian population. Secondly, Brouwer has rightly noted that 'if the extraterritorial jurisdiction or power of a [EU] Member State to prevent persons leaving a third state or international waters is to be recognized, why the same Member State cannot be held responsible for violations of human rights resulting from these preventive actions'.[153]

These actions also prevent migrants from exercising their fundamental right to seek asylum (Article 14 of the UDHR); the exercise of which is of course tightly linked to the right to emigrate and the possibility to leave one's own country of origin or residence. The participation of EU member states' patrols in border control activities of partner third states raises the same issue. Hathaway suggests that 'it could be claimed that the refusal to permit disembarkation and access to determination procedures could amount to an expulsion without a decision on the validity of a claim of asylum being made according to due legal process'.[154] It is provocatively possible to extend this reasoning to the forced redirection operated on the high seas when eventual individual claims for asylum are not submitted to adequate scrutiny by intercepting state authorities.

ii. The right to liberty and security

Article 5 of the ECHR guarantees to everyone the 'right to liberty and security of person'. This means that no one shall be deprived of his/her freedom except when

[150] General Comment No. 27, Freedom of Movement (Art. 12), UN Doc CCPR/C/21/Rev.1/Add.9, 2 November 1999, para. 16.

[151] Harvey and Barnidge, *supra* n 149, at 18.

[152] See *supra* n 135, at para. 3: 'La Cour relève que les mesures mises en cause par les requérants ne visaient pas à les priver du droit de quitter l'Albanie, mais à les empêcher d'entrer sur le territoire italien. Le second paragraphe de l'article 2 du Protocole n° 4 ne trouve donc pas à s'appliquer en l'espèce'.

[153] Brouwer, 'Extraterritorial Migration Control and Human Rights: Preserving the Responsibility of the EU and its Member States', in Ryan and Mitsilegas, *supra* n 32, at 225.

[154] J. C. Hathaway, *The Rights of Refugees under International Law* (2005), at 178 ff; see also Barnes, 'The International Law of the Sea and Migration Control', in Ryan and Mitsilegas, *supra* n 32, at 119.

lawfully decided by a competent court in compliance with relevant legislation. When arrested, a person shall be informed promptly of the reasons of the arrest and of the eventual charges, and shall 'be brought promptly before a judge or other officer authorized by law to exercise judicial power and shall be entitled to trial within a reasonable time or to release pending trial. Release may be conditioned by guarantees to appear for trial'.

EU law allows member states to hold in detention a person for identification purposes and pending the determination of his/her status, in particular when a demand for asylum has been submitted. Moreover, '[w]here an applicant for asylum is held in detention, Member States shall ensure that there is a possibility of speedy judicial review'.[155] Frontex JOs at sea may challenge these guarantees in two factual circumstances: when the irregular migrants are kept on board of their vessel or of the intercepting vessel; when they are disembarked and held in detention/reception camps in the participating third state.

In the first case, two hypotheses have to be analysed. First, as a consequence of an interception occurring on the high seas, either the vessel transporting the migrants is forcibly escorted or the irregular migrants are transferred to the warship and handed over in a section of the ship. In both situations, the migrants are under the strict control of the intercepting state while on the high seas and, pursuant to the above-mentioned ECtHR case-law, under its jurisdiction. However, in this case-law, the intercepted vessel was suspected of some criminal activities (ie drug trafficking) and thus the arrest was legally founded.[156] It is debatable whether at the moment of the interception on the high seas, the irregular migrant can already be considered 'irregular' as he/she has not yet crossed a border without the necessary documents; moreover, in order to eventually justify a preventive arrest, the intercepting state would have to prove that the intercepted migrants were actually headed towards its coast. Such an arrest might be lawful only for smugglers under the Palermo Protocol; irregular migrants would only suffer the consequences of this police activity.

Secondly, the intercepted vessel or the passengers are brought to a port and the coastal authorities refuse to authorize the disembarkation. As a consequence of this decision, the migrants spend an undetermined period of time on board without having the possibility of going elsewhere. Such a case has never been submitted to the ECtHR or other international bodies; neither does the author know of any such case brought in front of any domestic court of an EU member state. There is, however, an interesting case before the Federal Court of Australia, the case *Vadarlis v. Minister for Immigration and Multicultural Affairs and ors.*[157] On the fringes of the

[155] See Art. 18 Council Directive 2005/85, [2005] OJ L326/13, on minimum standards on procedures in member states for granting and withdrawing refugee status.

[156] See *Medvedyev and ors v. France, supra* n 139; see also *Rigapoulos v. Spain*, ECHR (1999) Appl. No. 37388/97, 12 January 1999.

[157] *Vadarlis v. Minister for Immigration and Multicultural Affairs and ors*, V 900 of 2001 FCA 1297, 11 September 2001; 'Refugees—Detention within Australian Territorial Sea—Pacific Solution—Migration Act' 21 *Australian Yearbook of International Law* (2001) 263.

well-known *Tampa* case,[158] the Federal Court of Australia inferred the detention of the passengers of the *Tampa* who were refused permission to disembark on the basis of an analysis of factual elements; among which was that the Australian authorities unilaterally decided where the *Tampa* could go or not go and that the passengers were completely isolated on board. Neither were they consulted on the question of their transfer to New Zealand and Nauru. The trial judge thus affirmed that:

> Where complete control over people and their destiny is exercised by others it cannot be said that the opportunity offered by those others is a reasonable escape from the custody in which they were held. The custody simply continues in the form chosen by those detaining the people restrained.[159] (para. 17)

Interception and diversion carried out during Frontex JOs might be subjected to the same claim. For the time being, measures linked with Frontex JOs have been challenged in front of the CAT Committee in the so-called *Marine I* case.[160] On 30 January 2007, the cargo vessel *Marine I* rescued about 370 people in the Senegalese SAR zone. Senegal asked Spain to deal with it and thus Spanish authorities received the distress call. Considering that the Mauritanian port of Nouadhibou was the closest one, Spain reached an agreement with Mauritania and the passengers of the cargo vessel were disembarked on 12 February 2007. In exchange, Spain agreed to pay €650,000 to Mauritania and to ensure that all passengers were repatriated from Mauritania within five days. The passengers were held in an abandoned former fish-processing plant, where they were under Spanish custody. The repatriation process took longer than expected; in particular a small

[158] The *Tampa* was a Norwegian merchant ship, which rescued an Indonesian fishing boat in distress on 26 August 2001 on the high seas. The *Tampa* had to keep all the 438 passengers of the Indonesian boat on board, notwithstanding that it was formally only allowed to transport a maximum of 50 persons. Having arrived at 13.5 nautical miles from the Australian Christmas Island, the master had to stop as the Australian authorities denied access into territorial waters. In light of the health conditions of the passengers, among them pregnant women and wounded men, the master took the decision to contravene the denial and entered the Australian waters looking for sanitary assistance. The vessel stopped four miles from the shore. The Australian government sent a special corps of the army to give first medical care and to avoid the disembarkation of the migrants. The *Tampa* then refused to leave the territorial waters because of the unsafe situation of the vessel due to the excess of people on board. Finally on 1 September, the Australian government declared that it had reached an agreement with New Zealand and transferred the passengers to a navy vessel bringing them to two Australian military bases in New Zealand. From there, the migrants arrived on the soil of New Zealand and Nauru. See Baillet, 'The *Tampa* Case and its Impact on Burden Sharing at Sea' 25 *Human Rights Quarterly* (2003) 741; Fornari, 'Soccorso di Profughi in Mare e Diritto di Asilo: Questioni di Diritto Internazionale Sollevate dalla Vicenda della Nave Tampa' 57 *La Comunità Internazionale* (2002) 61; White, 'Tampa Incident: Shipping, International and Maritime Legal Issues' 78 *The Australian Law Journal* (2004) 101; *idem*, 'Tampa Incident: Some Subsequent Legal Issues' 78 *The Australian Law Journal* (2004) 249.

[159] This judgment was then challenged on appeal and the Full Court of the Federal Court dismissed the decision and induced several critical opinions: *Ruddock and ors v. Vadarlis and ors* (2001) 66 A.L.D. 25 (V 1007 of 2001, FCA 1329), 18 September 2001, para. 5, in which the Chief Justice dissented on the admissibility of the appeal considering arbitrary the detention of the *Tampa* passengers.

[160] For relevant case-law see *J.H.A v. Spain*, 22 *International Journal of Refugee Law* (2009) 104. See also Klug and Howe, 'The Concept of State Jurisdiction and the Applicability of the *Non-refoulement* Principle to Extraterritorial Interception Meaures', in Ryan and Mitsilegas, *supra* n 32, at 83 and Wouters and Den Heijer, *supra* n 12.

group of them, the plaintiffs, remained in Mauritania for several months in precarious conditions. The CAT Committee affirmed that:

> [T]he State party [Spain] exercised, by virtue of a diplomatic agreement concluded with Mauritania, constant de facto control over the alleged victims during their detention in Nouadhibou. Consequently, the Committee considers that the alleged victims are subject to Spanish jurisdiction insofar as the complaint that forms the subject of the present communication is concerned.

The CAT Committee did not consider if the diplomatic agreement at issue provided for the exercise of such control. The lawfulness of the control was not relevant in order to determine the existence of the control, the (lawful or not) exercise of jurisdiction and the subsequent direct responsibility of Spain.[161]

Considering now a similar case in which Spain would not have had the control over the detention structure, would the CAT Committee have had any legal arguments to attribute to Spain (or any other EU member state) the responsibility for the perpetrated violations? In this context it is worth recalling Article 16 of the International Law Commission Articles on the responsibility of states for internationally wrongful acts (ILC Articles)[162] on 'Aid or assistance in the commission of an internationally wrongful act':

> A State which aids or assists another State in the commission of an internationally wrongful act by the latter is internationally responsible for doing so if:
>
> (a) that State does so with knowledge of the circumstances of the internationally wrongful act; and
> (b) the act would be internationally wrongful if committed by that State.

Consequently, it could be ascertained that indirect responsibility existed of any EU member state for violation of international obligations concerning the conditions of detention if it entrusts intercepted irregular migrants to a third state participating in the Frontex JOs, and if there are indications that the EU member state knows about the precarious situation, which exists with regard to the respect for fundamental rights in this third state. Similarly, Article 16 of ILC Articles may be invoked concerning the alleged violation of international obligations deriving from the law of asylum or from international protection.[163]

B. The effectiveness of asylum protection

i. EU common policy on asylum

According to the Council Decision 2010/252/EU of April 2010,[164] while performing the control of external borders, member states are bound by the provisions of the 'asylum *acquis*'. The EU asylum *acquis* sets a series of important guarantees for asylum seekers and refugees, but also for those in need of international protection.

[161] Wouters and Den Heijer, *ibid.*, at 11. [162] UNGA Res. 56/83, 12 December 2001.
[163] Fischer-Lescano, Löhr, and Tohidipur, *supra* n 42, at 280. [164] See *supra* n 127.

Here the instruments relevant with regard to border management are recalled briefly.

The Treaty of Amsterdam called for the adoption of minimum standards in accordance with the 1951 Geneva Convention on the Status of Refugee (hereinafter 1951 Geneva Convention)[165] and other relevant treaties (Article 63 of the ECT). The European institutions have then been particularly prolific in this field. In 2001 Council Directive 2001/55 was adopted on minimum standards for giving temporary protection in the event of a mass influx of displaced persons and on measures promoting a balance of efforts between member states in receiving such persons and bearing the consequences thereof.[166] This Directive provides for immediate and temporary protection in the event of a mass influx, or imminent mass influx, to displaced persons from third countries who are unable to return to their country of origin, in particular if there is also a risk that the asylum system of the destination country is unable to process this influx without adverse effects for its efficient operation (Article 2). The protection has a maximum duration of one year (Article 4), and can be extended with a decision of the Council on the proposal of the Commission or member state. This Directive creates a system through which a member state can ask the Council for assistance in order to deal with a mass flow of migrants. For the time being, this burden-sharing mechanism has not yet been activated.

Council Directive 2003/9 lays down minimum standards for the reception of asylum seekers.[167] According to its Article 3, the Directive 'shall apply to all third country nationals and stateless persons who make an application for asylum *at the border* or in the territory of a Member State as long as they are allowed to remain on the territory as asylum seekers, as well as to family members, if they are covered by such application for asylum according to the national law'(emphasis added). This Directive realizes the purposes expressed during the European Council of Tampere in 1999 regarding the fact that a Common European Asylum System should include common minimum conditions of reception for asylum seekers. The Directive provides that member states can confine an asylum seeker 'within a particular place, where the applicant is deprived of his or her freedom of movement' in order to ascertain his/her status. However, such a measure should be exceptional and provisional. Notwithstanding the *ratione loci* application clearly set in Article 3, the Commission highlighted how many member states do not apply this Directive in detention centres at the borders.[168]

Council Directive 2005/85 on minimum standards on procedures in Member States for granting and withdrawing refugee status[169] applies 'to all applications for

[165] 189 UNTS 150, at 137. [166] [2001] OJ L212/12. [167] [2003] OJ L31/18.

[168] Report from the Commission to the council and to the European Parliament on the Application of Directive 2003/9/CE of 27 January 2003 laying down minimum standards for the reception of asylum seekers, COM (2007) 745 final, 26 November 2007. See Den Heijer, 'Europe beyond its Borders: Refugee and Human Rights Protection in Extraterritorial Immigration Control', in Ryan and Mitsilegas, *supra* n 32, at 174–6.

[169] [2005] OJ L326/13.

asylum made in the territory, including *at the border or in the transit zones* of the Member States, and to the withdrawal of refugee status' (Article 3) (emphasis added). Accordingly, member states 'shall ensure that authorities likely to be addressed by someone who wishes to make an application for asylum are able to advise that person how and where he/she may make such an application and/or may require these authorities to forward the application to the competent authority' (Article 6(3)). Even if, at first glance, this Directive and the above-mentioned Directive 2003/9 do not seem to apply extraterritorially, their application cannot be excluded when border controls are performed beyond borders. The UNHCR suggested a reform of Directive 2005/85 in order to clarify its application to extraterritorial border procedures.[170] This suggestion was echoed by Council Decision 2010/252/EU, recalling in particular this Directive as part of the asylum *acquis*.

The entry into force of the Lisbon Treaty strengthens the asylum *acquis*. Article 78 of the TFEU calls for the adoption of 'a common policy on asylum, subsidiary protection and temporary protection with a view to offering appropriate status to any third-country national requiring international protection and ensuring compliance with the principle of *non-refoulement*'. This a very important step forward towards guaranteeing the effectiveness of international protection as its basic principles, in particular non-refoulement, have become EU treaty law. Moreover, the Lisbon Treaty does not ask for the adoption of minimum standards, but for the creation of a uniform status of asylum, a uniform status of subsidiary protection, and a common system of temporary protection in case of mass influx situations (Article 78(2) of the TFEU). The Lisbon Treaty also integrates the European Charter of Fundamental Rights, which includes a new fundamental right to asylum in Article 18. The Charter also reconfirms the fundamental status of the principle of non-refoulement within the EU legal system in Article 19.

ii. The principle of non-refoulement

Article 2 of the RABITs Regulation provides that the Regulation shall apply 'without prejudice to the rights of refugees and persons requesting international protection, in particular as regards non-refoulement'. The 2011 amendments insert four references to the respect of the principle of non-refoulement, in accordance with EU and international law.

The principle of non-refoulement is first set by Article 33 of the 1951 Geneva Convention which protects asylum seekers and refugees against being 'expel[led] or return[ed] ("refouler") ... in any manner whatsoever to the frontiers of territories where his life or freedom would be threatened on account of his race, religion, nationality, membership of a particular social group or political opinion'. This principle is at the core of asylum-seeker protection,[171] but it is also part of

[170] UNHCR, 'Response to the European Commission's Green Paper on the Future Common European Asylum System', September 2007, at 46; available at <http://www.unhcr.org/refworld/docid/46e159f82.html>.

[171] Lauterpacht and Bethlehem, 'The Scope and Content of the Principle of *Non-refoulement*: Opinion', in E. Feller, V. Türk, and F. Nicholson, *Refugee Protection in International Law* (2003) 87, at 107.

the international law of human rights. The non-refoulement principle in human rights law is guaranteed by Article 3 of the CAT which prohibits the removal of individuals to states where they risk being subjected to torture or other inhuman or degrading treatment. Article 7 of the ICCPR also affirms this. At the regional level, the protection against refoulement is guaranteed by Article 3 of the 1950 ECHR, Article 22(8) of the 1969 American Convention on Human Rights,[172] and Article 5 of the 1981 African Convention on the Protection of Human and Peoples' Rights.[173] Moreover, Article 45 of the 1949 Fourth Geneva Convention relative to the Protection of Civilian Persons in Time of War[174] provides that '[i]n no circumstances shall a protected person be transferred to a country where he or she may have reason to fear persecution for his or her political opinions or religious beliefs'. Because of its repetition in several instruments and considering the relevant practice, the principle of non-refoulement is today considered a customary norm both of human rights and humanitarian law.[175]

The principle of non-refoulement is the only guarantee that refugees will not be submitted again to the persecution which has caused their departure and responds to the refugee's need to enter in the asylum country. It does not, however, explicitly guarantee access to the territory of the destination state or admission to the procedures granting the status of refugee.[176] Actually, some authors have tried to support the existence of an additional obligation aimed at binding states to admit individuals applying for protection into their own territory but, for the time being, state practice cannot confirm these attempts.[177]

Noll gave a definition of the principle, which highlights its practical implications: '*Non-refoulement* ... could be described as a *right to transgress an administrative border*' (emphasis added).[178] On the one hand, Noll's definition

[172] 1144 UNTS 17955, at 123. [173] 21 ILM (1982), at 58. [174] 75 UNTS 973, at 287.

[175] Allain, 'The *Jus Cogens* Nature of *Non-refoulement*' 13 *International Journal of Refugee Law* (2001) 533; T. Gammeltoft-Hansen, *Access to Asylum, International Refugee Law and the Globalisation of Migration Control* (2011), at 44; Greig, 'The Protection of Refugees and Customary International Law' 8 *Australian Year Book of International Law* (1983) 106; Lauterpacht and Bethlehem, *supra* n 171, at 87; Mathew, 'Sovereignty and the Right to Seek Asylum: the Case of the Cambodian Asylum-seekers in Australia' 15 *Australian Year Book of International Law* (1994) 35; Salerno, 'L'obbligo Internazionale di Non Refoulement dei Richiedenti Asilo' 4 *Diritti Umani e Diritto Internazionale* (2010) 487, at 502.

[176] Salerno, on the contrary, affirms that the principle of non-refoulement implies the individual right of entry and stay in the territory for the time needed in order to have his/her status ascertained ('nel caso degli asilanti, il principio di *non refoulement* si congiunge con il diritto dell'individuo ad entrare e permanere nel territorio dello Stato per quanto necessario all'espletamento della procedura corredata delle necessarie garanzie giurisdizionali'); see Salerno, *supra* n 175, at 493.

[177] Not considered here are the issues related to the application of the principle of non-refoulement in a situation of expulsion from the territory of the host state, ie after the decision of the competent authorities not to admit the individual to the relevant procedures or the refusal to grant the status of refugee; situations implying other legal problems and consequences despite the phenomenon of seaborne asylum seekers. See G. S. Goodwin-Gill and J. Adam, *The Refugee in International Law* (3rd edn, 2007) at 257; J. C. Hathaway, *The Rights of Refugees under International Law* (2005), at 370; F. Lenzerini, *Asilo e Diritti Umani, L'evoluzione del Diritto d'asilo nel Diritto Internazionale* (2009), at 335.

[178] G. Noll, 'Seeking Asylum at Embassies: A Right to Entry under International Law?' 17 *International Journal of Refugee Law* (2005) 542, at 548.

integrates another very important obligation contained in Article 31 of the 1951 Geneva Convention: '[t]he Contracting States shall not impose penalties, on account of their illegal entry or presence, on refugees'. Consequently, the irregular arrival of an asylum seeker, for instance by sea, shall not hamper his/her right to seek asylum. Article 4(3) of the Schengen Border Code expressly provides that the application of penalties to persons who cross the external borders without authorization is 'without prejudice to [member states'] international protection obligation' and Article 13(1) states that Code's provisions concerning the right of asylum and international protection prevail over a decision to refuse entry at the external border.[179]

On the other hand, Noll's definition implies the application of the principle at the border, in its meaning of 'non rejection at the frontier'. This is mostly shared today,[180] but its application to interdiction operations on the high seas or within territorial waters of third countries is less clear. Non rejection at the frontier was included in the principle of non-refoulement in the instruments subsequent to the 1951 Refugee Convention, such as the 1967 Declaration on Territorial Asylum (1967 DTA)[181] and the 1967 OAU Convention on Refugees.[182] Since 1977,[183] the ExCom has brought forward this argument, restating it in relation to migration by sea in 1979 as follows:

> [I]t is the humanitarian obligation of all coastal States to allow vessels in distress to seek haven in their waters and to grant asylum, or at least temporary refuge, to persons on board wishing to seek asylum.[184]

And again in 1981, the ExCom recalled that:

> It is therefore *imperative to ensure that asylum seekers are fully protected in large-scale influx situations, to reaffirm the basic minimum standards for their treatment.* ... In all cases the fundamental principle of *non-refoulement—including non rejection at the frontier—must be scrupulously observed.*[185] (emphasis added)

Considering the several references contained in the legal texts (both of international and EU law) rooting and framing Frontex activities, and having ascertained the exercise of states' jurisdiction over intercepted migrants, the principle of non-refoulement certainly applies to Frontex JOs. Now it has to be discussed when and how Frontex JOs may violate this principle.

[179] Baldaccini, *supra* n 32, at 246.

[180] Lauterpacht and Bethlehem, *supra* n 171, at 113 *et seq*. Art. 3(1) Council Regulation 343/2003 includes the application of the principle in border situations (EC Regulation establishing the criteria and the mechanisms for determining the Member State responsible for examining an asylum application lodged in one of the Member State by a third-country national, [2003] OJ L50/1).

[181] UN Doc. A/RES/2312(XXII), 14 December 1967.

[182] OAU convention governing the specific aspects of refugee problems in Africa, 1001 UNTS 14691, at 45.

[183] ExCom, Conclusion No. 6 (XXVIII) 1977, para. (c): 'the fundamental importance of the observance of the principle of *non-refoulement*—both at the border and within the territory of a State'.

[184] ExCom, Conclusion No. 15 (XXX) 1979, para. (c).

[185] ExCom, Conclusion No. 22 (XXXII) 1981, reaffirmed during the crisis in Former Yugoslavia, in ExCom, Conclusion No. 74 (XLV) 1994, para. (r).

Frontex JOs may violate the principle of non-refoulement when the intercepted vessel and its passengers are forcefully diverted to an unsafe country where their life and liberty are threatened. The unsafeness of the country has to be determined on an individual basis, as the right to seek asylum has an individual nature. Therefore, the indiscriminate diversion of all the passengers of a vessel without a first screening in order to ascertain the presence of asylum seekers or of persons in need of international protection, constitutes a violation of the principle of non-refoulement.[186]

This interpretation is confirmed by the *Hirsi* case. The ECtHR affirmed that the principle of non-refoulement entails some positive obligations, such as the identification of the persons, even outside the territory, and 'to find out about the treatment to which the applicants would be exposed after their return';[187] moreover, 'the Italian authorities should have ascertained how the Libyan authorities fulfilled their international obligations in relation to the protection of refugees'.[188] In the view of the Court, these positive obligations apply even if the intercepted migrants failed to ask for asylum.[189]

The application of the principle of non-refoulement to police activities on the high seas implies also that the intervening state shall not preclude asylum seekers from seeking asylum elsewhere and, thus, force them back to their country of origin or to an unsafe third country. To simply repel vessels to the high seas, without a forced diversion, does not necessarily imply a violation of the principle of non-refoulement.[190] The intervening state shall, however, make sure that repelling them does not put their life in danger. Such behaviour would be in contrast with the duty to render assistance at sea.

The practical consequences of the application of the principle of non-refoulement at sea have been detailed in a pamphlet edited by the UNHCR and the IMO.[191] This document invites shipmasters—for cases in which people rescued at sea claim asylum—to 'alert the closest RCC (Rescue Co-ordination Centre); contact the UNHCR; [to] not ask for disembarkation in the country of origin or from which the individuals fled; [to] not share personal information regarding the asylum-seekers with the authorities of that country, or with others who might convey this information to those authorities'. It is regrettable that similar invitations are not repeated in the document concerning actions that have to be taken by governments. However, such an obligation already exists on the basis of the IMO Guidelines and Principles,[192] and on the basis of the application of the 1951 Geneva Convention and the relevant instruments on human rights. All these instruments are binding on EU member states, and on the EU with the explicit references integrated by the Lisbon Treaty.

[186] From the data reported in Frontex documents it is not clear whether such a screening has been performed by border guards during JOs.

[187] See *Hirsi* case *supra* n 12, para. 133. [188] *Ibid.*, para. 157. [189] *Ibid.*

[190] Trevisanut, 'The Principle of Non-Refoulement at Sea and the Effectiveness of Asylum Protection' 12 *Max Planck Yearbook of United Nations Law* (2008) 210, at 244.

[191] UNHCR and IMO, *Rescue at Sea, A Guide to Principles and Practice as Applied to Migrants and Refugees* (2007), available at <http://www.imo.org> and <http://www.unhcr.org>.

[192] See *supra* n 120 and n 122.

It is consequently unfortunate to find among the success stories reported by Frontex, a reference to the bilateral agreement between Italy and Libya,[193] thanks to which 'the number of people arriving from Libya, as well as the number of migrants [who] died at sea, decreased dramatically during Joint Operation Hermes 2009'.[194] This statement did not consider the questionable situation in Libya with regard to respect for human rights and the binding obligations falling upon member states in the field of human rights and asylum law; the ECtHR did consider these in the oft-mentioned *Hirsi* case.[195]

4. Which Governance for EU External Borders?

From the legal framework illustrated in these pages, it emerges that Frontex can be considered an 'intergovernmental agency'. Frontex structure and decision-making procedures make clear the central role that EU member states still play in this area. Member states' policy and legitimate interest in controlling their borders channel cooperative mechanisms, but 'compulsory solidarity' has not really been successful so far. Cooperation also means to share information and to be exposed to scrutiny or even to criticism. After days in which the Italian government and EU institutions had argued about the management of flows coming from Tunisia in February 2011,[196] Italy officially requested Frontex assistance.[197] However, Italy asked to strengthen the ongoing JO Hermes, not the activation of a RABIT, notwithstanding the emergency situation. Member states need help in managing their external borders, but are still reluctant to accept the intervention of any other actor on the basis of an institutionalized mechanism. In this context, to reach a balance between security imperatives and the need of guaranteeing fundamental rights seems difficult, but not impossible.[198]

The Lisbon Treaty provides some ambitious institutional proposals in this vein and may help in promoting coherence of actions and respect for international

[193] See *supra* n 142.

[194] Frontex General Report 2009, at 44. Also in the Council conclusions on 29 measures for reinforcing the protection of the external borders and combating illegal immigration (2998th JHA Council Meeting, Brussels, 25–6 February 2010), the cooperation with Libya is encouraged without any reference regarding the fact that Libya is not even a party to the 1951 Geneva Convention.

[195] See *supra* n 12.

[196] 'Press Statement on Sudden Increased Migratory Situation in Lampedusa', Frontex News Releases, 14 February 2011; 'Immigrati, Scontro tra UE e Maroni "Rifiutato Nostro Aiuto". "Falso" ', *Corriere della Sera*, 14 February 2011; 'UE: "L'Italia ha Rifiutato il Nostro Aiuto" Maroni: "Falso, ora Strategia Europea" ', *La Repubblica*, 14 February 2011.

[197] 'Request for Help over Migratory Pressure in Lampedusa', Frontex Press Release, 15 February 2011; 'Hermes 2011 Starts Tomorrow in Lampedusa', Frontex Press Release, 19 February 2011; both available at <http://www.frontex.europa.eu>.

[198] Barnes suggests, on the contrary, that such a balance is almost impossible, affirming that 'states have a legitimate interest in patrolling and maintaining the integrity of their borders to prevent illegal migration. To extend the application of the Refugee Convention to the outer limits of the territorial sea, or indeed any further, may render it practically impossible for coastal states to control illegal migration'; Barnes, *supra* n 154, at 121.

obligations.[199] The right to emigrate, the right to seek asylum, and the principle of non-refoulement should at least produce an obligation for states to grant asylum seekers access to an asylum determination procedure,[200] on their territory or in a safe third country. Moreover, both the law of the sea and human rights law complement each other and support the application of international protection obligations at sea. The 2011 amendments to the Frontex Regulation help to clarify the application of such obligations during Frontex JOs. The necessary yardsticks to states' actions already exist but they need to be strengthened in order to more efficiently push EU member states towards more integrated border management in compliance with international protection obligations.

[199] Carrera, *supra* n 1, at 30.
[200] Nessel, 'Externalized Borders and the Invisible Refugee' 40 *Columbia Human Rights Review* (2009) 625, at 678,

6

Integration of Immigrants in EU Law and Policy: Challenges to Rule of Law, Exceptions to Inclusion

Sergio Carrera

What is the legal landscape on the integration of immigrants in the European Union (EU)? One would be tempted to answer this question by saying that there exists no legal framework covering this domain at EU level. First impressions tend to oversimplify and offer a largely distant representation of the complexities and paradoxes inherent to any realities. This is also pertinent when reflecting on the relationship between integration and EU immigration law and policy. While it is true that integration remains a policy area where the (post-Lisbon) EU Treaties still recognize the predominance of national competence over that of the Union, preliminary presumptions about the limited (and even non-existent) EU role might prove to be deceptive when looking at the dynamism which has characterized the processes of policy convergence on issues related to integration of non-EU citizens during the last 12 years.

The integration of persons on the move has been at the core of European integration. The concept of integration has, however, remained largely undefined and can be said to be an indeterminate legal concept in the context of EU immigration law. Since the early 1970s, Europe has paid increasing attention to the legal status and rights of persons exercising mobility across internal frontiers and while doing so being guaranteed security of residence, socio-economic inclusion, family life, and non-discrimination. It was only since the transfer of the immigration domain to shared competence between the EU and its member states with the Amsterdam Treaty in 1999 that the Union commenced to develop a common immigration and integration policy covering certain aspects of the conditions of entry and residence of so-called third country nationals (TCNs) as a key component of the Union's Area of Freedom, Security, and Justice (AFSJ). The EU accounts now for an emerging transnational body of law and policy which, as this chapter will argue, presents various challenges both to its rule of law foundations as well as to the inclusion of TCNs.

The boundaries between law, soft law, and/or policy have remained contested in the Europeanization of integration policy. While the Council accorded a political direction in the 1999 Tampere Programme for the EU to progressively endow itself with a common immigration policy, the extent to which the Union had an express competence to legislate on integration has been subject to constant tensions emerging from a logic of intergovernmentalism anchored in appeals by certain member states' representatives to the principle of subsidiarity and the exclusivity of national competence. The heated discussions between the European Commission and the Council as to the extent to which former Article 63(3)(a) of the Treaty Establishing the European Community (TEC) granted the Union the necessary legal basis to have 'more Europe' on integration policy, did not, however, prevent the adoption in 2007 of the Council Decision establishing the European Fund for the Integration of TCNs, which constitutes the financial framework supporting the implementation of the EU's agenda on integration by the member states. It was also at the request of certain member states' representatives during the Council negotiations that 'integration conditions' and 'integration measures' were introduced in the body of Directives 2003/109 on the status of third country nationals who are long-term residents and 2003/86 on the right to family reunification. These two cases demonstrate that since 1999 the tensions between Europeanization and intergovernmentalism have not prevented the Council from adopting key legislative acts dealing directly with the integration of TCNs when member states' (political or financial) interests have been at stake.

The struggles surrounding the politics of integration at European level have perhaps most visibly resulted in the creation of a dual EU normative framework on integration consisting of EU immigration law and the EU Framework on Integration. While the former constitutes a typical example of ordinary EU secondary law, the latter needs to be understood as a quasi-Open Method Coordination making use of soft-policy/law tools, exchange of information mechanisms on 'best practices', evaluation of integration policies (benchmarking and indicators), and a multilayered system of experimental governance giving a central role to supranational networks of experts and practitioners. The EU Framework on Integration falls still formally outside the EU Treaties and defies the institutional and decision-making foundations envisaged within the remits of the Community method of cooperation: the Commission plays the role of coordinator in the exchange and evaluation of national integration policies; the policy outputs are not European law and, therefore, do not have any legally binding or enforceable effect upon the EU member states; the European Parliament has so far been excluded from the main decision-making processes and its interventions have been generally ad hoc; the Court of Justice has no recognized jurisdiction to interpret and review what is being adopted and implemented; and the decision-making procedures take place (and advance) through non-transparent and obscure processes in the form of (closed doors) expert seminars and inter-ministerial conferences where the role of networks of national experts and practitioners and civil society (the integration actors) have been central at times of creating a *doxa* and common EU discourse on what works for integration in the EU.

This chapter examines the legal and policy configurations on the integration of TCNs at EU level. It focuses on the effects stemming from the progressive

Europeanization of this domain—both in the context of EU immigration law and the EU Framework on Integration—in relation to rule of law principles as well as the inclusion of TCNs. Section 1 starts by studying the conceptions of integration predominating in the dual EU legal/policy framework of integration. It first examines the relation between integration and EU law by paying attention to the role exerted by integration conditions and measures in Directives 2003/109 on the status of TCNs who are long-term residents and 2003/86 on the right to family reunification. This is then combined with a study of the linkages between integration and the EU Framework on Integration. It is argued that in both supranational dimensions there has been a paradigm shift of the EU's approach(es) on integration from one that used to be focused on socio-economic inclusion and equal treatment/participation to another where insecurity, immigration, and identity control have become prioritized. Section 2 sketches the main substantive features of this new understanding of integration in EU law and policy and explores the main driving factors which have justified this transformation. Section 3 then moves into an analysis of the main implications that the multi-level Europeanization of integration over EU member states' discretion at times of using integration as an exception to inclusion, and more generally over the rule of law principles in prospect of the new institutional, decision-making, and legal setting emerging after the entry into force of the Treaty of Lisbon.

1. The Relation between Integration and EU Law and Policy

Narratives, policies, and laws dealing with the integration of persons exercising mobility across borders are far from being a new issue of policy attention at EU level. It is well known that one of the main driving motors of European integration was the establishment of an internal market.[1] Within this context, integration has functioned as a mechanism fostering the mobility of EU nationals' migrant workers (and their family members) across EU's internal borders and, while doing so, ensuring that they enjoy equality of treatment, non-discrimination, family reunion, and a secure legal status in the receiving EU member state.[2] Integration has therefore performed the role of a 'desecuritizing' tool in the internal market and the abolition of internal border checks by encouraging and facilitating cross-border mobility through the provision of non-discrimination, respect for family life, protection against expulsion, and socio-economic and legal inclusion in the receiving member state. Integration here has been conceived as a premise

[1] C. Barnard and J. Scott (eds), *The Law of the Single European Market: Unpacking the Premises* (2002).

[2] Groenendijk, 'Integration Policy and Community Law', in S. Carrera (ed.), *The Nexus between Immigration, Integration and Citizenship in the EU*, (2006) 9. Groenendijk, 'Access of Third-Country Nationals to Employment under the New EC Migration Law', in F. Julien-Laferriere, H. Labaye, and O. Edström (eds), *The European Immigration and Asylum Policy: Critical Assessment Five Years after the Amsterdam Treaty* (2005) 141. Refer to Council Regulation 1612/68 on freedom of movement for workers within the Community [1968] OJ L257/2.

for the materialization of the fundamental right to move and reside freely within the territories of the member states, and not as a mechanism to restrict free movement.[3] A conception of integration as an obligatory programme or a test on the society, values, or way of life and the language of the receiving state and conditioning the freedom of movement of EU citizens was alien to these past understandings, because it would have been conceived as a direct (and unacceptable) barrier to the free movement of persons and a violation of the principle of non-discrimination. It is true that the personal scope of these past debates mainly covered individuals holding the nationality of one EU member state (and therefore qualifying as European citizens). That notwithstanding, before the transfer of the domain of immigration in 1999 to shared EU competence, several EU law and policy responses and discourses were also concerned with the integration of TCNs and used a similar inclusionary understanding.

This has been evidenced by a genealogy of the main changing dynamics affecting the concept of integration in EU law and policy from the 1970s to the present day.[4] The various EU approaches to integration have been diverse and subject to a whole variety of official discourses, policies, and laws, some of which were often incompatible (or in conflict) with each other or difficult to frame into a bounded and coherent understanding of integration. While any genealogy presents its methodological limitations, the mapping revealed the existence of certain consistent and identifiable features in the public intended goal driving the EU's approach(es) to integration of TCNs from the 1970s until 1999. These features conceived integration (of EU nationals and TCNs) as a process concerned with the granting of a secured juridical status of residence, and driven by the principles of equality, non-discrimination, and parity of treatment.[5] The length of residence was a decisive connecting factor for conferring a secured legal status in the receiving state. This reflected a trend across Europe in the granting of an incremental degree of equality in relation to the duration of residence.[6]

Are these classical understandings of integration still the ones predominating in EU law and policy? As the next two sections will demonstrate, both in the scope of EU immigration law and the EU Framework on Integration there has been a mutation in the EU's paradigm on integration. The negotiations inside the Council of the first directives on regular immigration and the kick-off phase of the EU Framework on Integration marked a distinctive move from an approach framing integration as a process of inclusion to one where it functions as an insecurity, immigration, and identity-control tool. Integration is transformed into another

[3] As envisaged in the EU Charter of Fundamental Rights in Art. 45 (Freedom of movement and of residence), which according to its second paragraphs stipulates that 'Freedom of movement and residence may be granted, in accordance with the Treaties, to nationals of third countries legally resident in the territory of a Member State'.

[4] S. Carrera, *In Search of the Perfect Citizen? The Intersection between Integration, Immigration and Nationality in the EU* (2009).

[5] *Ibid.*; Groenendijk, 'Legal Concepts of Integration in EU Migration Law' 6 *European Journal of Migration and Law* (2004) 111.

[6] K. Groenendijk, E. Guild, and H. Dogan, *Security of Residence of Long-Term Migrants: A Comparative Study of Law and Practice in European Countries* (1998).

regulatory technique for the state to manage access by the foreigner to security and rights. Integration demands the immigrant demonstrate knowledge of the constructed identity façade and language of the receiving nation state as a condition for granting inclusion. The politics of integration at EU level during the last nine years have favoured the emergence of this new understanding of integration and its placement as one of the featuring components of EU law and policy.

A. EU immigration law and integration

The relation between integration and EU immigration law was officially launched with the negotiations of the first set of EU directives on regular immigration on the basis of former Articles 63(3)(a) and 63(4) of the TEC. These provisions called on the Council to adopt measures on the 'conditions of entry and residence ... including those for the purpose of family reunion' and 'defining the rights and conditions under which nationals of third countries who are legally resident in a Member State may reside in other Member States'. The legal basis for the enactment of a common immigration policy were accompanied by the political mandate agreed at the Tampere European Council Conclusions of 15 and 16 October 1999,[7] which in addition to being the first occasion when the Council agreed a multi-annual programme offering strategic guidelines on the EU's AFSJ, also contained an ambitious political agenda with the following four principles (the Tampere Milestones) which were intended to guide the EU's policy on immigration and integration: (1) The principle of fair treatment of legally residing TCNs; (2) The need to develop a more vigorous integration policy granting to legal TCNs rights and obligations comparable to EU citizens;[8] (3) The granting of rights which are 'as near as possible' to those of EU citizens to long-term resident TCNs;[9] and (4) The objective to approximate national legislations on the conditions for admission and residence.[10]

The Tampere Programme aimed at bringing some coherence to the piecemeal approaches which had characterized previous EU policies on integration since the 1970s by embracing the various Union understandings of integration under the same umbrella. The Programme constituted a tangible harmonization of the conception of integration rooted in previous EU policy, legal, and discursive responses. Except for some important reservations related to the undemocratic nature of its decision-making process,[11] the innovativeness inspiring the Tampere milestones received numerous supporters, not only across the EU policy-making spectrum but also in academia and civil society. As years passed, the excitement about the potentials of the Tampere Programme gradually became a shared nostalgia when these supporters witnessed how the principles remained, to a large extent, a mere

[7] Tampere European Council, Presidency Conclusions, SN 200/99, 15–16 October 1999.

[8] *Ibid.*, at para. 18, provides that 'A more vigorous integration policy should aim at granting them rights and obligations comparable to those of EU citizens. It should also enhance non-discrimination in economic, social and cultural life and develop measures against racism and xenophobia'.

[9] *Ibid.*, at 21. [10] *Ibid.*, at 20.

[11] T. Bunyan, 'The Story of Tampere: an undemocratic process excluding civil society', September 2003, available at <http://www.statewatch.org/news/2003/sep/tampere.pdf>.

political declaration of intent. Since then, many have looked back at Tampere as a benchmark for demonstrating the failures and gaps of current EU legal and policy responses on immigration. The materialization of the Tampere milestones into actual legislative outputs proved indeed to be more challenging than originally expected,[12] and this was particularly difficult to digest by the European Commission.

The Commission presented a package of legislative proposals putting Tampere's vision into practice. The legal and political elements donated in 1999 did not serve, however, to overcome the resistance by certain EU member states' representatives to have 'more Europe' in these domains. Intergovernmental resistance materialized most visibly in three factors: first, the arduous negotiations within the Council on the first Commission initiatives in the area of regular immigration and the nature (of minimums) of the final adopted texts; secondly, the failure of the Commission proposal on establishing an Open Method of Coordination for Community immigration policy, which is examined in section (B)(i) below; and finally, the cold welcome (and final withdrawal) of the 2001 Commission's proposal for a directive on economic migration,[13] which was intended to regulate the entry and residence conditions for all TCNs engaged in paid and self-employed activities. These factors fundamentally changed the working logic or ways of doing things by the Commission in relation to the EU member states.

The first of the factors is the most relevant for this particular section. The negotiations on the first legislative Commission proposals for a directive implementing the Tampere Programme—in particular Council Directives 2003/109 on the status of long-term residents who are TCNs of 25 November 2003 (LTR Directive)[14] and 2003/86 on the right to family reunification of 22 September 2003 (FR Directive)[15]—took years of long and intransparent discussions in the Council's rooms. We remind the reader that the decision-making processes which were applicable to regular immigration-related proposals fell outside co-decision (now ordinary legislative procedure), which actually meant that the Justice and Home Affairs Council was the main (and sole) legislator (with no binding intervention by the European Parliament) and the unanimity voting rule was applied for any of these initiatives to be adopted. These elements positioned the EU in a rather weak setting. The Commission put forward the FR Directive in 1999 and the LTR Directive in 2001, which respectively took five and four years of negotiations. The two acts need to be seen amongst the most relevant instruments so far adopted at EU level on the conditions for admission and residence to TCNs, not only in light of their effects on the discretionary powers enjoyed by national administrations in migration management, but also in light of the set of common EU rights,

[12] A. Wiesbrock, *Legal Migration to the European Union: Ten Years after Tampere* (2010).

[13] 'Proposal for a Council Directive on the Conditions of Entry and Residence for the Purpose of Paid Employment and Self-employment Activities', COM (2001) 0386 final. European Commission Proposal on withdrawal of commission proposals following screening for their general relevance, their impact on competitiveness and other aspects, 2006/C64/03, [2006] OJ C64/3.

[14] Council Directive 2003/109 concerning the status of third-country nationals who are long-term residents [2004] OJ L16/44.

[15] Council Directive 2003/86 on the right to family reunification [2003] OJ L251/12.

freedoms, and guarantees that they recognize for TCNs. The academic literature has paid a lot of attention to both Directives.[16] It is still of relevance for the purposes of this chapter to provide a synthesized overview of the ways in which they conceptualize and make use of integration.

The LTR Directive recognizes a common EU status of long-term resident to those TCNs who have legally and continuously resided for a period of five years in the territory of a member state. It harmonizes a number of socio-economic rights attached to this status, and foresees a reinforced protection against expulsion. The Directive also envisages a right to move to and reside (and to enjoy 'near-equality' of treatment) in a second member state.[17] As Kostakopoulou has argued,[18] the adoption of this Directive meant that TCNs who are permanent residents in the Union are no longer invisible subjects or non-citizens in the European polity. The Directive brought into the EU legal framework the status and rights of TCNs with durable residence in the Union by providing them with a number of rights and freedoms with a European-wide scope. Article 11(1) of the Directive states that long-term residents will enjoy equality of treatment (which in reality is near-equality in light of the exceptions which can be applied by the receiving state) with nationals as regards access to employment and self-employment, education and vocational training (including study grants), recognition of diplomas and other qualifications, social security, tax benefits, access to public goods and services (including housing), freedom of association and affiliation (including membership of employers' or workers' organizations), and free access to the entire territory.[19]

Integration appears in several venues of the Directive.[20] During the negotiations of the text, a new approach on integration emerged. The final text of the Directive foresaw a wider number of conditions on the TCN applicant to have access to the common EU status of LTR and the set of attached rights and guarantees.[21] These

[16] On the FR Directive, we can refer for instance to Oosterom-Staples, 'The Family Reunification Directive: A Tool Preserving Member State Interest or Conducive to Family Reunification Unity?', in A. Baldaccini, E. Guild, and H. Toner (eds), *Whose Freedom, Security and Justice? EU Immigration and Asylum Law and Policy* (2007) 451; Groenendijk, 'Family Reunification as a Right under Community Law' 8 *European Journal of Migration and Law*, (2006) 215; Peers, 'Family Reunion and Community Law', in N. Walker (ed), *Europe's Area of Freedom, Security and Justice* (2004) 143; and E. Guild, *The Legal Elements of European Identity: EU Citizenship and Migration Law* (2004). The literature on the LTR Directive has been equally substantial: K. Groenendijk, *et al., The Family Reunification Directive in EU Member States: the First Year of Implementation* (2007), at 17 and 18; S. Carrera, 'Integration as a Process of Inclusion for Migrants? The Case of Long-Term Residents in the EU', in H. Schneider (ed.), *Migration, Integration and Citizenship: A Challenge for Europe's Future* (2005) 109; Halleskov, 'The Long-Term Residents Directive: A Fulfilment of the Tampere Objective of Near Equality' 7 *European Journal of Migration and Law* (2005) 181; S. Boelaert-Suominen, 'Non-EU Nationals and Council Directive 2003/109/EC on the Status of Third-country Nationals Who are Long-term residents: Five Paces Forward and Possibly Three Paces Back' 42 *Common Market Law Review* (2005) 1011; and Guild, cited above in this footnote.

[17] Chapter III of the Directive, Articles 14–23.

[18] Kostakopoulou, 'Invisible Citizens? Long-Term Resident Third-Country Nationals in the EU and their Struggle for Recognition', in R. Bellamy and A. Warleigh (eds), *Citizenship and Governance in the European Union* (2001) 180.

[19] S. Peers and N. Rogers (eds), *EU Immigration and Asylum Law: Text and Commentary* (2006) 615.

[20] Recitals 4 and 12.

[21] Arts. 5, 6, and 7 of the Directive.

conditions act as derogative clauses in the hands of EU member state authorities. Surprisingly, integration represents one of the exceptions to the conferral of the EU LTR status, a function that has been denominated elsewhere as the conditionality of integration.[22] The lack of integration is framed as a ground for refusal of security of residence and equality of membership to the LTR foreigner. The use of integration as a condition and an exception becomes most visible in Article 5 of the Directive, which stipulates that 'Member States may require third-country nationals to comply with integration conditions, in accordance with national law'.

No definition is provided in the text concerning the actual scope and meaning of integration conditions. By using the 'may' clause, the article does not impose EU member states to apply integration conditions in the transposition of the Directive, but it has rather left that decision open to each national arena. However, during the Council negotiations there was a small group of EU member states which pushed for the introduction of this new approach to integration, and when asked during the discussions about what these integration conditions actually meant (due to the doubts raised by other member states' representatives as to the difficulty of finding objective criteria to evaluate this requirement), their answer was that it would actually mean the need to pass an integration programme as the actual condition for granting LTR status, which would include 'sufficient knowledge of the country'.[23] While this response shed some light on the actual scope of what integration conditions were intended to mean, this term has nonetheless confirmed itself as an indeterminate legal concept in the context of EU immigration law. The interpretation of the meaning of 'integration programme' and 'sufficient knowledge of the country' has been left to the national laws and practices of EU member states, something which has raised concerns due to the large margin of appreciation given to domestic authorities in the implementation phase.[24]

Moreover, the LTR Directive recognizes a right to move and reside in an EU member state different from the one which originally granted the EU LTR status.[25] It is also in this context where integration plays a new functionality. Article 15(3) stipulates that:

> Member States may require third-country nationals to comply with integration measures, in accordance with national law. This condition shall not apply where the third-country nationals concerned have been required to comply with integration conditions in order to be granted long-term resident status, in accordance with the provisions of Article 5(2). Without prejudice to the second subparagraph, the persons concerned may be required to attend language courses.

This provision means that those TCNs holding an EU LTR permit are entitled to move and reside in a second member state without being subject to integration measures there on the knowledge of society. The receiving state can only require them to participate in language courses as a condition for according them the

[22] Carrera, *supra* n 16. [23] Council of the European Union, 12217/02, 23 September 2002.
[24] S. Carrera (ed.), *The Nexus between Immigration, Integration and Citizenship in the EU* (2006).
[25] See Chapter III of the Directive, Arts. 14–23.

LTR status. The second member state has the obligation to treat these TCNs as if they are already civically integrated (in what concerns knowledge of society, way of life, history, and values) into their receiving societies. This provision therefore constitutes a *de jure* mutual recognition of civic integration decisions of long-term resident TCNs in the EU.[26] It has thus, for the first time, fostered a presumption in the scope of European law that a non-EU national who is integrated into 'the way of life and society' in one member state is to be considered automatically integrated into the societies of all the rest of EU member states, which constitutes a far-reaching contribution by the Directive.

The FR Directive, on the other hand, establishes common standards and criteria for TCNs residing lawfully in an EU member state to be reunited with their family members in the Union. It constituted the first legislative descendant of the common EU immigration policy. The Directive was equally subject to long and sensitive negotiations in the Council which lasted over seven different EU Presidencies and resulted in the adoption of a substantially toned down version of the act.[27] Its final shape included numerous derogations to rights which came along so-called 'stand-still clauses', whose main purpose was to ensure that EU member states would not instrumentalize them in order to lower already existing standards in their national legal systems at the time of adoption, or in some cases of implementation, of the Directive. As regards the personal scope, it applies where the sponsor[28] has a residence permit valid for at least one year and 'has reasonable prospects of obtaining the right of permanent residence'. The Directive has been said to recognize a distinctive EU right to family reunification and a set of derivative rights to certain categories of family members.[29] Several explicit references to the concepts of integration have also been included in its text.[30] The Tampere milestones are reflected, for instance, in Recital 4 which proclaims that 'Family reunification is a necessary way of making family life possible. It helps to create socio-cultural stability facilitating the integration of third country nationals in the Member State, which also serves to promote economic and social cohesion, a fundamental Community objective stated in the Treaty'.

The Tampere version of integration also contrasts here, with the conditionality of integration which resulted from the Council negotiations. By way of illustration, Article 7(2) stipulates that 'Member States may require third-country nationals to comply with integration measures, in accordance with national law'. With regard to refugees and/or their family members, the integration measures foreseen in this provision may only be applied once the persons concerned have been granted family reunification. Article 7(2) has in this way given the possibility

[26] Carrera and Wiesbrock, 'Civic Integration of Third Country Nationals: Nationalism versus Europeanisation in the Common EU Immigration Policy', CEPS Report, 2009.

[27] 'Proposal for a Council Directive on the Right to Family Reunification', COM (1999) 638 final.

[28] Art. 2(c) defines sponsor as 'a third country national residing lawfully in a Member State and applying or whose family members apply for family reunification to be joined with him/her'.

[29] Groenendijk, 'Family Reunification as a Right', *supra* n 16.

[30] Four of them appear in Recitals 3, 4, 12, and 15 of the Preamble, and the rest can be found in Arts. 4(1), 4(5), and 7(2).

to member states to apply integration measures to all other TCNs not falling within this legal category even before they have been granted family reunification, which includes the phase while they are still abroad in the country of origin. This Article constitutes a materialization of what has been denominated as integration abroad or the external dimension of integration, which finds its precursor in Dutch integration policy.[31] Integration experiences a process of externalization by which the requirement for the individual to be integrated moves beyond its territorial borders towards the country of origin. The would-be immigrant is subject to an evaluation and/or a course provided by the consular and diplomatic authorities of the EU member states in third countries about their way of life and values as well as language. Integration becomes here an additional criterion for having access to a visa for the purposes of family reunion.

The FR Directive has also included another provision on 'integration conditions'. According to Article 4, member states are under the obligation to authorize the entry and residence of the minor children of the sponsor and of her/his spouse. The minor children must be below the age of majority set by the law of the member state and must not be married. 'By way of derogation', Article 4(1) states that 'where a child is aged over 12 years and arrives independently from the rest of his/her family, the Member State may, before authorising entry and residence under this Directive, verify whether he or she meets a condition for integration provided for by its existing legislation on the date of implementation of this Directive'. The last part of the sentence is of central importance, as it exemplifies a standstill clause according to which member states were only allowed to introduce this exception in their national laws until the date of implementation of the Directive (3 October 2005). On the date of expiration of this deadline, there was not a single EU member state implementing this provision in their domestic legal system. The consequence of this is that Article 4(1) now represents an express prohibition on the introduction of 'integration conditions' to the family reunification for children over 12 years.[32]

The literature has engaged with the possible differences between the scope and effects of integration conditions and measures in both Directives. Groenendijk[33] has argued that integration conditions allow member states to introduce more far-reaching obligations to the TCNs such as passing an integration test and covering the financial costs/fees. Integration measures would only provide member states with the option of asking TCNs to make a certain effort by participating in language or societal courses. Another distinguishing feature between both terms could be the binding and/or voluntary nature of the integration programme and/or test.[34] The conditionality inherent to the category of integration conditions would in this way constitute another distinctive factor. Integration conditions offer

[31] Kostakopoulou, 'Introduction', in R. Van Oers, E. Ersboll, and D. Kostakopoulou (eds), *A Redefinition of Belonging? Language and Integration Tests in Europe* (2010); Carrera and Wiesbrock, *supra* n 26.

[32] Groenendijk *et al.*, *supra* n 16.

[33] Groenendijk, 'Family Reunification as a Right', *supra* n 16.

[34] Carrera, *supra* n 4.

member states the option to apply integration as a mandatory requirement, which in case of non-compliance would prevent access to the EU LTR status, the EU right to family reunification and/or all the other related rights and administrative guarantees foreseen by these Directives. The obligatory character would also imply that state authorities could apply financial penalties or sanctions on the applicant, such as the refusal of a permanent residence permit and family reunion, the non-renewal of the temporary residence permit, financial sanctions, and eventual expulsion. The concept of integration conditions would, therefore, foster an approach based on discipline, enforcement, and sanctions. Arguably, the next step would be to conclude that the reference to integration measures by Article 7(2) of the FR Directive and Article 15(3) of the LTR Directive would consequently prevent member states from introducing mandatory integration conditions and applying disciplinary measures against TCNs.

B. Integration and EU policy

The relationship between integration and the EU gets further enriched when looking at the policy developments which have emanated in the realm of the EU Framework on Integration. The origins of European policy interventions on the integration of TCNs find their official roots in 2001 with the adoption by the Commission of a Communication for an Open Method of Coordination for the Community Immigration Policy COM (2001) 387. The Communication did not receive any attention by the Council. Its failure did not reduce the ambition for Europeanization to move forward through alternative paths and the progressive establishment of a *sui generis* or a typical coordination mechanism at EU level. In fact, it may come as a surprise for some to notice that since 2002, the EU has dynamically built a common European framework of cooperation on integration. This Framework has been said to constitute a quasi-Open Method of Coordination falling outside the traditional EU decision-making procedure and making use of soft law/policy, networks of experts and other 'integration actors', exchange of information of integration policies and practices, and EU-wide evaluation mechanisms.

The kind of regulatory outputs, decision-making, and institutional arrangements characterizing the EU Framework on Integration challenge our knowledge on how the EU is supposed to work in theory and practice. The Framework simply does not fit anything that reputed EU law textbooks tell us about how the Union is supposed to function and develop. It makes experts, and especially lawyers (such as the one writing this chapter), feel rather uncomfortable because of the multiple ways in which it defies what we expect from the EU legal system and its various ways of working. This is precisely one of the grounds justifying its relevance not only at times of examining the relation of integration with EU law and policy, but also when analysing new modes or methods of policy-making at EU level in the immigration domain. This section examines the nature of the main substantive and financial elements of the EU Framework on Integration. It studies its origins and the main policy instruments adopted so far as well as the latest and forthcoming developments in the second phase of the EU's integration agenda. Our focus remains on the identification of novel approaches taken by these policy responses to conceptions of integration of TCNs.

i. The origins of the EU Framework on Integration

One example of the post-Tampere intergovernmental resistances which the Commission faced in its quest towards 'more Europe' in the domains of immigration and integration, was its unsuccessful attempt to launch an Open Method of Coordination on Immigration in 2001.[35] Open Methods of Coordination (OMC) have emerged at European level since 2000 as a key means by which the Commission can steer, support, and coordinate member states' policies in sensitive (nationally attached) areas (such as employment, social inclusion, education, etc) through the exchange of 'best practices', benchmarking, periodic reporting, and multilateral surveillance.[36] The academic literature has paid a wealth of attention to OMC and the Commission's proposal of an OMC on immigration.[37] The Commission was of the opinion that the development of a common immigration policy would require a coordinating mechanism which would be complementary to the enactment of the ordinary legislative framework. The Communication identified the integration of TCNs as one of the key areas around which coordination should focus.

In the Commission's view, such a method could be the most appropriate way to stimulate the gradual development of common European responses through coordination of, and experimentation with, national integration policies. The final objective would be the promotion of policy convergence of national policies and (in the long-run) the adoption of common standards and objectives. The OMC on immigration was envisaged to work on the basis of multi-annual guidelines adopted by the Council which would present timetables for the achievement of a list of shared goals. The proposal foresaw a central role for the Commission in overseeing its practical operability. The latter would be in charge of elaborating synthesis reports on common problems and concerns, and identifying those areas of intervention calling for common EU solutions. This would then pave the way for the preparation of European legislation. The coordination mechanism would involve wide consultation, and even the establishment of committees and working groups, with senior officials, experts, social partners, local and regional authorities, etc. However, such was the unwillingness of the member states to contemplate

[35] Commission Communication 'On an Open Method of Coordination for the Community Immigration Policy', COM (2001) 387.

[36] De la Porte, 'Is the Open Method of Coordination Appropriate for Organising Activities at European Level in Sensitive Policy Areas?' 8 *European Law Journal* (2002) 38.

[37] Velluti, 'What European Strategy for Integrating Migrants? The Role of the OMC Soft Mechanisms in the Development of an EU Immigration Policy' 9 *European Journal of Migration and Law* (2007) 53; Caviedes, 'The Open Method of Coordination in Immigration Policy: A Tool for Prying Open Fortress Europe' 11 *Journal of European Public Policy* (2004) 289; Bogusz, 'Modes of Governance for an EU Immigration Policy—What Role for the Open Method of Coordination', in B. Bogusz *et al.*, (eds), *Irregular Migration and Human Rights: Theoretical, European and International Perspectives* (2004) 221.

coordinating policies concerning the entry and treatment of legal migrants that the proposal did not even reach the Council table. The result was the emergence of the EU Framework on Integration.

ii. The EU Framework on Integration

The official point of departure of the EU Framework on Integration was the Justice and Home Affairs (JHA) Council meeting of 14–15 October 2002, which made reference to the need for a coordinated EU action and greater policy coherence in member states' integration policies.[38] The JHA Council underlined the relevance of exchange of information of national policies and the identification of 'best practices' at EU level. The EU Framework on Integration has ever since evolved in non-linear and multi-level fashions. Its main substantive and financial elements can be summarized around the four following streams: first, the national contact points on integration; secondly, the common basic principles on immigrants' integration; thirdly, the European integration fund; and fourthly, the European integration forum and the European website on integration.

a. The National Contact Points on Integration

The National Contact Points on Integration (NCPIs) constituted the first tangible output of the EU Framework on Integration. Their establishment originally resulted from the 2002 JHA Council meeting, which signalled the need to establish a network of experts drawn from the competent ministries of the member states, tasked with promoting information exchange, monitoring progress, and disseminating 'best practices' at both national and EU levels. The first meeting of the NCPIs took place in 2003. Since then, the NCPIs have consolidated themselves as a key supranational platform of EU politics on integration. The network, which is chaired by the Commission, counts the participation of representatives from all EU member states (including the UK, Ireland, and Denmark, as well as Norway in the capacity of observer). Its composition and the level of representation by member states are secretive, heterogeneous, and of an uneven nature.[39] Its inputs have been seminal in the provision of background information in the Commission's Annual Reports on Migration and Integration, which have provided

[38] Council Meeting 2455, Luxembourg, 14–15 October 2002.

[39] J. Niessen and T. Huddleston, *Handbook on Integration for Policy-makers and Practitioners* (3rd edn, 2010). The actual membership of the NCPIs is not public. The list of ministries represented by EU member states can only be found in the Annexes of the *Handbooks on Integration for Policy Makers and Practitioners*. Following distribution, it can be noticed that out of the 27 EU member states represented in the NCPIs first, there are now ten EU member states represented by experts from the Ministries of Interior (Cyprus, Czech Republic, Finland, France, Germany, Greece, Italy, Slovakia, and Slovenia), with the UK being represented by the UK Border Agency; secondly, six EU member states participate with their Ministries of Labour, Social Affairs, Social Solidarity, and Family Affairs (Belgium, Bulgaria, Lithuania, Malta, Poland, and Spain); thirdly, there are a few EU member states where the national contact point is a national organ directly covering 'integration' (this is the case for instance in Austria, Denmark, Ireland, and Sweden); finally, as regards the level of representation, some EU member states count two representatives from different ministries or institutions (Belgium, Italy, and Slovakia).

a comparative overview of developments and common trends of integration policies at national and EU level.[40]

The NCPIs have performed a decisive role in the three editions of the *Handbook on Integration for Policy Makers and Practitioners* published by the European Commission in 2004, 2007, and 2010, and which were carried out by the Brussels-based NGO the Migration Policy Group (MPG) on behalf of the latter.[41] The Handbook has established itself as one of the most relevant and recognizable policy tools of the EU's Agenda on Integration. It has structured the exchange of information in the EU Framework on Integration. Each of the three editions provides a selection of 'good practices' around a number of integration themes covering issues such as introduction of newly arrived immigrants and recognized refugees, civic participation, indicators, housing, economic integration, integration governance, media, acquisition of nationality, immigrant youth, education, and labour market, etc. The Handbooks have been the output (at the time of writing) of a total of 14 closed-doors technical seminars organized by the responsible national ministries for integration (NCPIs) in the hosting EU member state. The latter would propose the issues on integration policy or governance to be covered by the seminar, which was then fine-tuned and structured into specific (workshop) topics in collaboration with the Commission and the other NCPIs.

b. The common basic principles on immigrants' integration

Priority setting has been central to EU politics on integration. The second multi-annual programme on the EU's AFSJ—The Hague Programme—endorsed by the Council on 4 and 5 November 2004, placed integration policy at the centre of attention of the EU's political agenda.[42] The Hague Programme reinstated the need, previously accorded at the 2003 Thessaloniki European Council Conclusions,[43] to establish common basic principles underlying a framework on integration. It was at the JHA Council Conclusions of 19 November 2004, under the auspices of the Dutch Presidency of the EU, that the Council adopted by unanimity the Common Basic Principles for Immigrant Integration Policy (CBPs),[44] which aimed at:[45] first, assisting member states in formulating integration policies by offering them 'a simple non-binding guide of basic principles against which they can judge and assess their own policies', and to serve as a basis for the EU to explore how existing EU

[40] Commission Communication, 'First Annual Report on Migration and Integration', COM (2004) 508. Commission Staff Working Document, 'Second Annual Report on Migration and Integration', SEC (2006) 892. Commission Communication, 'Third Annual Report on Migration and Integration', COM (2007) 512.

[41] J. Niessen and Y. Schibel, *Handbook on Integration for Policy-makers and Practitioners* (2004); J. Niessen and Y. Schibel, *Handbook on Integration for Policy-makers and Practitioners* (2nd edn, 2007); Niessen and Huddleston, *supra* n 39.

[42] European Council, 'The Hague Programme: Strengthening Freedom, Security and Justice in the European Union', 2005/C53/01, [2005] OJ C53/1.

[43] Thessaloniki European Council, 19–20 June 2003, Presidency Conclusions, 11638/03.

[44] Council of the European Union, Justice, and Home Affairs, Council Meeting 2618, 'Common Basic Principles on Immigrants Integration', 14615/04, 19 November 2004.

[45] *Ibid.*, para. 8.

instruments on integration can be developed further; secondly, serving as a basis for the member states to explore how EU, national, regional, and local authorities can interact in the development and implementation of integration policies; and thirdly, assisting the Council to agree on EU level mechanisms and policies for the support of national and local level integration policy efforts, particularly through 'EU-wide learning and knowledge-sharing'. Their adoption was, therefore, in the hands of the Dutch Presidency, and only counted with the inputs from the NCPIs, the Strategic Committee on Immigration, Frontiers, and Asylum (SCIFA), and the Commission.

The full list of CBPs are provided in Annex 1 to this chapter. They aim to offer a common European understanding of integration at EU level, and reflect an attempt to flesh out a definition and interpretation of what integration means in the EU context. This goal, however, has been difficult to achieve in practice due to the lack of a common definition of integration in the scope of the EU Framework on Integration, where it would have been rather difficult to reach consensus amongst all EU member states.[46] The principles are so broad as to be largely symbolic, and could fit almost any national policy context across the EU. They are rather a general list of standards of a largely wide nature which could match (to a variety of degrees and levels) with any philosophies and modes of integration, ranging from the most classical assimilation and acculturation models to the those driven by multicultural, intercultural, and pluralist approaches. It is therefore difficult to argue that the CBPs provide a common EU model and definition on integration.

The CBPs have been also contaminated by the conditionality of integration. CBP 2 (Integration implies respect for 'the basic values of the EU') and CBP 4.1 (Basic knowledge of the host society's language, history, and institutions is indispensable for integration) transparently reflect a paradigm on integration which distances itself from previous classical EU approach(es). The Annex of the JHA Council Conclusions of 19 November 2004 further elaborated the meaning and scope of each of these CBPs. It stated that CBP 2 involves the obligation by every resident in the EU to adapt and adhere closely to the basic values of the Union and the laws of the member states, which include 'the principles of liberty, democracy, respect for human rights and fundamental freedoms, and the rule of law'. Furthermore, they include respect for the provisions of the Charter of Fundamental Rights of the Union, which enshrines the concepts of dignity, freedom, equality and non-discrimination, solidarity, citizens' rights, and justice. The Annex also requested EU member states to ensure that every resident understands, respects, benefits from, and is protected on an equal basis by the full scope of values, rights, responsibilities, and privileges established by the EU and member state laws. CBP 4 highlights the importance given by a majority of EU member states to 'basic linguistic, historical and civic knowledge' in introductory programmes, and stresses that '[a]cquiring the language and culture of the host society should

[46] M. Martiniello, *Towards a Coherent Approach to Immigrant Integration Policy(ies) in the European Union* (2008), retrievable from <http://www.oecd.org>.

be an important focus. Full respect for the immigrants' and their descendants' own language and culture should be also an important element of integration policy'.

c. The European Integration Fund

The EU Framework on Integration, and the actual relevance of the CBPs, cannot be understood without paying attention to the accompanying financial framework—ie the Decision establishing the European Fund for the Integration of TCNs (the EIF Decision).[47] The effects and potentials of the EU Framework on Integration cannot be comprehensively assessed without looking at the linkage between the policy outputs shaping the EU's agenda on integration (in particular the CBPs) and EU funding focused on putting the latter into practice. The EIF counts with a total of 825 million euros for the period 2007–13. It focuses on the co-financing of concrete actions supporting integration and has (according to Article 3 of Council Decision 2007/435/EC) the following four objectives: first, to facilitate the development and implementation of admission procedures relevant to and supportive of integration; secondly, to develop the integration of 'newly-arrived third country nationals' in the member states; thirdly, to increase the member states' capacity to develop, implement, monitor, and evaluate policies on integration; and fourthly, exchange of information, 'best practices', and European cooperation.

The Commission adopts strategic guidelines establishing a framework for intervention which gives priority to the implementation of the CBPs and to develop a common approach to the integration of TCNs in the EU. On the basis of the strategic guidelines, member states present a draft multiannual programme, which is then implemented into annual programmes after approval by the Commission.[48] When preparing their draft multiannual programmes, member states are requested to target at least three of the priorities identified by the Commission. Among these, those dealing with the implementation of actions designed to put the CBPs into practice (Priority 1) and those of evaluation mechanisms and indicators (Priority 2) are mandatory in nature. According to the EIF Decision, pre-departure and introductory (civic integration) programmes are actions that may be supported.[49] It is noticeable that the EIF expressly covers the financing of 'integration abroad'

[47] Council Decision establishing the European Fund for the Integration of Third-Country Nationals for the Period 2007 to 2013 as part of the General Programme 'Solidarity and Management of Migration Flows', 2007/435/EC, [2007] OJ L168/18.

[48] European Commission, Decision Implementing Council Decision 2007/435/EC as regards the adoption of strategic guidelines for 2007/2013, 21 August 2007. Two units within Directorate B for Immigration, Asylum, and Borders are in charge of oversight, with one focusing on policy aspects (B.1) and the other on financial aspects (B.4). The European Commission has also adopted a Commission Decision laying down rules for the implementation of the EIF Decision regarding the management and control structures in the member states, the rules for administrative and financial management, and the eligibility of expenditures. See European Commission, Decision 2011/151/EU of 3 March 2011 amending Decision 2008/457/EC of 5 March 2008 laying down rules for the implementation of Council Decision 2007/435/EC establishing the European Fund for the Integration of Third-country Nationals for the period 2007 to 2013 as part of the General Programme 'Solidarity and Management of Migration Flows' as regards member states' management and control systems, the rules for administrative and financial management, and the eligibility of expenditure on projects co-financed by the fund, [2011] OJ L62/32.

[49] Arts. 4(1)(c) and 4(2)(a) of the EIF Decision.

measures and, therefore, also ascribes to the new EU understanding of integration as insecurity, immigration, and identity control. In particular, Article 1(2) establishes that TCNs who are in a third country and who are complying with 'pre-departure measures and/or conditions set out in national law, including those relating to the ability to integrate in the society of this Member State fall under the scope of this Decision'. Currently, discussions are being held inside the Commission on new ways of improving the current operability of the EIF coinciding with its mid-term (political) evaluation which is expected to be delivered before summer 2013.

d. The European Integration Forum and the European Website on Integration

One of the distinctive features of the EU Framework on Integration has been the contributions by supranational networks of 'integration actors' in the sharing of experiences and information. The Framework has evolved along with a series of tools and alternative institutional venues allowing for active inputs from national experts from relevant ministries, civil society actors, and EU umbrella NGOs as well as other EU level organizations. The involvement of 'stakeholders' materialized in the setting up of a European Integration Forum and a European Website on Integration (EWSI) in 2009. Both instruments need to be seen as the two last steps foreseen for the implementation of the first phase of the EU Agenda on Integration outlined by the European Commission in its Communication on a Common Agenda for Integration COM (2005) 389.[50]

The Commission requested that the European Economic and Social Committee (EESC) adopt an Opinion concerning the establishment of the Forum, which was adopted on 9 July 2008.[51] Since its first meeting in April 2009, the plenary of the Forum has come together on four occasions. It has constituted itself as a European platform for dialogue and representation of civil society and migrants' organizations. The tasks attributed to the Forum are those of consultation, exchange of expertise (technical 'know-how' and 'good practices'), and drawing up recommendations, which are fulfilled through the drawing of reports and conclusions. It is composed of 100 members representing EU umbrella organizations, as well as consultative bodies and platforms established at the national level with each member state sending between one and four representatives.[52] The Forum also counts with the participation of the NCPIs and the main EU institutions and agencies as well as external experts (academics and researchers) working on integration issues.[53] The CBPs constitute the core thematic guide of its activities, but it can also address other relevant issues falling within the scope of the EU Framework on Integration.

[50] Commission Communication, 'A Common Agenda for Integration—Framework for the Integration of Third Country Nationals in the European Union', COM (2005) 389.

[51] EESC, Elements for the Structure, Organization and Functioning of a Platform for the Greater Involvement of Civil Society in the EU-level Promotion of Policies for the Integration of Third Country Nationals, Opinion, SOC/281, CES1208/2008.

[52] *Ibid.*, para. 3.6.5.

[53] See Press Release, 'European Integration Forum and European Website on Integration', available at <http://ec.europa.eu/ewsi/en/policy/legal.cfm#>.

Its agenda is decided by a Bureau composed by the Commission, the EESC, and two members of the Forum, which at present are Caritas Europa and the Council of Ethnic Minorities in Denmark. The kick-off of the European Integration Forum coincided with the official launch of the EWSI, where the Forum's activities and reports are publicly available.[54] The website has been developed by the MPG together with UNISYS, Social Change Online, and Eurocities. The EWSI's main goal is to offer a better and more solid structure for the exchange of information and 'good practices' on integration between practitioners and policy-makers at EU level.

iii. Latest and upcoming policy developments: towards the EU second integration agenda

The end of 2009 marked a new phase for the Union and, perhaps more substantially, for its political elements embodied in the EU's AFSJ. The entry into force of the Treaty of Lisbon along with endorsement by the European Council of the third multiannual programme on FSJ—the Stockholm Programme—in December 2009 provided a renewed Treaty-based and political framework for the development of common European policy responses and strategies over immigration and integration. The Stockholm Programme—'An Open and Secure Europe Serving and Protecting the Citizen'—which presents the EU's policy agenda for the period 2010–14,[55] identified the integration of TCNs as one of its political priorities. The Programme called for the further development of structures and tools for 'knowledge exchange and coordination' and proposed the following three specific measures:

First, the establishment of a 'common coordination mechanism' understood as a common reference framework to improve structures and tools for European knowledge exchange. No further details were provided by the Programme as to its actual meaning, scope, and reach. The Commission is currently working on a new Communication which could perhaps give further hints by outlining some of the fundamentals and specific policy steps to guide the second phase of the EU's agenda on integration. The Communication will hopefully bring some clarity as regards the shapes and scope that such 'mechanism' could be expected to have in the future.

Secondly, the European Modules for Migrant Integration (EMMIs). The Commission has on several occasions considered the EMMIs as 'the building blocks for comprehensive integration strategies' which would 'start by addressing organization of language and civic courses on the host society's history, institutions and the common shared values of the EU'.[56] The processes resulting in the publication

[54] Available at <http://www.integration.eu>

[55] Council of the EU, 'The Stockholm Programme—An Open and Secure Europe Serving and Protecting the Citizen', 5731/10, 3 March 2010.

[56] European Commission, 'Strengthening Actions and Tools to Meet Integration Challenges: Report to the 2008 Ministerial Conference on Integration', Commission Staff Working Document, SEC (2008) 2626.

of three editions of the *Handbooks on Integration for Practitioners and Policy Makers* will constitute the basis for the EMMIs. According to the Commission,[57] the modules aim at representing an established point of reference that can be adapted to different contexts and can contribute to the design of integration programmes across Europe. They should be a tool at the disposal of policy-makers and practitioners. With the support of technical assistance, European modules will enhance the mutual learning process, systematize existing expertise, and benefit further from the existing European standards which form part of the Common Basic Principles and the EU legal framework. They can be used to design and improve integration strategies within member states at both national and local level.

The EMMIs are currently under construction following a similarly obscure and multilayered decision-making process, ie steering the process forward through closed-doors expert seminars organized by NCPIs in cooperation with external contractors and with the involvement of the usual integration actors. There have been three Expert Conferences organized around this issue since the end of 2010. One of these events took place on 15–16 December 2010 under the Belgian Presidency of the Council of the EU. Discussions were not focused on the actual added value of such an initiative but rather on already developing a first conceptual input for the development of the EMMIs. The Modules have been envisaged to cover the following three integration-related areas: introductory (civic) and language courses, 'strong commitment by the host society', and 'active participation of immigrants in all aspects of collective life'. The background of the Conference's discussions was provided by a concept paper on 'Integration Modules: New Tools for European Co-operation' prepared by the MPG, which aimed at contributing to moving things forward by proposing the following working definition of the integration modules: 'Integration modules can be described as negotiated standards comprised of [a] set of specifications and qualifications which deal with essential aspects of integration'.[58] According to an additional Working Document distributed at the event by the NCPI Belgium,[59] which provided a number of framing key questions to be addressed in the different working sessions composing the event, the European modules need to be seen:

> as a standardised concept on a given topic. Each module contains a number of 'building blocks' or components which Member States may draw upon when developing integration policies and actions within their specific national context ... [T]he modules ... will provide focussed, detailed and practical non-binding guidelines to the Member States ... Moreover, the modules are to provide quality standards and may inspire Member States to set indicators and targets to measure the impact of these policies and practices.

[57] European Commission, 'The Consolidation of the EU Framework on Integration—Report to the 2010 Ministerial Conference on Integration', Commission Staff Working Document, SEC (2010) 357 final, at 8.

[58] Niessen and Kirshberger, 'Integration Modules: New Tools for European Cooperation', concept paper prepared at the request of the Belgian EU Presidency as an input for the Conference on Integration Modules, 2010.

[59] Belgian Presidency of the EU, Expert Conference on European Integration Modules, Working Document, 2010.

The third initiative put forward by the Stockholm Programme was an invitation to the Commission 'to support' EU member states' actions through the development of core indicators for monitoring and evaluating results of integration policies and increasing their comparability. The evaluation of the information and practices being exchanged within the scope of the EU Framework on Integration has been at the heart of the Union's priorities. One of the eleven CBPs deals specifically with this matter, in particular CBP 11 which calls for the development of European criteria (indicators and benchmarks) for adjusting policy and to evaluate progress on integration and make the exchange of information more effective. Evaluation constitutes also one of the mandatory areas of intervention for the EU member states in the implementation of the EIF, which requests national governments to foresee the development of indicators and evaluation methodologies to assess progress, adjust policies and measures, and to facilitate coordination of comparative learning. It was at the JHA Council Conclusions on 'Strengthening of Integration Policies in the European Union by promoting Unity in Diversity' of 12–13 June 2007 when the political mandate was conferred upon the Commission to promote the development of common indicators.[60] In the meantime, the Commission had already funded several studies and research projects destined to 'benchmark integration of TCNs'.[61] A case in point has been the MIPEX (The Migrant Integration Policy Index) carried out since 2005 by the MPG in cooperation with the British Council and external migration experts,[62] which has been critically examined elsewhere.[63] The MIPEX provided the first EU-wide comparative exercise evaluating (in a rather obscure methodological fashion) national integration policies against a set of 'European standards' using a number of indicators which lead to the identification and selection of 'best practices'.

The Swedish Presidency of the EU (in the second half of 2009) paid attention to the integration indicators debate, which led to the adoption of Presidency Conclusions on indicators and monitoring of the outcome of integration policies in December 2009.[64] The Conclusions were again based on an expert meeting format with the aim of identifying core indicators for monitoring integration policies in the following policy areas: employment, education, social inclusion, and active citizenship. The long-term goal was said to be 'full comparability' between the integration policies of all EU member states. The indicators, which were elaborated by the NCPIs and the Commission, were presented in the Annex of the

[60] Council of the European Union, Justice and Home Affairs Council Meeting 2807, Luxembourg, 12–13 June 2007, Press Release, 10267/07.

[61] H. Entzinger and R. Biezeveld, *Benchmarking Immigrant Integration* (2003), available at <http://ec.europa.eu/justice_home/funding/2004_2007/doc/study_indicators_integration.pdf>.

[62] A. Geddes and J. Niessen, *European Civic Citizenship and Inclusion Index*, (2005); J. Niessen, T. Huddleston, and L. Citron, *Migrant Integration Policy Index* (2nd edn, 2007). The third edition of the MIPEX was expected to be launched at the end of February 2011, but its website (available at <http://www.integrationindex.eu>) was still under construction in October 2013.

[63] S. Carrera, *Benchmarking Integration in the EU: Analysing the Debate on Integration Indicators and Moving it Forward* (2008).

[64] Presidency Conclusions on Indicators and Monitoring of the Outcome of Integration Policies, 14–16 December 2009, Malmö, Sweden.

Presidency Conference Conclusions.[65] The next step in the process of identification of 'EU reference indicators' was the European Ministerial Conference on Integration organized in Zaragoza under the auspices of the Spanish Presidency of the EU in April 2010.[66] The Conference came out with a Declaration emphasizing the Ministers' agreement on deepening the integration agenda and the launching of a pilot project focused on putting into practice the indicators for evaluation of integration policies.[67] One of the indicators provided by the Declaration was titled 'Active Citizenship' and included: the share of immigrants that have acquired citizenship; the share of immigrants holding permanent or long-term residence permits; and the share of immigrants among elected representatives. It is noticeable that in a small footnote of the Declaration it was said that '[t]here is currently no unified view among Member States on indicators in the area of civic citizenship. Member States' views differ in relation to different views, goals and regulatory frameworks of integration policies in the respective Member States'.

2. Understanding the Paradigm Shift of Integration in EU Law and Policy: Scope and Driving Factors

The various changes affecting the concepts of integration in EU law have not passed unnoticed by the literature.[68] One of the main findings emerging from the analysis conducted in section 1 has been that both in EU immigration law and the EU Framework on Integration, the concept of integration has mutated into a legal criterion conditioning access by TCNs to social inclusion, security of residence, and EU rights. The functionality of 'integration conditions' and 'integration measures' inside the LTR and FR Directives is one conferring the option on national governments to use integration as an exception or derogative clause (in the form of an integration programme or a test on knowledge of society and language) to the granting of the EU rights and guarantees recognized to TCNs in EU immigration law. A similar move is also visible in the EU Framework on Integration, particularlyin CBPs 2 and 4.1. The conditionality inherent to this notion of integration demands that foreigners demonstrate knowledge on the way of life, values, culture, and history of the receiving state as a *sine qua non* for their actual inclusion.

The EU is now promoting an approach on integration which puts an emphasis on the control side of mobility and identity. This conception reinvigorates its

[65] *Ibid.*, at 10 and 11.

[66] Council of the EU, European Ministerial Conference on Integration, 15–16 April 2010, Zaragoza, Declaration, 8771/10.

[67] *Ibid.*, at 15.

[68] E. Guild, K. Groenendijk, and S. Carrera (eds), *Illiberal Liberal States: Immigration, Citizenship and Integration in the EU* (2009) (and especially Kostakopoulou, Carrera, and Jesse, 'Doing and Deserving: Competing Frames of Integration in the EU', at 167); Carrera, *supra* n 4; Oger, 'Integration in Tension in Immigration Law: Mirror and Catalyst of the Inherent Paradox of Nation-States', EUI Working Paper No. 1, 2005; Groenendijk, *supra* n 5.

linkages with the conditions of admission and residence stipulated by immigration law. It is one reflecting a predominantly nationalistic focus, as it is based on (and serves as a catalyst to) integration policies and programmes of certain EU member states which have been powerful, and strategically wise, in transferring their own integration philosophies towards EU policy arenas. The scholarly literature has demonstrated how in a significant number of cases the political justifications and/or intended (or even unintended) effects given by those EU member states making use of mandatory civic integration tests in immigration law (for example the Netherlands, Germany, France, and Austria) have been a reduction in the total number of foreigners and/or entries for family reunification purposes.[69] Integration serves as a tool for a restrictive immigration policy. As Guild[70] has argued, the proliferation of the testing exercise from the national arenas towards the EU has signified the emergence of a new ground for exclusion of foreigners into EU immigration law, based on the security risk of failure to integrate. Integration becomes a ground of exclusion of TCNs. Integration no longer functions as a *desecuritization* tool for the promotion of socio economic inclusion, non-discrimination, and equal participation/membership of TCNs, but rather as an *insecuritization* mechanism strengthening the managerial imagination of the nation state over mobility and feelings of belonging by TCNs. By focusing on the obligation for TCNs to integrate, this new approach raises four major consequences and issues of concern.

First, it nuances the relevance of (the length of) residence as one of the crucial connecting factors playing a role at times of determining the access by TCNs to rights and equality of treatment. Residence is no longer the main component in the delivery of integration to TCNs.

Secondly, it weakens the scope and impact of EU rights and guarantees on the level of protection against expulsion envisaged in European immigration law by making dependent their granting to an indeterminate legal concept whose actual interpretation and implementation is to a large extent left to the discretion of national authorities. It confers a high margin of manoeuvre to the state authorities at the moment of deciding whether or not to confer EU rights to TCNs depending on the distance that they might show from their own imagined society and citizenry.

Thirdly, it takes us to a distant terrain which until recently used to be only paradigmatic of nationality laws. Integration into the constructed national culture and values has been used in some European states' legal systems as a test for acquiring nationality via naturalization.[71] A similar testing exercise has been now transferred to the confinements of immigration law. The nation state demands a citizenship level of cultural allegiance and integration to those TCNs who might not necessarily

[69] Guild, Groenendijk, and Carrera, *ibid*; Carrera and Wiesbrock, *supra* n 26.

[70] Guild and Carrera, 'Are Integration Tests Liberal? The "Universalistic Liberal Democratic Principles" as Illiberal Exceptionalism', in R. Bauböck and C. Joppke (eds), *How Liberal Are Citizenship Tests?*, EUI Working Paper No. 41, 2010.

[71] De Groot, Kuipers, and Weber, 'Passing Citizenship Tests as a Requirement for Naturalisation: A Comparative Perspective', in E. Guild, K. Groenendijk, and S. Carrera (eds), *Illiberal Liberal States: Immigration, Citizenship and Integration in the EU* (2009), 51.

aim at the acquisition of nationality, but who rather claim security or legality of residence in its territory. TCNs are required to be 'naturalized' to be granted residence and family reunion.

Fourthly, this new understanding of integration stands in contrast to CBP 1 of the EU Framework on Integration according to which integration is a dynamic, two-way process of mutual accommodation by all immigrants and residents of the member states. The conditionality of integration favours a unidirectional process of acculturation according to which the TCN, whom the state presumes to be alien to liberal democratic principles and fundamental values, has the obligation to know (and in some cases disappear into) the national values, principles, and way of life supposed to be reigning in its societies. Integration imposes the heaviest burden of proof on the foreigner's shoulders to demonstrate their assimilation into a homogeneous framing of the pure societal self, which ideally exists at the foundations of the nation.[72] Liberal democratic principles and values become exceptions (or instruments of 'exceptionalism') for foreigners to benefit from (and be protected by) the very same liberal democratic entitlements.[73] The mandatory nature of integration implies that the TCN's failure to comply with the obligation to integrate justifies the application of sanctions by the state, which range from financial penalties to the non-granting of a visa or a residence permit, or the non-renewal of the latter, falling into irregularity and/or the consequent expulsion from its territory.

The Council negotiations on the LTR and FR Directives and the building of the EU Framework on Integration since the early 2000s have marked a 'break in contiguity' in the Union's relation with immigration and integration policy.[74] This break has signified a shift in the rooted perspectives that used to inspire previous EU discourses, policies, and acts on integration. The intergovernmental barriers and tensions faced by the incursion of the Union into the immigration and integration domains certainly provided the general contextual background for this shift to propagate both in EU law and policy. Yet, the following three specific factors might have played a more determinant influence: first, the unanimity voting rule; secondly, the Directorate General Home Affairs (DG Home) of the Commission; and thirdly, the multi-level networked expert framework fostering the EU Framework on Integration.

A. EU immigration law and unanimity

The institutional and decision-making procedures envisaged by the 1999 Amsterdam Treaty have marked one of the factors determining the transition of the EU conception of integration towards nationalistic and insecurity venues. The old Article 67 of the TEC had envisaged a transitional period of five years (1999–2004) during which the decision-making procedures applicable to legislative acts falling within the umbrella of Title IV of the TEC would remain outside co-decision (now the

[72] C. Joppke and E. Morawska (eds), *Toward Assimilation and Citizenship: Immigrants in Liberal Nation-States* (2003).

[73] Guild and Carrera, *supra* n 70. [74] Kostakopoulou *et al.*, *supra* n 68.

ordinary legislative procedure) and qualified majority voting in the Council. This would be the case for measures adopted under Articles 63(3)(a) and 63(4) of the TEC which covered 'the conditions of entry and residence and the standards for issuing long-term visas and residence permits, including those for family reunification', as well as the adoption of common rules defining the rights and conditions under which TCNs 'legally resident in one Member State' may reside in another. The negotiations of the LTR and FR Directives occurred precisely during that transitional period where the JHA Council was the sole legislative actor holding the ownership and ultimate decision (on unanimous vote by all its members) on the destiny of any legislative proposal.[75]

The years of negotiations which proved to be necessary for these Directives to be adopted during the Greek Presidency of the EU in the second half of 2003,[76] and the EU level institutional and member states diplomatic strategies which surrounded them have been subject to academic attention.[77] The role played by a small group of representatives from the Ministries of Interior of certain EU member states, and that of the EU Presidency itself, was decisive in order to understand the final outputs of these measures, as well as the agreement which was finally reached on the framing of integration as a 'condition' or a 'measure'. It is nonetheless important to recall that the original versions of these two acts closely followed the fair and equality of treatment milestones enshrined in the 1999 Tampere Programme. Both instruments, however, were later on substantially watered down in the Council, which included the injection of nationally oriented integration provisions into their components.

The outcome of the Council debates led to the introduction of express references to integration measures and conditions on the initiative of Austria, Germany, and the Netherlands. These three EU member states managed to transfer to EU immigration law integration policies existing in their respective national immigration laws (which in the case of the Netherlands were at that time still under debate in parliament) and which conceived integration as an insecurity, immigration, and identity control tool for TCNs to have access to a long-term residence permit and family reunification. The decisiveness of the influence of these member states' representatives in the change of integration paradigm is evidenced when looking at the Council debates. Austria, Germany, and the Netherlands were in favour of adding the term integration conditions to the main text of the Directives. As we have seen in section 1(A) above, the only justification that was given for the need to insert these clauses into the body of the Directives was that this would make the

[75] It is also noticeable that, on the basis of the second paragraph of Art. 67 TEC, the Council took a Decision on 22 December 2004 by which all the immigration-related fields contained in Title IV TEC, with the exception of those dealing with regular immigration, were moved to the co-decision procedure. Council Decision 2004/927/EC of 22 December 2004 providing for certain areas covered by Title IV of Part Three of the Treaty establishing the European Community to be governed by the procedure set out in Art. 251 of that Treaty, [2004] OJ L396/45.

[76] This was proudly adopted in para. 28 of the Thessaloniki European Council Conclusions, *supra* n 43.

[77] See, eg, G. Papagianni, *Institutional and Policy Dynamics of EU Migration Law* (2006).

Directives compatible with their respective national laws, where newcomers had to follow mandatory integration programmes from the moment they were legally residing, and the degree of integration was used as one of the conditions for granting the settlement permit and family reunion.

The resulting scenario was one where EU policy served as a vehicle for legitimizing and promoting the integration policies of these EU member states, which were making use of integration in a conditional fashion in their respective immigration legislations. The use of integration conditions and measures taking the form of obligatory integration programmes, courses, contracts, or tests not only reflected a trend at national level in these three specific member states. By accommodating it into EU immigration law, the Union legitimized and (to a certain extent) supported its expansion across other national arenas. The literature has paid increasing attention to the ways in which ever since there has been a gradual proliferation of integration programmes, courses, and tests in a large number of EU member states.[78] Comparative academic contributions have pointed out the tensions raised by integration tests when putting in relation their public intended goals with the aims of the Directives and the EU general principles of proportionality, non-discrimination, and fundamental rights of TCNs.[79]

B. The European Commission

The prevailing intergovernmental logic influencing EU level decision-making processes also had repercussions on the internal working methods of the Commission, which in turn also affected the Union's vision on the goals and fundamentals of its agenda on integration policy. As anticipated above, the final results of the Council debates on the LTR and FR Directives—along with the failure of 2001 initiatives such as an OMC on immigration and the proposal for a directive on the admission and residence of TCNs for reasons of employment and self-employment—caused a certain internal trauma to the former DG Justice, Freedom, and Security (DG JLS) of the Commission. The DG got closer to certain national immigration and integration policy agendas. It often chose to privilege member states' interests and made substantial concessions in the development of common European rules and standards as early as in the proposal phase.[80] The watering down of European standards started to occur not only inside the Council's rooms but at an earlier stage, with the Commission supporting and/or favouring initiatives constituting already low minimum denominators following certain national policy or political priorities of particularly powerful EU member states.[81]

[78] Guild *et al.*, 'Challenges and Prospects for the EU's Area of Freedom, Security and Justice: Recommendations to the European Commission for the Stockholm Programme', CEPS Working Document No. 313, April 2009; Kostakopoulou, *supra* n 31.

[79] Carrera and Wiesbrock, *supra* n 26.

[80] See, eg European Commission, 'Communication on a Policy Plan on Legal Migration', COM (2005) 669 final.

[81] Guild *et al., supra* n 78.

The focus on immigration and identity control and integration was also favoured by the predominantly Ministry of Interior-like approach inspiring the work and priorities of the DG JLS, which has since its establishment tended to give preference to management and control (prevention) of the phenomenon of immigration, rather than facilitating access to socio-economic inclusion and non-discrimination of vulnerable groups. The home affairs rationale inspiring the integration agenda of this DG has not been alleviated by the subsequent split of DG JLS into two different Directorates in July 2010 with the new (Barroso II) Commission—DG Justice, Fundamental Rights and Citizenship led by Reding and DG Home Affairs led by Malmström. The integration dossier has nonetheless remained under the responsibility of the DG Home Affairs. Since 2005 the DG JLS (now DG Home) has contributed to the support of the new approach on integration as insecurity, immigration, and identity control. This is illustrated, for instance, when looking at the 'Communication on A Common Agenda on Integration' (2005) 389, where the Commission put forward concrete measures to strengthen the practical applicability of the CBPs at national and EU levels.[82] As we have seen above, CBP 2 and CBP 4.1 constitute a clear expression of the shift in the integration paradigm in EU policy. Surprisingly, the following specific actions were proposed by the Communication to put them into practice. First, in relation to CBP 2, it recommended that the EU member states emphasize civic orientation in introduction programmes and other activities for newly arrived TCNs with a view to ensuring that immigrants understand, respect, and benefit from common European and national values. Secondly, for the implementation of CBP 4.2, the Commission called for the organization of introduction programmes for newcomers, offering courses on 'previous knowledge of the country' and recommending:

> strengthening the integration component of admission procedures, e.g. through predeparture measures such as information packages and language and civic orientation courses in the country of origin ... organising introduction programmes and activities for newly arrived third-country nationals to acquire basic knowledge about language, history, institutions, socioeconomic features, cultural life and fundamental values.

Another example was the Commission Staff Working Document 'Strengthening Actions and Tools to meet Integration Challenges' SEC (2008) 2626,[83] which was prepared on the occasion of the Third EU Inter-Ministerial Conference on Integration organized by the French Presidency of the EU in November 2008 and which led to the adoption of the so-called 'Vichy Declaration'.[84] The Commission identified as a priority the establishment of the above-mentioned EMMIs, which amongst other issues were expected to focus on standards for the organization

[82] European Commission, 'Communication on a Common Agenda for Integration—Framework for the Integration of Third Country Nationals in the European Union', COM (2005) 389.

[83] European Commission, 'Strengthening Actions and Tools to Meet Integration Challenges: Report to the 2008 Ministerial Conference on Integration', Commission Staff Working Document, SEC (2008) 2626.

[84] European Council, European Ministerial Conference on Integration (Vichy 3–4 November 2008)—Declaration, 14898/08, 9 December 2008.

of introductory (civic) and language courses which would 'start by addressing organization of language and civic courses on the host society's history, institutions and the shared values of the EU'.[85]

C. A multi-level networked expertise

The role played by networks of experts and practitioners (the integration actors) and the various multilevel decision-making ways in which Europeanization works in the EU Framework on Integration, which are analysed in detail in section 3(B), have also contributed to the break in continuity in the EU's integration paradigm. Since its origins in 2002, the EU Framework on Integration has heavily depended on the active inputs by supranational networks of experts coming from national ministries responsible for integration policies in the exchange of information and the identification of 'good and/or best practices' on integration policies. A number of EU member states' representatives have been more successful than others in channelling and propagating their national integration programmes and policies to the European level as 'lessons learned'. They have tended to be those considered to have more experience in the management of the phenomenon of immigration (often denominated as 'traditional immigration countries'), which unsurprisingly have coincided (yet not always) with those very same states which proved to be more influential during the Council discussions on the LTR and FR Directives. The most visible effect has been the privileging and legitimization of civic integration programmes and tests inside and abroad as 'good practices' and CBPs.

The NCPIs have played a seminal role in the exchange of information and the evaluation of national practices and policies on integration, as well as in the identification of 'best practices'. They have been particularly successful in facilitating the development of a distinctive way of speaking about integration at EU level. This has been further strengthened by the participation of certain civil society organizations, such as the MPG, which have also actively steered forward the process. The interaction between the DG Home of the Commission, the NCPIs, civil society actors, and other integration stakeholders has led to the emergence of a common discourse on what works and does not work on integration. It has also favoured a strong (nationally oriented) policy agenda, catapulting domestic integration programmes, favouring philosophies of integration as insecurity, towards the European realm. This has been possible as a result of the way in which decisions are taken in the EU Framework on Integration, which suffer from a high level of unaccountability and lack of transparency. The NCPIs expert seminars and technical meetings were always closed to the public and, even though they counted the participation of a diverse range of actors from policy–making and civil society, their format has been one mainly interested in 'moving things forward' and 'showing results' without always allowing any critical reflection as regards its added value, coherency, and potential implications.

[85] European Commission, *supra*, n 83.

The EU Framework on Integration has not only brought legitimacy to the new understanding of integration as an insecuritization mechanism by framing it as CBPs. This EU standard setting has additionally unveiled an exchange of ideas promoting the diffusion of this new understanding of integration as a 'best practice' beyond particular national arenas and across a larger number of EU member states. The Framework has become a supranational forum prioritizing certain integration policies, programmes, and practices at the national level considered to be 'good' or in need of promotion in the entire EU. In addition to the recommendations highlighted by the above-mentioned Commission Communication of 2005 for EU member states to implement CBP 2 and 4.1, the way in which the first *Handbook on Integration* published in 2004 encouraged the organization of integration programmes including 'socio-cultural' (value-related) elements may also be added.[86] Some EU governments have consequently practised what we call 'politics of mimetics' by using the 'good practices' generated by the EU Framework on Integration, which were often directly imported from other EU member states such as the Netherlands,[87] in order to justify the introduction of integration tests in their own national legislations and policies.[88]

3. Integration and Rule of Law

Integration has, therefore, been subject to dynamic policy-making at EU level. This dynamism has come at a price, consisting of a deep paradigm shift of the classical conceptions of integration in EU immigration law and policy towards unexpected venues, capitalizing integration as an insecurity, immigration, and identity-control tool with an inherent nationalistic nature and fundamentals. The next question is the extent to which the very same Europeanization which has provoked this conceptual transition poses at the same time limits to the implementation of this new approach of integration by EU member states. Perhaps unexpectedly for some national governments and authorities, the gradual incursion by the Union into immigration and integration policy, and the consequent transfer of legislative and coordination powers to the EU, goes along with a diminution of the level of discretion enjoyed by the member states in the application of integration as a mechanism for 'exceptionalism' and exclusion of TCNs. As this section will demonstrate, this is the case when moving within the remit of EU immigration law and the LTR and FR Directives, where the role of the Commission (infringement proceedings) and the Court of Justice (preliminary rulings and the general principles of EU law) are deemed to be central at times to ensuring EU member states' compliance with EU rights and standards and scrutinizing the application of any exceptions to the

[86] Niessen and Schibel, *supra* n 41.

[87] Besselink, 'Integration and Immigration: The Vicissitudes of Dutch "*Inburgering*"', in E. Guild, K. Groenendijk, and S. Carrera (eds), *Illiberal Liberal States: Immigration, Citizenship and Integration in the EU* (2009) 241.

[88] Carrera and Wiesbrock, *supra* n 26.

latter. A different scenario, however, emerges in the EU Framework on Integration. Its *sui generis* legal nature prevents the display of basic rule of law principles upon which the EU system has been constructed.

A. Integration as an exception in EU immigration law

EU immigration law is not a peculiar sort of European law. While the shapes of the LTR and FR Directives have been considered to be of minimums—leaving a wide margin of appreciation to national authorities at times of national implementation, EU immigration law is as legally binding upon EU member states as the rest of the directives covering other policy domains. Some of the provisions stipulated in the LTR and FR Directives are also sufficiently clear and precise as to benefit from the legal doctrine and judicial interpretation on direct effect.[89] The legitimate number of interferences or derogations exercised by national authorities in what concerns the package of EU rights and freedoms foreseen by these directives needs to remain within specific frontiers. EU member states are under the obligation to abstain from adopting any national measure or practice that would jeopardize their objectives, rights, and common administrative criteria.

The LTR and FR Directives constitute an EU-wide immigration legal framework limiting the degree of discretion of member states and providing a ceiling of common standards and EU-wide rights and guarantees. As Groenendijk[90] has pointed out, many administrative techniques and barriers previously applied in immigration law, such as disproportionally high fees, exclusion of judicial control, or excessively one-sided interpretations of general rules of administrative law, are no longer acceptable within the remits of the Directives. They offer a European set of rights and freedoms to TCNs that all participating EU member states need to uphold in the phases of transposition and practical implementation. Any exceptions applicable to those, including the use of 'integration conditions and measures', are monitored by the Commission and would be expected to be increasingly subject to judicial scrutiny by the Court of Justice. By inserting this new approach of integration into some of the articles of the Directives, member states' actions must now not only comply with the objectives and provisions thereby stipulated, but also with the general principles of EU law developed by the jurisprudence of the Court of Justice in Luxembourg, which include amongst others those of proportionality and non-discrimination.[91]

Since 1999, the Court of Justice has enjoyed jurisdiction to review and interpret EU legislative measures on regular migration falling within the umbrella of the former Title IV of the TEC ('Visas, Asylum, Immigration and Other Policies

[89] P. Craig and G. de Búrca, *EU Law: Text, Cases and Materials* (2007), at 268–304.

[90] Groenendjik, 'Citizens and Third Country Nationals: Differential Treatment or Discrimination?', in J. Y. Carlier and E. Guild (eds), *The Future of Free Movement of Persons in the EU* (2006) 79.

[91] De Witte, 'Institutional Principles: A Special Category of General Principles of EC Law', in U. Bernitz and J. Nergelius (eds), *General Principles of Community Law* (2000) 143; T. Trimidas, *The General Principles of EU Law* (2nd edn, 2006).

related to the Free Movement of Persons'). Its interventions concerning the LTR and FR Directives have so far not been very prolific due to the limitations which were envisaged by the treaties, which stipulated in Article 68 of the TEC that only those national tribunals against whose decisions there is no judicial remedy under national law could present a preliminary ruling before Luxembourg.[92] As we will see in section 3(C), the expansion of the Court of Justice's competence by the Treaty of Lisbon sheds light on the increasing relevance that it is expected to gain in reviewing and interpreting member states' actions, and the application of exceptions such as the one of integration, in the scope of EU immigration law. So far, the landmark case where the Court embarked on the interpretation of one of the integration-related provisions envisaged in a directive on regular immigration was Case C-540/03, *EP v. Council*.[93] In that case, the European Parliament presented an action for annulment against the validity of three provisions envisaged by the FR Directive because of their alleged incompatibility with fundamental rights and non-discrimination, in particular the right to family life and the right not to be discriminated against on grounds of age. One of the contested provisions was Article 4(1) of the FR Directive, which gave the possibility to EU member states to evaluate whether a child over 12 years old (and arriving independently from the rest of the family) met an 'integration condition'.[94] We remind the reader that the insertion of this and the other integration-related references in the Directive constituted a central point in the political compromise which allowed the final unanimous adoption of the Directive inside the Council.

One of the issues was the extent to which the partial annulment of the contested provisions was in fact possible (their severability), or whether their annulment would affect the substance of the Directive. The Court used this as an opportunity to enter into a review of the substance of the case and each of the derogative clauses being challenged by the Parliament. While the Court finally held that these provisions were non-severable and the Directive was in compliance with fundamental rights, the ruling was of a special significance because of the proactive and expansionist way in which the Court interpreted the guarantees offered by fundamental rights to the family life of TCNs, and the boundaries that it settled to the applicability of exceptions by EU member states to the rights prescribed by the Directive.[95] The ruling started by stressing that the provisions under examination impose 'precise positive obligations, with corresponding clearly defined individual rights, on the Member States'.[96] Further, while the Court considered that Article 4(1) was not contrary to fundamental rights, it stated that the objective of this provision was (or rather should be) the one provided in Recital 12 of the Directive, of

[92] S. Peers, 'The Jurisdiction of the Court of Justice over EC Immigration and Asylum Law: Time for a Change?', in A. Baldaccini, E. Guild, and H. Toner (eds), *Whose Freedom, Security and Justice? EU Immigration and Asylum Law and Policy* (2007) 85.

[93] Case C-540/03, *European Parliament v. Council*, [2006] ECR I-5769. Refer also to the Opinion of Advocate General Kokott delivered on 8 September 2005, Case C-540/03, *European Parliament v. Council*, at 43 and 45.

[94] The other two articles were Arts. 4(1) and 8.

[95] Carrera, *supra* n 4.

[96] Para. 60 of the judgment.

'facilitating the integration of third country nationals in Member States by making family life possible through reunification'. By doing so, the Court confirmed the relevance of the Preamble when interpreting the undefined concept of integration conditions and measures. The judgment acknowledged the possibility that some national transposition of integration conditions could potentially be in violation of fundamental rights, and called national tribunals facing difficulties in the interpretation or validity of the Directive to refer a preliminary ruling should a question of incompatibility potentially arise in practice.[97]

The difficulties experienced by EU member states in the transposition of the FR Directive have been examined by several studies commissioned by the European Commission.[98] While acknowledging that directives are only binding as to the result to be achieved and that they leave the choice to national authorities on the form and methods for transposition, the Commission confirmed the limited margin of manoeuvre enjoyed by EU member states in the transposition of integration-related provisions in its Report on 'The Application of Directive 2003/86/EC on the Right to Family Reunification', COM (2008) 610.[99] Here the Report followed the jurisprudence of the Court by stating that the objective of any national integration measures should be to facilitate the integration of TCNs' family members and added that their admissibility under the main text and preamble of the Directive depends on whether they serve this purpose. To this it added that the lawfulness of the application of integration measures under the Directive depends on whether:

> they respect the principle of proportionality. Their admissibility can be questioned on the basis of the accessibility of such courses or tests, how they are designed and/or organised (test materials, fees, venue, etc.), whether such measures or their impact serve purposes other than integration (e.g. high fees excluding low-income families). The procedural safeguards to ensure the right to mount a legal challenge should also be respected.

B. The EU Framework on Integration and the rule of law

There is a tension between the EU Framework on Integration and the rule of law. This, in turn, nuances the potential influences or limitations that the EU legal system could inflict on the proliferation of the new approach(es) to integration in the context of EU policy-making. Section 1(B) above has studied the substantive and financial elements composing the EU's Integration Agenda. It has been argued that these elements make of the EU Framework on Integration a quasi-OMC which falls outside the traditional decision-making and institutional arrangements

[97] D. Martin, 'Comments on *European Parliament v. Council* (Case C-540/03 of 27 June 2006)' 9 *European Journal of Migration and Law* (2007) 144.

[98] European Migration Network, *Family Reunification* (2008), available at <http://emn.intrasoft-intl.com/html/index.html>; H. Labayle and Y. Pascouau, *Directive 2003/86 on the Right to Family Reunification: Synthesis Report* (2008), available at <http://ec.europa.eu/home-affairs/doc_centre/immigration/immigration_studies_en.htm>.

[99] European Commission, 'Report on the Application of the Directive 2003/86/EC on the Right to Family Reunification', COM (2008) 610.

foreseen by the Treaties. The EU Framework on Integration constitutes an alternative policy-making method, moving Europeanization forward through soft law/policy, networks of 'integration actors', as well as the exchange and evaluation of integration practices/policies. This kind of 'experimental governance' causes several issues of concern because it develops through patterns of cooperation presenting a blurred legal nature and effects, and therefore standing in a difficult relationship with rule of law principles at the foundation of the EU legal regime, in particular those of legal certainty, transparency, democratic accountability, and judicial control.

The principle of legal certainty remains at stake when examining the very nature of the EU Framework on Integration and its instruments and outputs. The failure of the 2001 Commission proposal on an OMC on immigration provoked the emergence of something different from any already known path of European cooperation in the context of European law and/or policy. If OMCs can be generally viewed as multi-level frameworks of governance falling in between law and politics,[100] the EU Framework on Integration takes us even further into the realm of politics. A point in common between OMCs and the EU Framework on Integration is that the two 'methods' are meant to influence EU member states through informal discussions and exchanges of practices, the participation of networks of practitioners, and supranational coordination and evaluation. However, the EU Framework on Integration presents major differences in contrast with other OMCs, which make it an atypical coordination mechanism. The powers of the Commission are significantly weaker when monitoring the implementation by EU member states of the CBPs and the EIF. Neither are member states under an obligation to deliver National Action Plans (NAPs) on the implementation of the CBPs, allowing for review by the Commission and the identification of common issues of concern and shared solutions. The Framework does not aim at (at least primarily) legislative harmonization, but rather at being complementary to the enactment of EU law.

The nature and effects of the instruments and outputs which have flourished in the EU Framework on Integration are also not of an undisputed character. They do not correspond with any usual secondary sources of EU law (Regulations, Directives, Decisions, Recommendations, and Opinions),[101] but rather they have adopted the shape of Annual Reports, Handbooks, Communications, Commission Staff Working Documents, Council Conclusions, and the like, whose actual legal nature and effects call for closer critical reflection, especially when used in domains so sensitive from a fundamental rights perspective such as those of immigration and integration. By way of illustration, the CBPs (adopted in the form of Council Conclusions) are supposed to offer a non-binding guide against which EU member states can assess and evaluate their own integration policies and programmes.

[100] Trubek and Trubek, 'The Open Method of Coordination and the Debate over "Hard" and "Soft" Law', in J. Zeitlin and P. Pochet (eds), *The Open Method of Coordination Action: The European Employment and Social Inclusion Strategies* (2005) 83; Hatzopoulos, 'Why the Open Method of Coordination is Bad for You: A Letter to the EU' 13 *European Law Journal* (2007) 309.

[101] Refer to Art. 288 TFEU.

They also seek to facilitate 'EU-wide learning' and 'knowledge-sharing' through exchanges of information on 'best practices' identified through benchmarking and indexing techniques. The softness inherent to the CBPs has, however, been strengthened after the adoption of the EIF, which positioned their national implementation at the heart of its funding priorities. The linkage between policy and funding enables the reframing of political opportunities using the tools of the EU Framework on Integration. It also allows for unexpected impacts and disruptive venues at national, regional, and local governance levels.

Another central question for consideration is the extent to which these outputs can be considered as law or policy. One could argue that they should be viewed as soft law. The scholarly debates have been already succinct on the adequacy of using the labels of 'soft law' or 'hard law' when looking at alternative methods of governance at EU level.[102] Some have alluded to the inherent contradiction of using the term soft law: ie soft law without legal effects cannot be considered as law, and soft law with legal effects should be viewed as law itself. A similar line of argumentation could be applicable to other labels such as 'soft policy' or 'hard policy'. Policy is by definition soft in nature and effects, and hard policy would imply having some sort of legal effects which would make it close to law. The use of either conceptual categorization would still not fade away with the uncertainties concerning their legal nature and effects. While the tools of the EU Framework on Integration are not legally binding, one should not underestimate their potential for having incidental legal effects and affecting (directly or indirectly) the legal position—rights and obligations—of TCNs. Moreover, their legal value could also be developed through their potential use as interpretative sources in hands of European tribunals of integration-related provisions incorporated into EU Directives on regular immigration.

The EU Framework on Integration additionally challenges the institutional (and decision-making) arrangements underpinning the Community method of cooperation and the EU Treaties. The EU multi-stakeholder (networked) framework driving it has enabled a dynamic level of policy convergence, often at the expense of general principles of transparency, scrutiny, and accountability. EU clubs of integration experts and practitioners have been central in steering forward the processes on the exchange of information, the identification of 'best practices', the adoption of the key substantive elements, and the identification of current and near future political priorities of the Framework. The ways in which Europeanization advances, allows for few critical and democratic debates on added value, necessity, and any negative repercussions of the tools being developed. The fact that discussions have too often occurred in closed-doors meetings and inter-ministerial conferences has not helped to ensure the transparency and proper scrutiny of decisions and results.

These concerns become reinforced when taking into consideration the limited involvement by the European Parliament in the negotiations and adoption of the most important decisions surrounding the EU Framework on Integration. The

[102] L. Senden, *Soft Law in European Community Law: Its Relationship to Legislation* (2003).

Framework has only ensured plural democratic debates on its components and agendas in a rather ad hoc fashion.[103] The CBPs, for example, were adopted only between the Dutch Presidency of the EU, the NCPIs, the SCIFA in the Council, and the Commission through opaque and secretive procedures. To this we may add the uncertainty concerning the extent to which the Court of Justice has jurisdiction to review and interpret the adopted instruments. As a consequence of its special legal nature, one could conclude that the outputs of the EU Framework on Integration remain outside the scope of review of the validity of their provisions, and even more so as regards any national implementation. That notwithstanding, it would in our view all depend on the eventual legal effects that these 'soft tools' might prove to exert over the rights and responsibilities (status) of TCNs in a context where a particular national, regional, or local public integration policy would be based on (or justified by making reference to) the EU Framework on Integration.

C. The Treaty of Lisbon and integration

The entry into force of the Lisbon Treaty in December 2009 has introduced a renewed institutional and substantive landscape of European cooperation over domains falling under the umbrella of the EU's AFSJ, including those of immigration and integration of TCNs.[104] In fact, the AFSJ has been considered to be amongst those policy areas where Lisbon has inflicted a more far-reaching overhaul.[105] The new Treaty framework has brought the following three overarching innovations to the relation between integration and EU law and policy: first, the provision of an express legal competence for the EU to intervene on integration policy; secondly, the application of the Community method of cooperation or ordinary legislative procedure for the adoption of common European measures; and thirdly, a substantial institutional reshaping leading to a new relational power architecture on immigration and integration policies.

First, the Treaty on the Functioning of the European Union (TFEU), which has taken over from the former TEC, now provides one unique Title V covering the previously fragmented or 'pillarized' (EC First Pillar and EU Third Pillar) AFSJ.[106] The TFEU has for the first time envisaged a provision granting express legal competence to the Union to legislate on measures covering the integration of TCNs. It is worth recalling here the debates which have been witnessed since 1999 on the

[103] One of the few inputs by the European Parliament on the EU Framework on Integration can be found in its report, Committee on Civil Liberties, Justice, and Home Affairs, 'Strategies and Means for the Integration of Immigrants in the European Union', 2006/2056/INI, A6-0190/2006.

[104] Consolidated versions of the Treaty on European Union and the Treaty on the Functioning of the European Union, [2010] OJ C83/01.

[105] Carrera and Geyer, 'The Reform Treaty and Justice and Home Affairs: Implications for the Common Area of Freedom, Security and Justice', in E. Guild and F. Geyer (eds), *Security versus Justice? Police and Judicial Cooperation in the European Union* (2008) 289; Dougan, 'The Treaty of Lisbon 2007: Winning Minds, not Hearts' 45 *Common Market Law Review* (2008) 617.

[106] Arts. 67–89 TFEU.

extent to which the Union actually had the legal competence to intervene in this policy area. As signalled in the introduction to this chapter, the tensions between certain EU member state representatives and the European Commission, however, did not prevent the Council from adopting, on the basis of the former Article 63 of the TEC, the EIF and introducing 'integration measures' and 'conditions' in the main body of the LTR and FR Directives, which in our view exemplified a recognition by the EU legislator of the existence of legal competence for Union intervention. The TFEU has in any case put an end to these debates. The new Article 79(4) of the TFEU provides that:

> [t]he European Parliament and the Council, acting in accordance with the ordinary legislative procedure, may establish measures to provide incentives and support for the action of Member States with a view to promoting the integration of third-country nationals residing legally in their territories, excluding any harmonisation of the laws and regulations of the Member States.

The most immediate consequence of this provision is that the current soft law/ policy multilevel (networked) setting on integration has been granted a clear legal basis in the Treaty. The following two general elements regarding its material and personal scope can be underlined: first, the Article offers the possibility to bring into the realm of the Treaties and European law the current and future components substantiating the EU Framework on Integration. Any harmonization of laws, however, remains excluded from its scope, which emphasizes that any measure which will be adopted on this basis will primarily aim at providing 'incentives and support for the action of Member States'. This confirms the predominance of national competence over the domain of integration. Secondly, the personal scope of European measures will remain limited to the integration of TCNs who are legally residing in EU member states' territories. This in principle excludes the possibility of enacting measures covering other vulnerable groups such as asylum seekers and recognized refugees, undocumented immigrants, Roma, etc.

Article 79(4) of the TFEU also expands the Community method of cooperation to the EU's agenda on integration by making allusion to the application of the ordinary legislative procedure (formerly co-decision procedure) currently foreseen in Article 294 of the TFEU. This procedure recognizes the right of initiative of the Commission, the application of qualified majority voting (QMV) inside the Council, and the transformation of the Parliament into co-legislator. In contrast to the current configuration of the EU Framework on Integration, the second phase of the EU's integration agenda now counts with a solid decision-making scenario which could lead to a higher degree of efficiency, legal certainty, accountability, and democratic control of the laws and policies to be developed in the years to come. An optimist would, therefore, expect that the obscurity, lack of transparency, and secrecy that has so far affected European cooperation on integration will be partially overcome. The application of QMV could also prevent situations such as those experienced during the negotiations of the LTR and FR Directives, in particular strategies such as those practised by Germany, Austria, and the Netherlands. The positive implications of QMV in the migration domain have been illustrated during the negotiations of the Regulation extending the provisions of Regulations 883/2004 and 987/2009 on the coordination of social security systems to TCNs,[107] which was finally adopted against the negative votes by Germany, Austria, and Bulgaria.[108]

Moreover, the European Commission holds a reinforced role as initiator of legislation, which could be expected to increase its powers as coordinator and evaluator in future EU policy steps. The new role of the European Parliament as co-legislator might also diversify and provide new venues for EU mobilization beyond hesitations and nationalistic positions advocated by certain EU member states' representatives in this policy domain. As regards the Council, a direct effect of Article 79(4) of the TFEU has been the renaming of the Council Working Party on Migration and Expulsion, which is composed by EU member states' representatives dealing with the negotiations of migration-related legislative initiatives (in particular those covering non-EU nationals' entry residence and expulsion), to the Working Party on Integration, Migration, and Expulsion. The formal incursion of the Council on integration policy now leaves the question open as regards the actual role and added value of the NCPIs. All this without forgetting the expansion of the Court of Justice's jurisdiction to review and interpret measures adopted under Article 79 of the TFEU by overcoming the previous limitation restricting the presentation of preliminary rulings to last instance national courts or tribunals. The liberalization of the Court of Justice jurisdiction may lead to an increase in the number of cases reaching Luxembourg on the interpretation and validity of national measures falling within the scope of EU immigration law and strategic litigation on the national implementation of integration conditions and measures. Also, any future legal measure to be adopted in the context of the EU Framework on Integration, and proving to have legal effects affecting rights and freedoms of TCNs falling within the scope of EU law should, of course, be also expected to benefit from EU judicial control.

Finally, the subsidiarity principle check has also become salient through the enhanced role recognized to national parliaments and the Committee of the Regions. Article 6 of the Protocol on the application of the principles of subsidiarity and proportionality states that any national parliament (or any chamber of a national parliament) can, within eight weeks from the date of transmission of a draft legislative act, send to the European Parliament, the Council, and the Commission a reasoned opinion stating the reasons why it considers that the legislative draft is

[107] Proposal for a Regulation of the European Parliament and of the Council extending the provisions of Regulation (EC) No. 883/2004 and Regulation (EC) No. 987/2009 to nationals of third countries who are not already covered by these provisions solely on the ground of their nationality COM (2007) 439 final. Refer also to the Commission Communication, 'Consequences of the Entry into Force of the Treaty of Lisbon for Ongoing Interinstitutional Decision-making Procedures', COM (2009) 665 final.

[108] Council of the EU, Voting Result—Proposal for a Regulation of the European Parliament and of the Council extending the provisions of Regulation (EC) No. 883/2004 and Regulation (EC) No. 987/2009 to nationals of third countries who are not already covered by these provisions solely on the ground of their nationality—Adoption of the Council's position 3028th meeting of the Council of the EU (General Affairs), 26 July 2010, Council Document 12801/1/10, 20 October 2010.

not in conformity with the principle of subsidiarity. The role of the Committee of Regions has been also strengthened by Article 8 of the same Protocol, which grants it the possibility to present an action before the Court of Justice on grounds of infringement of the principle of subsidiarity against legislative acts for the adoption of which the TFEU provides its consultation.[109]

4. Conclusion

This chapter has examined the legal landscape on the integration of TCNs in the EU. It has revealed how complex and dynamic the relationship is between integration and EU immigration law and policy. During the last 12 years, and in light of the political milestones adopted in 1999 by the Tampere Programme, the EU has endowed itself with an emerging body of legislation and policy directly and/or indirectly engaging with the integration of TCNs. The progressive Europeanization of these domains, however, has not been exempted from frictions emerging from certain EU member states' representatives, which have persisted in their struggles to delimit the boundaries of Union's intervention. These logics of intergovernmentalism, which have to a great extent prevented the accomplishment of the political agenda originally envisaged by the Tampere Programme, have in turn led to the bifurcation of the normative framing of integration policy at EU level into a new dual setting, ie EU immigration law and the EU Framework on Integration.

Through an examination of the relation between integration and the Directives on LTR and FR as well as the current state of affairs (and near-future policy developments) in the EU Framework on Integration, the chapter has demonstrated how in both frameworks the EU's traditional approach(es) or conceptions of integration have shifted from an understanding of integration as a desecuritization tool centred on the facilitation of socio-economic inclusion, non-discrimination, equality and fair treatment, towards new venues conceiving it as an insecuritization mechanism primarily aimed at the management of immigration and belonging of TCNs in the context of immigration law. Integration has mutated into a legal criterion conditioning access by TCNs to social inclusion, security of residence, and rights. It now takes the shapes of a mandatory civic integration programme, course, test, or contract demanding TCNs to show knowledge and to adhere to a set of constructed societal and liberal democratic values and a way of life adjusted to the perfection and homogeneity presumably existing in the national citizenry. The immersion of integration into assimilation and acculturation waters, and the demand to demonstrate naturalization into the citizenship of the receiving state, has surprisingly become a criterion for the individual to be granted legality and security of residence and family reunion.

[109] S. Carrera, *The Role and Potential for Local and Regional Authorities in the EU Framework on the Integration of Immigrants* (study commissioned by the Commission for Constitutional Affairs, European Governance, and the Area of Freedom, Security and Justice of the Committee of the Regions) (2009).

This paradigm shift has its foundations in the beginning of the 2000s, during the arduous Council negotiations of the LTR and FR Directives and the gradual development of the EU Framework on Integration as a *sui generis* coordination mechanism. The applicability of the unanimity voting role inside the Council enabled the transfer by a small group of EU member states of their own national integration approaches to the legislative body of the LTR and FR Directives through the insertion of 'integration condition' and 'measures' clauses conditioning access by TCNs (and functioning as an exception) to EU rights, freedoms, and guarantees. A similar nationalistic drive can be perceived in the EU Framework on Integration, where the exchange of information by networks of 'integration actors' on national policies has facilitated the promotion of certain domestic integration programmes using a similarly restrictive conception of integration by qualifying them as 'best practices' and finding their place in CBPs 2 and 4.1.

The dynamic expansionism of 'more Europe' in the domain of integration of TCNs has in this way come at a high cost to the Union, which has mainly consisted in a far-reaching distancing from the traditional EU approach(es) of integration towards neo-nationalistic terrains giving the opportunity to national governments to use the latter as an exception to inclusion and a condition to rights. That notwithstanding, the chapter has demonstrated how the increasing Europeanization of immigration law has come along with a diminution in the degree of autonomy enjoyed by EU member states in the implementation of integration as an insecurity, immigration, and identity control mechanism. The practice by the state of integration as an exception to the common set of rights and administrative standards provided by the LTR and FR Directives needs to comply with their goals and fundamentals. The lawfulness of the practical transposition of integration measures and conditions is now monitored by the Commission and potentially subject to judicial control by the Court of Justice. Here the role and impact of the general principles of EU law, such as those of proportionality, legal certainty, and non-discrimination, is expected to be increasingly relevant in the years to come.

The EU Framework on Integration presents, however, a number of deficits and unresolved dilemmas which are inherent to the ways in which it has developed so far, and which present various challenges to EU rule of law principles, especially those of legal certainty, transparency, democratic accountability, and judicial control. The Treaty of Lisbon, however, offers interesting prospects for overcoming some of these vulnerabilities, yet it does not resolve all of them. One of the central questions which will still remain for the second phase of the EU's integration agenda is the kind of incentives and national integration approaches and policies that the Union will support and promote. It is to be hoped that the next generation of the EU Framework on Integration will be one fully reconciled with EU law general principles and capable of proving its added value by going beyond neo-national understandings of civic integration as an exception to inclusion and rights in immigration legislation and policy. The second phase of the EU's agenda on integration could signify a unique opportunity to come back to (and further consolidate) the classical EU conceptions of integration as an inclusionary process, where the socio-economic and legal inclusion of TCNs would regain a more central stance in the Union's policy priorities.

ANNEX 1

Common Basic Principles for Immigrant Integration Policy[110]

1. Integration is a 'dynamic, two-way process of mutual accommodation' by all immigrants and residents of the member states.
2. Integration implies respect for 'the basic values of the EU'.
3. Employment is a key part of the integration process and participation of immigrants.
4. 1. Basic knowledge of the host society's language, history and institutions is indispensable for integration; 2. enabling immigrants to acquire this basic knowledge is essential to successful integration.
5. Efforts in education are critical to preparing immigrants, and particularly their descendants, to be more successful and more active participants in society.
6. Access for immigrants to institutions, as well as to public and private goods and services, on a basis equal to national citizens and in a non-discriminatory way.
7. Frequent interaction between immigrants and EU citizens is a fundamental mechanism for integration. Shared forums, inter-cultural dialogue, education about immigrants and immigrants culture, and stimulating living conditions in urban environments enhance the interactions between immigrants and Member States citizens.
8. 1. The practice of diverse cultures and religions is guaranteed under the Charter of Fundamental Rights and must be safeguarded, 2. unless practices conflict with other inviolable European rights or national law.
9. The participation of immigrants in the democratic process and in the formulation of integration policies and measures, specially at the local level, support their integration;
10. Mainstreaming integration in all relevant portfolios and levels of government and public services; and
11. Developing clear goals, indicators and evaluation mechanisms to adjust policy, evaluate progress on integration and to make the exchange of information more effective.

[110] Council of the European Union, Justice and Home Affairs Council Meeting 2618th, Common Basic Principles on Immigrants Integration, 14615/04, 19 November 2004.

7

Analysing European Case-Law on Migration: Options for Critical Lawyers

Thomas Spijkerboer[1]

This chapter is about three strategies which lawyers may use when they want to criticize a court decision, or a set of court decisions ('case-law'). I will presume that they will criticize court decisions within legal discourse. Of course, they might do otherwise and criticize court decisions in other discourses. They might, for example, argue that the court decisions do not reflect the will of the democratic majority which drafted the legal rule which was applied (political critique), or that the court decisions are immoral (moral critique), or inefficient (law and economics critique). However, the influence a lawyer has stems from the notion that legal discourse is—to some extent—technical in nature, which gives it certain legitimacy. If a critical lawyer wants to rely on this source of legitimacy, the critique must be legal. I will presume that that is what critical lawyers want to do.

In order to point out other options than the one the court has taken, critical lawyers will either have to argue that the court was simply wrong, or that the court had another option which was preferable on some ground. In this text, I will largely ignore the first possibility. Although, obviously, it does happen that courts produce arguments which would be plain wrong in a law school exam, this does not happen very often, and it certainly does not happen much in the courts on which I focus here, the European Court of Human Rights (ECtHR) and the Court of Justice of (now) the EU (ECJ).

I am aware that terms like critique and critical lawyers have a progressive, leftist ring. However, the case-law of the European courts may be criticized both from a progressive position (in the present-day migration context: they give too much space to state sovereignty and give insufficient protection to individual rights) as well as from a more state-oriented position (the courts have gone way beyond what states have agreed to and infringe on the possibilities of national communities to rule themselves[2]). Although no doubt the following will expose me as belonging to

[1] I thank Louis Middelkoop for his research assistance and Herbert Schilthuis for his medical insights.

[2] See, in this vein, eg M. Bossuyt, *Strasbourg et les demandeurs d'asile: des juges sur un terrain glissant* (2010).

the first variety of critics, my aim in this text is more limited, and for that reason coincidentally more neutral. I want to inquire into three common strategies which critical lawyers of any political colour may use when they criticize case-law in the terms of legal discourse. The theoretical interest of this inquiry is that critical lawyers have to deal with the inconsistency at the heart of legal reasoning, being that legal reasoning, through its technical nature, claims to lead to determinate outcomes (at least in the great majority of cases) while at the same time the critique will point out that legal reasoning allows for more than one legitimate outcome.[3]

In order to distinguish the political positions one may take on immigration, I rely on a grid representing four ideal typical positions.[4] In the context of migration, familiar ways of linking general political views to particular positions on migration do not seem to work. If we loosely define leftists as people primarily concerned with equal distribution of wealth and rightists as people primarily concerned with freedom from government constraints, we cannot predict the positions of these persons on migration issues. There are leftists who defend migrants' rights, advocate freedom of cross-border movement, and embrace multiculturalism. But there are also leftists who plead for restricted migration as this seems necessary for defending the achievements of the labour movement over the past century or so. There are rightists who argue for free migration because they consider restrictions on migration as labour market distortions. But there are also rightists who champion migration restrictions on the basis of cultural-nationalist assumptions. In other words the political spectrum is warped on migration issues.

Table 7.1 Political positions on migration

	Left	Right
Libertarian	Multicultural rights advocates	Laissez-faire liberals
Statist	Welfare nationalists	Cultural nationalists

In this contribution, I will argue that this warped character of the political spectrum constitutes an opportunity for engaged lawyers who care about the outcome of their legal arguments, and about the decisions of courts. In the first part of my contribution, I will show how case-law that at first sight seems to be consistent, can be approached in such a way that when analysed more rigorously, it turns out to be inconsistent. This can be done by including in the analysis cases which were considered to be about something else in the more conventional approach. This opens up the possibility of suggesting to the judiciary more consistent ways of addressing the issues at stake. This section will use the ECtHR's case-law on the intensity of judicial scrutiny in asylum cases as an example. In section 2, I will show how case-law may be contrasted with a potential alternative which is just as valid from a legal-technical position as the one adopted in standing case-law.

[3] This is inspired to a great extent by D. Kennedy, *A Critique of Adjudication (Fin de Siècle)* (1997).

[4] This is loosely inspired by Marie-Bénedicte Dembour's four human rights schools, see M.-B. Dembour, *Who Believes in Human Rights? Reflections on the European Convention* (2006).

When the standing case-law has been downgraded to merely one of the possible alternatives, this creates space for the court to adopt the alternative. In this second section, the ECJ's case-law on family reunion of EU citizens will be used as an example. Section 3 will address the possibilities of focusing on something that participants in the legal debate consider as an uncontested, evident issue (which I will call a background issue). Reframing the background issue may affect the likely outcomes of legal debates. The example in this chapter will be the Strasbourg case-law about HIV positive aliens and Article 3 of the European Convention on Human Rights (ECHR).

1. Constructing Consistency: the Intensity of Judicial Review in Asylum Law

The first argumentative move I want to discuss is one that identifies inconsistency in the law as it stands, and develops a more coherent approach which is presented as better from a technical-legal point of view. And—lo and behold!—the improved, more coherent approach invariably tends to be closer to the political position of the person making the move. This is obvious, because identifying the inconsistency and reconstructing a more coherent approach is a lot of work, which one will only undertake if one has a reason to do so. People who are more or less pleased with the law as it stands will not devote their time and energy to trying to change it.

The example I will use is the position of the ECtHR on the intensity of judicial review in asylum law.[5] When faced with a case concerning a government act (such as deportation), courts can ask themselves roughly two questions. They can ask the question whether the government was *correct* in finding the act legal. The object of enquiry is the government decision to undertake that act. In this case, the domestic court will replace the government's opinion with its own. However, courts may ask themselves another question, which leads to a significantly less intense form of review. In this case, the domestic court asks whether the government could *reasonably* decide to undertake the act. The domestic court will only intervene if the decision is unreasonable, either in substance (for example, the balance of interests should clearly have been decided otherwise), or procedurally (for example, the individual did not have a fair hearing). Whereas in response to the first question only one outcome will be acceptable to the domestic court (namely, the correct one), in response to the second question several outcomes may be acceptable (namely, all reasonable ones).

Faced with case-law of the ECtHR which seemed to accept a less intense scrutiny by domestic courts, I will argue that this is inconsistent with its case-law about its own assessment in asylum cases. Having identified the inconsistency, I will suggest a way to remedy it.

[5] This is based on T. Spijkerboer, 'Subsidiarity and "Arguability": the European Court of Human Rights' Case Law on Judicial Review in Asylum Cases' 21 *International Journal of Refugee Law* (2009) 48, at 63–9.

Interestingly, the ECtHR uses the same term for the scrutiny which it applies itself in asylum cases as for the scrutiny it requires domestic courts to apply in asylum cases on the basis of Article 13 of the ECHR. Since its *Vilvarajah* judgment, the ECtHR has consistently held that its own examination of the existence of ill-treatment in breach of Article 3 of the ECHR must necessarily be a rigorous one in view of the absolute character of this provision, and the fact that it enshrines one of the fundamental values of the democratic societies making up the Council of Europe.[6] This was reconfirmed in the Grand Chamber judgment in the *Saadi* case.[7] Since *Jabari*, the ECtHR has held that, given the irreversible nature of the harm that might occur if the risk of torture or ill-treatment materialized, and the importance of Article 3, the notion of an effective remedy under Article 13 requires independent and rigorous scrutiny of a claim under Article 3.[8] The fact that the ECtHR uses the term 'rigorous scrutiny' both for its own scrutiny and for the scrutiny it requires from domestic courts, suggests that these should be identical. However, that idea becomes problematic when one pays close attention to the ECtHR's case-law.

A. Rigorous scrutiny by the Court

In its case-law, the ECtHR acknowledges the difference between more and less intense forms of scrutiny. For example, in cases concerning Article 6 of the ECHR, the ECtHR has developed the position that its duty is to ensure the observance of the ECHR by states, not to deal with errors of fact or law allegedly committed by a national court, 'unless and in so far as they may have infringed rights and freedoms protected by the Convention'.[9] It has ruled, in contrast, that notwithstanding its subsidiary role, in cases concerning Articles 2 and 3 of the ECHR, 'the Court must apply a particularly thorough scrutiny, even if certain domestic proceedings and investigations have already taken place'.[10]

[6] *Vilvarajah and ors v. UK*, ECHR (1991) Series A, No. 215, para. 108.

[7] *Saadi v. Italy*, ECHR (2008) Appl. No. 37201/06, para. 128.

[8] *Jabari v. Turkey*, ECHR RJ&D 2000-VIII, para. 50.

[9] *García Ruiz v. Spain*, ECHR (1999) RJ&D 1999-I, 28; compare with *Herbst v. Germany*, ECHR (2007) Appl. No. 20027/02, para. 83; *Tamminen v. Finland*, ECHR (2004) Appl. No. 40847/98, para. 38; *K-H. W. v. Germany*, ECHR (2001) Appl. No. 37201/97, para. 44; P. van Dijk and G. J. F. van Hoof, *Theory and Practice of the European Convention on Human Rights* (2006) 585, fn 512. In a number of Art. 6 cases the ECtHR attached importance to the fact that judges in the UK have particular knowledge of, and experience with, the jury system, see *G.C. v. UK*, ECHR (2001) Appl. No. 43373/98, para. 36, cited in *Snooks and Dowse v. UK*, ECHR (2002) Decision on Appl. No. 44305/98, equally an Art. 6 case; cited in *Betson and Cockram v. UK*, ECHR (2002) Decision on Appl. No. 12710/04.

[10] *Aktas v. Turkey*, ECHR (2003) RJ&D 2003-V; compare with *Ribitsch v. Austria*, ECHR (1995) Series A, No. 336; *Avsar v. Turkey*, ECHR (2001), Appl. No. 25657/94. Unusual, however, is the admissibility decision in the *Damla* case (*Damla and ors v. Germany*, ECHR (2000) Decision Appl. No. 61479/00). Here, the Court considered both that its examination in cases concerning Art. 3 must necessarily be a rigorous one, and that factual matters are primarily a matter for national courts (its general, distantial position developed in cases concerning Art. 6). Because the facts had already been evaluated carefully by national courts in three asylum procedures, and in the absence of indications of arbitrariness in this respect, the Court concluded that no substantial grounds had been shown for believing the applicants would face a real risk of treatment contrary to Art. 3 upon return to the country of origin. One explanation for this departure from its Art. 3 case-law may be that the Court

In two 1991 asylum judgments, the ECtHR seemed not to apply a rigorous scrutiny, but instead to supervise national fact finding in a more distant way. In the *Cruz Varas* judgment it attached importance to the experience of the Swedish authorities in evaluating asylum claims, and to the fact that the national authorities had conducted a thorough examination.[11] The *Vilvarajah* judgment contains a similar passage.[12] Notwithstanding its deference to national authorities in its *Cruz Varas* and *Vilvarajah* judgments, in these and many other cases the ECtHR at the same time explicitly held that its examination of a risk of ill-treatment in breach of Article 3 of the ECHR must necessarily be a rigorous one in view of the absolute character of Article 3.[13] From a more recent judgment, it appears that the ECtHR sees no tension between, on the one hand, attaching special importance to the findings of national authorities, and making its own assessment on the other:

> [The Court] accepts that, as a general principle, the national authorities are best placed to assess not just the facts but, more particularly, the credibility of witnesses since it is they who have had an opportunity to see, hear and assess the demeanour of the individual concerned. However, in the circumstances of this case, the Court does not share the conclusion of the Government that the information provided by the applicant was such as to undermine his general credibility and it notes that one of the Migration Court's lay judges considered that the applicant had given a credible account of events and that he ought to have been granted asylum.[14]

The ECtHR's assessment of the facts is indeed often rigorous, as can be further illustrated by a number of cases. Specifically, when the credibility of the statements of an asylum seeker is at stake, the ECtHR itself will assess the credibility:

> [I]n the opinion of the Government, the applicant's account of his arrest, of the reasons for it, and of his escape, is so implausible as to invalidate his claim of having deserted from the army. This being so, the Court must proceed, as far as possible, to an assessment of the general credibility of the statements made by the applicant before the Netherlands authorities and during the present proceedings.[15]

erroneously used a standard text block from Art. 6 cases for an Art. 3 case. However, for this explanation it is puzzling that in *Damla*, the Court formulated a standard that seems even more restrictive (fact finding by national courts cannot be reviewed by the Court 'unless there is an indication that the judges have drawn grossly unfair or arbitrary conclusions from the facts before them') than the standard position in Art. 6 cases (the Court will not deal with errors of fact and law by national courts 'unless and in so far as they may have infringed rights and freedoms protected by the Convention', see n 9). Because of the eccentricity of the Court's considerations when compared to the rest of its case-law, I hold the considerations from the *Damla* decision to be an error.

[11] *Cruz Varas and ors v. Sweden*, ECHR (1991) Series A, No. 201, para. 81.

[12] *Vilvarajah v. UK, supra* n 6, para. 114.

[13] *Vilvarajah v. UK, supra* n 6, para. 108; *Chahal v. UK*, ECHR (1996) RJ&D 1996-V, 96; *D v. UK*, ECHR (1997) RJ&D 1997-III, 49; *T. I. v. UK*, ECHR (2000) RJ&D 2000-III, 'The Court's Assessment'; *Bensaid v. UK*, ECHR (2001) RJ&D 2001-I, 34. Compare the Court's case-law in French, 'Pour déterminer s'il y a des motifs sérieux et avérés de croire que l'intéressé court un risque réel de traitements incompatibles avec l'article 3 en cas d'extradition, la Cour adopte des critères rigoureux et s'appuie sur l'ensemble des éléments qu'on lui fournit ou, au besoin, qu'elle se procure d'office', *Chamaiev v. Georgia and Russia*, ECHR (2005) RJ&D 2005-III, 336.

[14] *R.C. v. Sweden*, ECHR (2010) Appl. No. 41827/07, para. 52.

[15] *Said v. The Netherlands*, ECHR (2005) RJ&D 2005-VI, 50.

In its *Hilal* judgment[16] the ECtHR dealt extensively with the credibility of the applicant's statements, as well as with the authenticity of the documents submitted, and on both points ruled in favour of the applicant. The same proactive attitude is clear from the *N v. Finland* judgment,[17] where the ECtHR, 'in order to carry out its own assessment of the facts', appointed two delegates[18] who went to Finland and took testimony from the applicant, his common-law wife, another asylum seeker, and a Finnish civil servant. The ECtHR, after considering that the applicant's own testimony before the delegates was evasive on many points, reached detailed conclusions. It was not prepared to accept every statement of the claimant as fact, and found the core of N's motivation to flee credible, but not his account of his journey to Finland.[19] In the *Nasimi* decision, the Court assessed the statements of the applicant in a similarly detailed manner, did not find them credible, and hence dismissed the application as inadmissible.[20]

In the *Salah Sheekh* judgment, the Court considered:

> In its supervisory task under Article 19 of the Convention, it would be too narrow an approach under Article 3 in cases concerning aliens facing expulsion or extradition if the Court, as an international human rights court, were only to take into account materials made available by the domestic authorities of the Contracting State concerned, without comparing these with materials from other reliable and objective sources. This further implies that, in assessing an alleged risk of treatment contrary to Article 3 in respect of aliens facing expulsion or extradition, a full and *ex nunc* assessment is called for as the situation in a country of destination may change in the course of time.[21]

This consideration is in line with what the ECtHR actually does in its decisions, and judgments. It is true that the ECtHR finds it relevant when the national authorities have engaged in extensive and thorough assessment of facts as well as collection and evaluation of evidence (*Cruz Varas* and *Vilvarajah*). However, its main point is that it has to be 'satisfied that the assessment made by the authorities of the Contracting State is adequate and sufficiently supported' by relevant sources.[22] In this, the thoroughness of the national asylum procedure is one factor, but the crucial issue is not a procedural one, but the substance: was the assessment right?

[16] *Hilal v. UK*, ECHR (2001) RJ&D 2001-II.

[17] *N v. Finland*, ECHR (2005) Appl. No. 38885/02, 152.

[18] See Rules of Court, Art. A1.

[19] *N v. Finland, supra* n 17, paras 154–6. In a confusing consideration, the Court apparently sought to limit the gap between its own findings and those of the Finnish authorities. In para. 157 it stated: 'The Court would note in this connection that the Finnish authorities and courts, while finding the applicant's account generally not credible, do not appear to have excluded the possibility that he might have been working for the DSP. Moreover, the Finnish authorities and courts did not have an opportunity to hear K.K.'s testimony with regard to the applicant's background in the DRC. It cannot be said therefore that the position of the Court contradicts in any respect the findings of the Finnish courts.' This is surprising, because the Court's finding that N's statements are credible does contradict the Finnish outcomes. More specifically, in para. 154 the Court stated that the testimony of the other asylum seeker was available to the Finnish authorities when they considered N's application (para. 154), while it now holds that they did not have an opportunity to hear her testimony.

[20] *Nasimi v. Sweden*, ECHR (2004) Appl. No. 38865/02; compare with *A. J. v. Sweden*, ECHR (2008) Appl. No. 13508/07.

[21] *Salah Sheekh v. The Netherlands*, ECHR (2007), Appl. No. 1948/04, para. 136.

[22] *Ibid.*

In sum, we can see that the requirement of rigorous scrutiny, which the ECtHR applies in its own assessment of asylum cases, means that the ECtHR replaces the view of the national authorities with its own view when it sees reason to disagree with the national authorities. The ECtHR does attach special importance to the position of the national authorities, but accords their view no formal deference of any kind.

B. Rigorous scrutiny under Article 13

Although the ECtHR uses the term rigorous scrutiny both for its own activity in Article 3 of the ECHR cases and for what it demands from domestic courts in Article 3 cases, under Article 13 it has accepted the UK judicial review system in asylum cases, which may well apply a form of scrutiny which is less intense than the ECtHR's own.[23] As was explained in the *Vilvarajah* judgment, UK judicial review occurs on the basis of the Wednesbury principles, and consists of an examination of the exercise of discretion by the authorities to determine whether they left out of consideration a factor that should have been taken into account or took into account a factor that should have been ignored, or whether they came to a conclusion so unreasonable that no reasonable authority could have reached it.[24] This gives the impression that UK judicial review in asylum cases is relatively distanced, and quite marginal. However, the ECtHR then went on to cite a then leading asylum decision of the House of Lords as to the extent and effect of judicial review. The Lords considered that the Wednesbury principles must be applied in such a way as to subject the refusal of asylum 'to the more rigorous examination to ensure that it is in no way flawed' and had to be subjected to 'the most anxious scrutiny' and to 'rigorous examination' (para. 91). In later case-law, the ECtHR cited the UK Court of Appeal, which held that in asylum cases the domestic court must subject the refusal of asylum to rigorous examination 'and this it does by considering the underlying factual material for itself to see whether it compels a different conclusion'. The Court of Appeal held that, notwithstanding that domestic law places asylum decisions in a discretionary area of judgment, no special deference had to be paid by the domestic courts to the authorities' conclusion on the facts. According to UK case-law, '[i]n circumstances such as these, what has been called the "discretionary area of judgment"—the area of judgment within which the Court should defer to the Secretary of State as the person primarily entrusted with the decision on the applicant's removal ... —is decidedly a narrow one'.[25] Thus, the ECtHR has consistently emphasized that the fact that judicial scrutiny in UK asylum cases takes place against the background of the criteria applied in judicial review of administrative decisions, namely, rationality and perverseness,

[23] I am aware that domestic law in the UK has changed as a consequence of the 1998 Human Rights Act. However, the focus here is not the compatibility of UK domestic law with the ECtHR, but the case-law of the ECtHR. As a consequence, UK domestic law is only relevant in as far as, and in the way in which, it is perceived by the Court.

[24] *Vilvarajah v. UK, supra* n 6, para. 90.

[25] *Bensaid v. UK, supra* n 13, para. 28; *Hilal v. UK, supra* n 16, para. 37.

does not deprive the procedure of its effectiveness. The ECtHR found it sufficient that UK courts can 'effectively control the legality of executive discretion on substantive and procedural grounds', and that they can quash a decision 'where it was established that there was a serious risk of inhuman or degrading treatment'.[26]

One may argue that, in these cases, the ECtHR has accepted the UK judicial review system in asylum cases because, against the background of legal standards formulated in terms of domestic law, in fact a 'most anxious scrutiny', a 'rigorous examination' is applied, which 'ensures' that the denial of asylum is 'in no way flawed'. In this understanding of the ECtHR's case-law, the marginal form is accepted because of the rigorous substance.[27] Another view, however, holds that a judicial review which applies a marginal test on important points (concretely, on the assessment of credibility) still constitutes a rigorous scrutiny in the sense of Strasbourg case-law.[28] The body of case-law on Article 13 of the ECHR in itself leaves some room for this view. In its *Hilal* decision, the ECtHR found that a UK court 'would not form its own independent view of the facts which would then necessarily prevail over whatever view has been formed' by the authorities.[29] Also, the ECtHR has never explicitly stated that it accepted application of the Wednesbury principles *because*, in actual practice, they are applied in a way which leaves the administration barely any discretionary freedom. Furthermore, the ECtHR has not ruled that a judicial scrutiny which is less intense than the one in UK judicial review cases would be in violation of Article 13. The ECtHR has, in other words, never stated that the UK review system constitutes the bottom line of what is still acceptable.

To summarize this point, although it is not entirely clear to what extent the ECtHR accepts that domestic courts allow a meaningful discretionary area of judgment, it is clear that it has not required domestic courts to replace the view of the administration by their own view if they see reason to do so.

C. The meaning of rigorous scrutiny

At this point in the argumentation, the inconsistency has been established. In the context of Article 3 of the ECHR, the ECtHR holds that 'rigorous scrutiny = replace domestic position by Court's own view' but in the context of Article 13 of the ECHR, the Court holds that 'rigorous scrutiny ≠ replace administrative position by court's own view'.

If one accepts that one term used by one single court in the context of the same set of cases should have the same meaning, there is a problem to be resolved.

[26] *Bensaid v. UK, supra* n 13, paras 55–6; *Hilal v. UK, supra* n 16, paras 77–8.

[27] S. Essakkili, 'Marginal Judicial Review in the Dutch Asylum Procedure', VU University Migration Law Papers, No. 2, 2005, at 46–51.

[28] This is the view of the Dutch *Afdeling Bestuursrechtspraak van de Raad van State* (Council of State Administrative Jurisdiction Division), 15 June 2006, JV 2006/290. For the details of the Dutch marginal judicial scrutiny see Essakkili, *ibid.*, at 13–41.

[29] *Hilal v. UK, supra* n 16, para. 74.

It is, however, not easy to reconcile the ECtHR's clear position on its own rigorous scrutiny, and its ambiguous position on the rigorous scrutiny required from domestic courts in asylum cases. Clearly, the ECtHR cannot require that domestic courts examine by themselves whether or not deportation is contrary to Article 3. This is what the ECtHR does. Domestic courts in many, if not most, European countries work in a system in which the object of their scrutiny is not the deportation, but the decision to deport. This object of scrutiny in itself allows for either a full, or a marginal, judicial scrutiny, as explained above. It would be contrary to the ECtHR's subsidiary role if it were completely to rewrite national law of administrative procedure. It must limit itself to the way in which the procedure is applied.

As a consequence of the ECtHR's subsidiary role, it will not object in the abstract to the form of judicial review. This means that it will not question the criteria which are to be applied before national courts even when, as in the UK case, these criteria prescribe a marginal rationality test. The ECtHR can only intervene if the way in which the national test is applied in practice leads to judicial scrutiny which gives fewer guarantees for conformity of deportations with Article 3 of the ECHR than the ECtHR's own examination. If one interprets the ECtHR's case-law on Article 13 in such a way that domestic courts can apply a less intense scrutiny than the ECtHR itself, this implies that the Court would apply a kind of scrutiny to asylum cases which has not been applied by domestic courts. This is incompatible with the subsidiary role of the ECtHR, which requires that domestic courts apply a scrutiny which is at least as comprehensive and intense as the one applied by the Court.[30]

Only such a systematic analysis of the term rigorous scrutiny can take away the ambiguity in the ECtHR's case-law on the meaning of Article 13 of the ECHR in asylum cases. The scrutiny by domestic courts must dispel any doubts as to the unsoundness of the claim (compare with *Saadi*), regardless of the formal criterion applied, be it full scrutiny or a marginal rationality test. The ECtHR itself has not drawn this conclusion, and has even sidestepped the issue.[31] But if the Court wants to repair this open inconsistency, and if it wants to end the situation in which many asylum seekers approach the ECtHR in order to get a level of judicial scrutiny which they were unable to get at the domestic level, then the Court must impose on states the obligation to put in place judicial scrutiny in asylum cases which has the same substance (ie the same intensity, although it may have a different form) as the scrutiny which it exercises itself. Alternatively, the ECtHR could relax its own scrutiny—but such a restriction of the Court's supervision of the application of Articles 2 and 3 ECHR would be without precedent, and for that reason seems unlikely to occur.

[30] This interpretation also fits with an aspect of the *Chahal* judgment, where the ECtHR found that a remedy in which the central question is actually an incorrect one constitutes a violation of Art. 13; *Chahal v. UK, supra* n 13, para. 153.

[31] *Mir Isfahani v. The Netherlands*, ECHR (2008) Appl. No. 31252/03 (struck out of the list).

D. Constructing consistency: concluding observations

We can safely presume that welfare nationalists and cultural nationalists (ie the statists, be they on the left or the right), who both favour migration control, will favour marginal judicial scrutiny in asylum cases, because this gives optimal space for democratically legitimized governments to execute those asylum policies which they see as being in the interest of the national population. As a consequence, they do not have many problems with the permissive attitude of the ECtHR towards judicial scrutiny by domestic courts in asylum cases. They may even pressure the ECtHR to relax its own scrutiny. We can also safely assume that the multicultural rights advocates will insist on full judicial scrutiny at the domestic as well as at the European level. This simply increases the chances that asylum seekers will be accepted. Laissez-faire liberals do not have political stakes in asylum as such, although they may view asylum seekers with some sympathy. However, they have two reasons for sympathizing with the multicultural rights advocates: (1) more admitted asylum seekers means more competition on the labour market, which they favour; (2) laissez-faire liberals need courts to curb government intervention in markets; especially during a phase of government intervention in the market, they will favour judicial control as such, regardless of the subject, and consequently will be sympathetic to full judicial scrutiny in asylum cases—without, as a rule, joining the multicultural rights advocates on the barricades.

Table 7.2 Political positions on judicial scrutiny in asylum cases

	Left	Right
Libertarian	Strict scrutiny	Strict scrutiny
Statist	Marginal scrutiny	Marginal scrutiny

So whereas the statists will not make too much of the inconsistency (they will relate it to the different contexts of domestic courts and the ECtHR, and argue it is more a difference than an inconsistency) the multicultural rights advocates will expose it and champion a more coherent position, as shown above. They will be supported by laissez-faire liberals, whose main function will be that they will not speak out against the multicultural rights advocates (and may speak in favour of them in passing).

It should be noted that not only critics, but courts as well use the potential of inconsistency—or at least vagueness as to consistency. In the judgment in *A and others*,[32] for example, the ECtHR set rules for the admissibility of secret evidence in the context of Article 5 of the ECHR (detention, in this case on national security grounds). It referred to its case-law under Articles 6 and 13, thus signalling the broader relevance of its judgment. However, it gave no clues as to whether, and if so how, the rules specified in the rather specific context of national security detention would apply in the context of asylum or family migration cases. The combination

[32] *A and others v. UK*, ECHR (2009) Appl. No. 3455/05.

of, on the one hand, signalling the broader importance of the judgment, while, on the other hand, leaving unclear how different sets of case-law concerning secret evidence might relate to each other has as an effect, that litigation will follow at the domestic level as to the application of the ECtHR's rules in different contexts. After a while, the ECtHR will get a picture of how its rules have been received at the domestic level, and it can elaborate more detailed rules without running the risk of being unacceptable to domestic courts.

2. Exposing Choice: Family Members of European Workers

The second argumentative move I want to discuss consists of showing how a given position of a court is not a necessary application of law as it exists. Standing case-law is contrasted with an alternative application of the law, which is just as good from a legal-technical point of view, but yields a different outcome. If the existence of the alternative has been made plausible, it turns out that for one and the same legal issue there are two correct, but different outcomes. Preferring one outcome over the other then must be the result of a conscious or unconscious choice, which is not legitimate on account of being the right legal answer. Usually, the person making this argument will then argue that the alternative option (ie the one not presently adopted by the courts) is superior, because it is more efficient, more in line with human rights, or some such. If a person is satisfied with the choices that have been made in case-law, that person will not spend time on making it subject to critical debate.

The example I will use for this is case-law of the ECJ concerning the family members of European citizens. Even when these family members are not themselves EU citizens (so-called third country nationals (TCNs)), they can rely on EU law if they are family members of an EU citizen who has exercised his right of freedom of movement of workers. The problem that has come up in case-law is that in this way, in particular circumstances, TCNs may acquire a residence right on the basis of EU law which they would not have on the basis of the legislation of any EU member state. They may be considered as using EU law in order to evade national migration law. Interestingly, the ECJ itself has taken two fundamentally different positions on this issue, so we can analyse the choice it has made without having to construct the alternative.

A. *Levin*: motives for using freedom

Levin was a UK national who had married a South African man. After his asylum application in the UK had failed, they moved to the Netherlands.[33] When the couple was threatened with removal, she started working part-time as a room maid in Amsterdam, earning less than the social minimum.[34] A Dutch court sent

[33] Case 53/81, *D.M. Levin v. Staatssecretaris van Justitie*, [1982] ECR 1035.

[34] The particulars of this case are based on the case comment of Kees Groenendijk on the *Levin* judgment in T. P. Spijkerboer (ed.), *Rechtspraak Vreemdelingenrecht in 100 uitspraken* (2001), at 592.

preliminary questions to the ECJ, focusing on, first, the question whether someone earning an income below the social minimum could be considered as a worker in the sense of European law (then Article 48 of the Treaty Establishing the European Economic Community) and, secondly, if so, whether such a worker would have a right to reside in another member state if it was apparent that the chief motive was not the pursuit of an economic activity. On the first point (which is not directly relevant in our context), the court famously held that part-time employment may make someone a worker in the sense of European law, but that these rules:

> cover only the pursuit of effective and genuine activities, to the exclusion of activities on such a small scale as to be regarded as purely marginal and ancillary. It follows both from the statement of the principle of freedom of movement of workers and from the place occupied by the rules relating to that principle in the system of the treaty as a whole that those rules guarantee only the free movement of persons who pursue or are desirous of pursuing an economic activity.[35]

The ECJ then went on to discuss the relevance of the motives of a European national for becoming a worker in the sense of European law. It referred to four provisions in European legislation stipulating that free movement is granted 'for the purpose of' or 'in order to' take up employment. It goes on to say that these formulations 'merely' express that free movement may be relied upon 'only by persons who actually pursue or seriously wish to pursue' employment (the reference to persons wishing to pursue employment concerns the right of free movement of job seekers[36]). But they do not mean that this freedom 'may be made dependent upon the aims pursued' by the person concerned. Therefore, 'the motives which may have prompted the worker to seek employment in the Member State concerned are of no account and must not be taken into consideration'. This meant that it did not matter that, so to speak, Levin worked in Amsterdam in order to get her husband asylum which had been denied in her own country. Together with the later *Surinder Singh* judgment,[37] which had the effect of giving persons in the situation of Levin and her husband a right to return to the UK, this meant that restrictive national immigration and asylum law could be evaded by taking up work in another European country, getting the TCN spouse a European law residence right there, and taking that European residence right back to the home country which had denied that right in the first place.

The ECJ reached this result by relying on a classical notion of a freedom: the essence of a freedom is that why the freedom is exercised is not to be questioned. Otherwise, the freedom in question may be made void. For example, if one holds that freedom of expression can only be used to express views which reflect the real interests of the person concerned (and not deluded views which have been implanted by, say, capitalist alienation or fundamentalist indoctrination), then

[35] *Levin, supra* n 33, Rec. 17.

[36] Case 292/89, *R. v. Immigration Appeal Tribunal, ex parte Gustaff Desiderius Antonissen*, [1991] ECR 1-00745.

[37] Case 370/90, *Surinder Singh*, [1992] ECR I-4265.

in fact the freedom of expression is denied. Comparably, the underlying idea of the ECJ in *Levin* seems to be that the freedom of movement of workers would be undermined if it could only be used for reasons of industriousness, as would be the result of a reasoning based on the 'for the purpose of/in order to' wording. The freedom of movement of workers, the Court decided, could be used in order to earn money, but also out of love (as in *Levin*), curiosity or for other motives—as long as the European national worked.[38]

B. *Akrich*: freedom versus access[39]

This line of thought was reversed in the *Akrich* judgment, where the ECJ—in the footsteps of the national court which had submitted the prejudicial questions—recast the issue at stake.[40] The central issue in these cases was not seen as whether particular motives for using the freedom of movement could be disqualified, but whether the freedom of movement of European nationals could be used in order to get non-European nationals entry into a European country through the back door.

Akrich, a Moroccan national, entered the UK as a tourist in 1989. A residence right as a student was refused. In 1990 he was convicted for attempted theft and use of a stolen identity card, and he was deported to Algeria in 1991. In 1992 he returned to the UK using a false French identity card. He was arrested and again deported five months later. He clandestinely returned to the UK shortly after. In 1996 he married a citizen of the UK. He was taken into immigration detention in 1997 and deported to Dublin, at his request, where his wife had moved two months earlier. In 1998 Akrich asked for permission to enter the UK. The couple argued that the UK spouse had worked for half a year in Ireland and that as a consequence Akrich had a European law-based residence right in Ireland (*Levin*) and could accompany his wife back into the UK (*Surinder Singh*). The national court wanted to know whether, in a situation where a European national moves to another member state in order to claim a residence right for her spouse upon return to her own country, the intention of the couple could be regarded as reliance on European law in order to evade the application of national legislation. The follow-up question was whether, if that was the case, this would be a ground for refusing a residence right.

The ECJ started out by stating that the preliminary questions were mainly about the scope of the *Surinder Singh* judgment, ie about the right to return with a TCN

[38] For a long time, European law emphatically encouraged persons (women in particular) to join the labour market. M. Kraamwinkel, 'The Imagined European Community: Are Housewives European Citizens?' in J. Conaghan, R. M. Fischl, and K. Klare (eds), *Labour Law in an Era of Globalization, Transformative Practices and Possibilities* (2002), at 321. Although explicit requirements on this point are less prevalent now, the economic rationale of European law still strongly suggests that 'the European citizen works'.

[39] See, for a different perspective on *Akrich*, P. Boeles *et al.*, *European Migration Law* (2009), at 76–82.

[40] Case 109/01, *Akrich v. Secretary of State of the Home Department*, [2003] ECR 1-9607.

spouse from another European state to the country of origin (Rec. 46). The Court then explained that this right follows from the right to freedom of movement (Recs 47–8). But it then redefined the issue at stake in the case before it. It made a distinction between 'freedom of movement within the Community', which is covered by European law, and on the other hand 'access [of third country nationals] to the territory of the Community' (Rec. 49). It then formulated the crucial consideration:

> In order to benefit in a situation such as that at issue in the main proceedings from the rights provided for in Article 10 of Regulation No. 1612/68 [now Directive 2004/38], the national of a non-Member State, who is the spouse of a citizen of the Union, must be lawfully resident in a Member State when he moves to another Member State to which the citizen of the Union is migrating or has migrated. [Rec. 50]

The ECJ argued for this position on a free movement rationale. First, it stated that freedom of movement implies that if a European national moves to another member state, 'that move must not result in the loss of the opportunity lawfully to live together' [Rec. 52]. However, the ECJ found that when the third country spouse had no right to reside in a European country to begin with, the fact that the spouse will not have that right in another European country either does not constitute a barrier to the free movement of the European national. Using freedom of movement should not result in the loss of an opportunity, but the fact that it does not lead to the creation of a new right does not deter European nationals from exercising their rights (Recs 52–4).

The ECJ then turned to the issue of abuse. It first repeated the passages from *Levin* holding that the motives for seeking employment in another member state were of no account (Recs 55–6). But it then overturned *Levin* (where the ECJ found the motive of the couple, to acquire a residence right for the South African husband, of no account) by holding:

> Conversely, there would be an abuse if the facilities afforded by Community law in favour of migrant workers and their spouses were invoked in the context of marriages of convenience entered into in order to circumvent the provisions relating to entry and residence of nationals of non-Member States. [Rec. 57]

It then pointed to Article 8 of the ECHR which protects 'genuine' marriages [Recs 58–60]. The concept of marriage of convenience which the ECJ employs here is not entirely clear. In the normal usage of the term, it refers to marriages which are not contracted out of love, but in order to get one of the spouses a residence right. What does the ECJ mean to say here? Does it equate a marriage of convenience to marriages entered into in order to circumvent migration law? These may include marriages concluded out of love (but the lovers would not have married if the foreign partner could have acquired a residence right without marrying). Does it suggest that couples which move to another member state in order to get the foreign spouse a residence right are involved in marriages of convenience? This may also involve true love couples (as, apparently, in the *Levin* case).

In any case, the crux of the ECJ's argument in *Akrich* consists of holding that the case is about access to the EU, and invoking the freedom of movement is not hindered if a European national does not have a right in the member state of destination which he or she also did not have in the member state of origin.

C. *Metock*: the text of the law

In 2008, the ECJ revisited the question whether a TCN who is the spouse of a European worker can rely on European law to create a residence right (as opposed to transporting an already existing residence right from one member state to another). The case concerned failed asylum seekers who were spouses of European nationals who had moved to Ireland and worked there. The central question was whether European law stands in the way of national legislation which requires previous lawful residence in another member state in the context of the case.[41]

The ECJ set out by stating that no provision of the relevant Directive 2004/38 'makes the application of the directive conditional on [family members] having previously resided in a Member State' (Rec. 49). It then pointed out that Article 3, which stipulates the beneficiaries of the Directive, does not distinguish according to whether or not family members have lawfully resided in another member state. It then referred to three other provisions in the Directive, which confer the right of entry and residence to TCN family members who accompany *or join* European citizens, 'without any reference to the place or conditions of residence they had before arriving in that member State' (Rec. 51). It also pointed to a provision providing that TCN family members have a visa, thus providing for entry into a member state of family members who do not possess a residence card in another member state (Rec. 52). And yet another provision, which lists exhaustively the documents which TCN family members may be required to present, does not mention documents demonstrating prior lawful residence in another member state (Rec. 53). Therefore, it concluded that the right to reside with a European national who works in another member state than his or her own applies to all TCNs, 'without distinguishing according to whether or not the national of a non-member country has already resided lawfully in another member State' (Rec. 54). This finding is in accordance with the ECJ's earlier case-law (Recs 55–7), except the *Akrich* judgment, the conclusion of which, however, 'must be reconsidered' (Rec. 58).

The ECJ then began a second line of argument, focusing on the division of competences between the member states and the Community. The contested issue here is whether there is European competence regarding the first admission of TCNs; member states have argued that this has remained a national competence, which they have not abandoned by adopting Directive 2004/38. The ECJ stated that it is common ground that the Community is competent to legislate on the free movement of European nationals. It then stated that it would interfere with the freedom of movement of Europeans if they would not be able to be accompanied or joined by family members (Recs 62–4, and, worded slightly differently,

[41] Case 127/08, *Blaise Baheten Metock and ors v. Minister for Justice, Equality and Law Reform*, [2008] ECR I-6241.

Recs 67–8). The ECJ did not deal with the issue that it said the opposite in Recs 52–4 of *Akrich*. The ECJ rejected the interpretation that the member states have retained exclusive competence to regulate the first access of TCN family members of European nationals (Rec. 66). Then it mentioned that it would be paradoxical if member states were free to refuse entry and residence to the spouse of a European national while it would be obliged to admit that person on the basis of Directive 2003/86 (Family Reunification) (Rec. 69). Then followed some paragraphs reassuring member states that they can apply public policy, public security, or public health grounds in these cases, as well as combating abuse (Recs 74–5).

We can see that the Court uses two lines of argument. The first is literalism: the use of the word join, the reference to visa, the lack of reference to documents showing prior legal residence—this is a very black letter-law positivist way of applying legal provisions. But one can easily understand the ECJ's arguments on this point. The second line of argumentation relies on the argument that requiring a previous residence right would interfere with freedom of movement. Despite the ECJ's repetitions and its emphasis on this point, it is hard to follow its arguments. Because, indeed, as the ECJ itself argued in *Akrich*, if someone does not have a right in one member state, how can free movement possibly be affected by the fact that that same right will not be granted in another member state either? Why does the ECJ find it paradoxical to hold that a TCN should first be admitted to a European country on the basis of national laws (which are harmonized by, inter alia, Directive 2003/86), and can only after that invoke the right to accompany a spouse to another member state?

D. Emphasizing choice

In the two judgments, the ECJ plays with the object of scrutiny. In *Akrich*, the ECJ argued that what in fact is at stake is the right of access of a TCN to European territory, not free movement of European citizens. In *Metock*, the Court stated that free movement of Europeans can only materialize if Europeans have the right to be joined by TCN family members—and therefore the case is, essentially, about free movement.[42]

Also, the ECJ situates the issue in a different field of law. The *Akrich* Court found the issue one of immigration law (which is a field of harmonized, but nevertheless national law), while the *Metock* Court found the issue one of European law on free movement of citizens (of which the ECJ is the supreme supervisor and guardian).

In this case, it is easy to see the choice the Court made, because the Court itself followed one line of argument up until *Akrich*; then implicitly reversed its view in *Akrich*; subsequently wavered a bit (see *Eind*[43] and *Jia*[44]); and finally explicitly

[42] In Duncan Kennedy's terms, this issue is one of nesting, ie of locating the issue at hand in a broader and familiar legal dispute. See Kennedy, *supra* n 3, at 219.

[43] Case 291/05, *Minister voor Vreemdelingenzaken en Integratie v. R. N. G. Eind,* [2007] ECR I-10719.

[44] Case 1/05, *Yunying Jia v. Migrationsverket*, [2007] ECR I-00001.

rejected its *Akrich* position in *Metock*, thereby returning to the earlier *Levin/Surinder Singh* position. It is undeniable that there are two conceivable positions, both apparently good enough for an institution no less reverend than the ECJ to take. Relying on the same legal rules (but see the excursion below) the ECJ took two different views. Therefore, the difference between the two positions cannot be legal in nature, and must be related to the people taking the two positions.

i. Excursion

I make a small excursion here. When you work in the mode I am writing in at the moment (exposing choices by judges which cannot be based on legal necessity), you will resist the idea that, as a matter of fact, there were compelling legal reasons for the ECJ to change course. What would an argument holding that, in fact, there were compelling reasons for the ECJ's changes of opinion look like? It would go as follows. Before *Akrich*, the ECJ had never been asked directly whether European law could *create* a residence right for a TCN family member. Admittedly, the ECJ had suggested that this could be the case, in particular because *Levin* was precisely about such a case. But the idea that a TCN could acquire a residence right in a European country on the basis of European law had been implicit, and it was not clear that the ECJ was willing to accept such a rule were it confronted with a direct question. In Akrich, Advocate General Geelhoed submitted a brilliant and compelling opinion.[45] He argued that the case was at the juxtaposition of two areas of competence, namely immigration law (national sovereignty) and free movement (almost complete harmonization). Although from a free movement perspective it is evident that a spouse must be able to accompany a European citizen who moves to another member state, it is—Geelhoed argued—'less self-evident also to grant a right of residence under Community law to spouses from non-Member States who have not yet been so admitted or who, as in the case of Mr Akrich, are within the territory of the European Union without leave to remain' (Rec. 7). Notice that Geelhoed does not start out by denying the possibility of a residence right for *Akrich*, but by questioning it. But also notice that Geelhoed uses his crucial argument here: he refers to 'the territory of the European Union', thus framing the issue as whether European law creates a residence right in Europe without a prior residence right based on national law. Although Geelhoed will take several pages to get to it, the answer is already clear: such a right is nowhere to be found in European law. Geelhoed rephrases the question several times, culminating in:

> Thus I come to the dilemma to which the Court must find a solution. Must the Court's extensive case-law, as expressed, *inter alia*, in the *Singh* judgment, entail the consequence that national immigration legislation must always remain inapplicable where spouses from outside the European Union who are married to Community nationals, were not, at the time when they were entitled to derive rights from Community law, legally within the territory of the European Union? That dilemma is all the more pressing since in regard to

[45] Advocate General Geelhoed in *Akrich v. SSHD, supra* n 40.

freedom of movement for persons EC law does not verify the nature and duration of the marriage whilst that test is of considerable significance under national immigration law in order to prevent marriages of convenience. [para. 10]

After this introduction, it is clear where Geelhoed is headed. Relying both on competence (immigration is a national, not a European competence) and on the purpose of free movement (no obstacles, but no need for rewards in the form of creating a new immigration right) he argues for the conclusion which was adopted by the ECJ. So, the argument supporting *Akrich* as a non-political judgment would go, Geelhoed's analysis convinced the Court of not going where its case-law until then possibly was headed, but where it had not yet arrived. One can defend *Akrich* by admitting that it was a change of tone, of attitude, possibly a rejection of implications of earlier case-law—but not a change in something the ECJ had already decided explicitly. And, both from the point of view of competence as well as from the point of view of free movement, Geelhoed's reasoning was superior to the alternative—so the argument goes.

Now that we have gotten rid of the idea that *Akrich* constituted a choice of the ECJ to change direction (motivated by politics, ethics, or whatever one wants to call it—but not by compelling legal arguments), we also have to get rid of the explicit change of direction in *Metock*. *Metock* is a Grand Chamber judgment, unlikely to be an incident. It may be noticed that only one judge sitting in *Metock* was also a member of the *Akrich* chamber (the Dutch judge, Timmermans). But that does not imply that *Metock* did not constitute a change. An argument that *Metock* did not constitute a change would go something like this. Earlier case-law of the Court concerned Regulation 1612/68.[46] *Akrich*, to the contrary, concerned a new piece of European legislation, entailing a recodification of the free movement of persons—Directive 2004/38. This recodification did involve changes. First, the legal instrument was not a Regulation any more (ie not European legislation that by its very nature has direct effect in member states), but a Directive (ie European legislation creating an obligation for member states to adopt national legislation in accordance with the Directive). Secondly, the applicable rules were not, strictly speaking, identical. None of the provisions of Directive 2004/38 the ECJ referred to were identical to provisions in Regulation 1612/68, even where there were roughly equivalent provisions (like Article 3(2) of Directive 2004/38 and Article 1 of Directive 1612/68; Article 2(2) of Directive 2004/38 and Article 10(1) of Directive 1612/68). As a consequence, the ECJ was not bound by case-law concerning Regulation 1612/68.

Are these arguments convincing? The first one (*Akrich* was not a change of direction) was made by Geelhoed in such a delightful way that I find it hard to resist. Given the outcome he prefers, he faces a difficult position because the Court's case-law seems against him. However, the facts of the case are good for Geelhoed's position—Akrich is a criminal. He succeeds in accepting all the Court's case-law, but shows that the ECJ has never given a ruling on this particular issue. This

[46] Council Regulation 1612/68, [1968] OJ L257/2.

creates an opening where he can deploy his heavy statist artillery: Europe should not take away competence from member states without their consent and free movement should not be allowed to become a ploy for illegal immigration. All these arguments are fine, but Geelhoed had to ignore a crucial thing. In *Levin*, three decades earlier, the ECJ had been faced with the same issue. Sure, the questions were worded differently, but it was clear that the national court in that case wanted to know whether free movement could be used in order to get a TCN a residence right which he did not have before. The ECJ gave a clear answer, which was reversed in *Akrich*. So regarding *Akrich*, I admire the argument that the ECJ did not change course, but I am unconvinced.[47]

The argument holding that *Metock* does not represent a change of direction, but merely reflects new legislation is unconvincing for more than one reason. Most importantly the Court does not say that *Akrich* is not in line with the new Directive, but it says that *Akrich* 'must be reconsidered'. Apparently, the ECJ itself thought it was changing course. Secondly, the ECJ abundantly referred to case-law about the old Regulation in order to justify its conclusion. This underscores the third point, namely that the new wording of the Directive does not reflect substantively new positions, but merely reflects the desire to combine different pieces of secondary legislation into one comprehensive legal instrument, and to incorporate the ECJ's case-law about the Regulation in explicit legislation. So it seems clear that the *Metock* Court was of the opinion that the law had not changed in substance, and that it wanted to change its position about the law.

One might use another argument for defending *Metock* as legally necessary. It requires outsmarting the ECJ, which did not use this argument itself. The Directive was intended, among others, to codify case-law. *Akrich* was given on 23 September 2003. The Directive was adopted on 29 April 2004. Because *Akrich* was not incorporated in any way in the text of the Directive, the ECJ had to do something with the fact that the European legislator did not do so. This argument would be convincing if the Court indeed had given its judgments about the Directive as if its case-law about the Regulation were irrelevant. As I noted above, it did not do this. If it had presented this argument as decisive for the outcome of *Metock*, it would have lost its standing case-law as a source of legitimacy in any situation where new legislation has been adopted. Clearly, that is not where the ECJ is going.

To summarize, *Metock* clearly represents a change of direction of the ECJ; in that judgment, the ECJ in so many words abandoned the *Akrich* position. Was *Akrich* a change? Geelhoed did an admirable job in creating space for a judgment reflecting his views by arguing that the ECJ had not yet ruled on the creation of a residence right for a TCN family member by European law. But the fact that it

[47] See D. Martin, 'Comments on *Förster* (Case C-158/07 of 18 November 2008), *Metock* (Case C-127/08 of 25 July 2008) and *Huber* (Case C-524/06 of 16 December 2008)' 11 *European Journal of Migration and Law* (2009) 95; A. P. Van der Mei, 'Comments on *Akrich* (Case C-109/01 of 23 September 2003) and *Collins* (Case C-138/02 of 23 March 2004)' 6 *European Journal of Migration and Law* (2004) 277; E. Fahey, 'Going Back to Basics: Re-Embracing the Fundamental of the Free Movement of Persons in *Metock*' 36 *Legal Issues of Economic Integration* (2009) 83; C. Costello, '*Metock*: Free Movement and Normal Family Life in the Union' 46 *CMLR* (2009) 587.

needed such an admirable job in the end merely underscores that the outcome actually was at odds with earlier case-law.

ii. End of excursion

The point I want to make is that, even if a court has not changed position, it is possible to construct an alternative legal argument which is just as good as standing case-law. This may require a bit of work (as Geelhoed did in his opinion, or as the Court in *Metock* had to undertake), but it is always possible. If one has constructed a rivalling position, a court can be challenged for not taking that option. The argumentative move I try to illustrate here consists of four steps: (1) the court has position A; (2) but position B is just as convincing from a legal point of view; (3) the difference between A and B therefore is not legal in nature, but political, moral, ethical, etc; (4) so let us discuss politics, morality, ethics, etc.

This argumentative move can make sense if it seems impossible to win a case by more mainstream, less confrontational tactics. In this instance, the different constructions affected the support both positions could get. The left libertarians are against requiring prior legal residence in both constructions, and the right statists are for it in both constructions. If the issue is constructed as being about immigration, the leftist statists will be for requiring prior legal residence, because admission of a TCN will mean an extra person potentially burdening the redistributive system. The right libertarians will hesitate. Their global labour market perspective will make them inclined not to require prior legal residence, but they will be hesitant because from an immigration perspective the behaviour of the TCN looks too much like abuse. The right libertarians attach too much importance to respectability to openly side with possible abusers. Once the issue is reconstructed as being about free movement, the hesitations of the right libertarians vanish. Free movement is exactly what they are for, and proudly so; they will not want prior legal residence to be required. The hesitation is passed on to the left statists. Instead of arguing for a requirement of prior legal residence, they will hesitate. The free movement of workers (and of others who are economically active or self-supporting) is not problematic for them because sufficient guarantees against undermining redistributive policies were built into the free movement system. Because they are entitled to equal labour standards, they are not a source of unfair competition and do not undermine the system of redistribution, but merely expand it. But instead of openly not requiring prior legal residence, they will hesitate because they are beginning to be insecure about those guarantees. Their hesitation is not caused by third country national family members, but by workers from the member states admitted since 2004. Is there not replacement of the local workforce by Eastern Europeans?[48] Is their influx not enlarging the pool of potential workers, with downward pressure on labour standards as a result?

[48] These concerns might be increased by Case C-438/05, *International Transport Workers' Federation and Finnish Seamen's Union v. Viking Line ABP and OÜ Viking Line Eesti*, [2007] ECR I-10779 and Case C-341/05, *Laval un Partneri Ltd v. Svenska Byggnadsarbetareförbundet, Svenska Byggnadsarbetareförbundets avd. 1, Byggettan, Svenska Elektrikerförbundet*, [2007] ECR I-11767.

Table 7.3 Immigration perspective

	Left	Right
Libertarian	Prior legal residence not required	Hesitation
Statist	Prior legal residence required	Prior legal residence required

Table 7.4 Free movement perspective

	Left	Right
Libertarian	Prior legal residence not required	Prior legal residence not required
Statist	Hesitation	Prior legal residence required

In this context, European law has two competing perspectives at the disposal of anyone who wants to make an argument. The cases discussed here can be brought under both, because they are related both to immigration and free movement. The different perspectives bring along different applicable rules, and they have a different appeal for two of the four ideal typical positions on migration.

3. Exposing Background Rules: Expulsion of HIV-Positive People

The last argumentative move I want to discuss is exposing the background rules of legal argumentation. These background rules are usually taken for granted, but they are very important to the outcome of legal argument. Background rules are the legal version of 'normality'—the things that go without saying, and mostly are not noticed. People will only expose the background rules if they think they cannot make a successful argument in the existing context, and therefore have to question that existing context. The example I will use is, in fact, a bad one, because the background that I will expose and question is not a rule, but a situation. The situation is that of the possibilities for HIV/AIDS treatment in Africa which, in the case I will discuss, is considered as given, while it can be argued that it is related to the outcome of that case.

A. *St Kitts*: the compassionate court

In its famous *St Kitts* judgment,[49] the European Court of Human Rights ruled that the removal of a man (D) dying of AIDS to the Caribbean island of St Kitts, where AIDS treatment was not available and where most likely nobody would take care

[49] *D v. UK*, ECHR (1997) RJ&D 1997-III, para. 37.

of him, would constitute a violation of the right not to be subjected to inhuman treatment (Article 3 of the ECHR). What was so remarkable about the judgment was that if the man had lived on St Kitts, no human rights violation would have taken place. Therefore, the *St Kitts* judgment was not yet another application of the line of case-law developed by the ECtHR since *Soering*,[50] according to which a person cannot be expelled or removed to a country where that person faces a real risk of being subjected to inhuman treatment. If D was removed to St Kitts, his treatment on St Kitts would not constitute inhuman treatment. The behaviour of poor countries towards ill people whose medical care they cannot afford does not constitute inhuman treatment. Then how could the ECtHR conclude that D's removal was contrary to Article 3?

The ECtHR notes that, until then, it has found the removal of aliens contrary to Article 3 where the risk of inhuman treatment 'emanates from intentionally inflicted acts of the public authorities in the receiving country or from those of non-state bodies in that country where the authorities there are unable to afford him appropriate protection' (para. 49). The ECtHR implies that in these situations, the public authorities in the country of origin are directly (by meting out the inhuman treatment) or indirectly (by failure of protection) responsible for the situation of the individual concerned. It contrasts this to 'other contexts' in which the public authorities of the country of origin do not infringe the standards of Article 3 (para. 49), and where 'it cannot be said that the conditions confronting him in the receiving country are themselves a breach of the standards of Article 3' (para. 53). But, 'given the fundamental importance of Article 3 in the Convention system, the ECtHR must reserve for itself sufficient flexibility to address the application of that Article in other contexts which might arise' (para. 49). To limit the application of Article 3 to contexts in which there is direct or indirect responsibility of the receiving state 'would be to undermine the absolute character of its [i.e. Article 3] protection'.

What the Court then focused on, was whether D's removal would be contrary to Article 3 in view of his present medical situation (para. 50). D's (limited) quality of life results from the sophisticated treatment, medication, care, and counselling he was at that moment receiving in the UK (para. 51). The abrupt withdrawal of the facilities would 'entail the most dramatic consequences for him', being a reduction of his already limited life expectancy (which was discussed in terms of months), and acute mental and physical suffering (para. 52). The Court emphasized that the UK had assumed responsibility for treating D's condition since 1994, and that he had become reliant on the care given to him. The Court's conclusion was that 'his removal would expose him to a real risk of dying under most distressing circumstances and would thus amount to inhuman treatment'. [para. 53]

The ECtHR hastened to add that aliens who have served their prison sentence cannot in principle claim continuation of medical, social, or other forms of assistance, and that this case concerned 'very exceptional circumstances' and 'compelling humanitarian considerations' (para. 54).

[50] *Soering v. UK*, ECHR (1989) Series A, No. 11.

The ECtHR's reasoning becomes more obvious if we ignore the immigration context. If D were a legal resident of the UK, it would be a violation of Article 3 of the ECHR if he were denied medical treatment, or if medical treatment were terminated, if he clearly needed medical treatment and if the decision to exclude him from medical treatment was not taken on medical grounds.[51] This would violate Article 3, because it amounts to the infliction of suffering. In the *St Kitts* judgment, the ECtHR held that, because of the special circumstances of the case, the right to continuation of medical treatment 'trumps' the right of the UK to expel an alien who has no right of residence.

B. *Bensaid*: the torn court

In *Bensaid v. UK*,[52] the ECtHR had to decide about the removal of an Algerian national who had been in the UK since 1989, and who had been treated with medication for schizophrenia since 1994–5. Deterioration in his illness could involve relapses into hallucinations and psychotic delusions involving self-harm and harm to others, as well as restrictions in social functioning. The Court considered that the suffering associated with such a relapse could, in principle, fall within the scope of Article 3 of the ECHR (para. 37). The circumstances of the case made it less likely that he would receive adequate treatment in Algeria (the ECtHR spoke of circumstances which are 'less favourable', (para. 38)). The circumstances mentioned by the Court are the following:

- The village where Bensaid's family lived was 75–80 km from the nearest hospital where treatment could be provided (para. 36);
- In that part of Algeria, at that time there was violence and active terrorism (para. 37);
- If he was an outpatient, the drug he was receiving was not free, but was 'potentially available on payment', as was other medication 'used in the management of mental illness' (para. 36);
- Bensaid's family did not have a car, and as devout Muslims they 'would urge him to rely on faith rather than medicine' (paras 30 and 39).

Bensaid, in short, argued that it was likely that he would not be treated. The ECtHR did not deny this, but essentially found the causal link between deportation and a relapse insufficient. To this end, it considered that there was a risk of relapse even if Bensaid remained in the UK and was given treatment (para. 38),

[51] Denial of medical treatment in a non-migration-related setting is usually dealt with under Art. 2 ECHR. The ECtHR has held on several occasions that 'an issue may arise under Article 2 where it is shown that the authorities of a Contracting State put an individual's life at risk through the denial of health care which they have undertaken to make available to the population generally' (*Cyprus v. Turkey*, ECHR (2001) RJ&D 2001-IV, 219; *Nitecki v. Poland*, ECHR (2002) Appl. No. 65653/01; *Pentiacova and ors v. Moldova*, ECHR (2005) RJ&D 2005-I; *Makuc and ors v. Slovenia*, ECHR (2007) Appl. No. 26828/06).

[52] *Bensaid v. UK*, *supra* n 13.

while Bensaid not receiving sufficient care and treatment in Algeria was 'to a large extent speculative'. Apparently, the fact that removal from the UK to Algeria made it rather more likely that a relapse would occur was not a sufficiently direct effect of the removal.

However, no less than three out of the seven judges, including President Costa, in a separate opinion appealed to the UK authorities:

> Nevertheless, on the evidence before the Court, there exist powerful and compelling humanitarian reasons in the present case which would justify and merit reconsideration by the national authorities of the decision to remove the applicant to Algeria.

We see the Court distinguishing this case from *St Kitts*. The relationship between removal and suffering is less direct than in the *St Kitts* context, therefore—according to a unanimous ECtHR—removal to Algeria was not a violation of Article 3 of the ECHR. But we can see the hesitation of the ECtHR in the concurring opinion. Until the passage quoted above, the concurring opinion merely explains why the judgment is correct. The quoted passage is superfluous from a legal point, and even dubious. The ECtHR has competence to decide whether an expulsion would violate Article 3; that is what the complaint is about. The Court has no competence to adjudicate on 'compelling humanitarian reasons'. What the opinion states here is superfluous, does not fall within the ECtHR's competence, and therefore does not bind the UK or anybody else. Then why do three of the seven judges involved take the effort of writing a concurring opinion, the only use of which is this passage? It seems likely that these judges fear that the ECtHR will seem harsh, and they want to signal to the reader that, although the law is harsh, they are not harsh persons. They feel torn between morality and law.

C. *N v. UK*: the split court

In 2008, the Court referred a case to the Grand Chamber in order to restate its position on the removal of HIV-positive aliens.[53] The facts of the case resemble those of *St Kitts*, as it also concerns an HIV-positive person who claims that ending her medical treatment by removal will lead to intense suffering. N had entered the UK in 1998 under an assumed name, and was admitted to a UK hospital shortly after, being seriously ill with AIDS-related illnesses (para. 9). She had been treated in the UK. It was accepted that without medical treatment her condition would 'deteriorate rapidly and she would suffer illness, discomfort, pain and death within a year or two' (paras 23 and 47). If treatment were continued, she would be in good health for decades (para. 17). In Uganda, the country of origin of N, antiretroviral medication is available, 'although through lack of resources it is received by only half of those in need' (para. 48). N claimed that she would not be able to afford the treatment; that it would not be available to her in the rural area from which she came; and that her relatives would not be willing to care for her (para. 48). Five of her six siblings had died of AIDS (para. 27).

[53] *N v. UK*, ECHR (2008) Appl. No. 26565/05.

The majority of the ECtHR followed the same logic as in *Bensaid*, and found that the removal of N to Uganda would not be contrary to Article 3, because 'the rapidity of the deterioration which she would suffer and the extent to which she would be able to obtain access to medical treatment, support, and care, including help from relatives must involve a certain degree of speculation, particularly in view of the constantly evolving situation as regards the treatment of HIV and AIDS worldwide' (para. 50). Because of the fierce dissenting opinion of three judges, the judgment is more explicit on some points than *Bensaid*.

Put bluntly, the problem which the ECtHR faced was this. If it accepted that there was a 50 per cent chance that N would not get treatment in Uganda, and applied the normal criteria, N would win her case in Strasbourg. Without a doubt, a 50 per cent chance that someone will be subjected to inhuman treatment after removal will lead to a successful application. The ECtHR could only stop short of that conclusion by holding, as it did in both *St Kitts* and *Bensaid*, that this is not a normal case concerning Article 3 and removal. It repeats the passages from the earlier judgments where, after referring to case-law concerning removal and Article 3, there may be 'other contexts' where Article 3 may stand in the way of removal. In the normal cases, the harm emanates from intentionally inflicted acts or omissions of public authorities or non-state bodies; but here, it emanates from 'naturally occurring illness and the lack of sufficient resources to deal with it in the receiving country'. That is why the high threshold set in *St Kitts* must be maintained (para. 43). A second characteristic of this kind of case which distinguishes it from other cases, according to the ECtHR, is that this case concerned social and economic issues, while the Convention 'is essentially directed at the protection of civil and political rights' (para. 44). Thirdly, the Court stated, a fair balance must be found between the demands of the general interest of the community and the fundamental rights of individuals. Advances in medical science, together with social and economic differences between countries, entail that the level of medical care varies considerably. 'Article 3 does not place an obligation on the Contracting State to alleviate such differences through the provision of free and unlimited health care to aliens without a right to stay in its jurisdiction. A finding to the contrary would place too great a burden on the Contracting States' (para. 44).

The dissenting opinion is unusual in tone. On a technical point which is not relevant in this context, it states that the majority could 'neither legally nor morally' take a certain position (para. 26). On all three points in the majority opinion identified above, the dissenters disagree. First, they disagree that a high threshold should be set. They point to case-law of the ECtHR indicating that inhuman treatment may include the suffering which is the result of illness. It is unclear to them why the usual criterion (is there a real risk that the applicant will be exposed to inhuman treatment?) should not apply (para. 5). Secondly, on the issue of socio-economic rights, the dissenters accuse the majority of giving an 'incomplete and thus misleading quotation' from the judgment dealing with the implications of the ECHR for social and economic rights. In addition, the minority points out that, on this point, the majority's position is circular or, as they put it, the *N* case *is* about a civil right, namely the one guaranteed by Article 3 (para. 6). Thirdly, the dissenters point out that just a few months earlier, in the Grand Chamber judgment in the *Saadi v. Italy* case, the Court had ruled that the protection of Article 3 is absolute and does not allow for balancing. It is inconsistent with this principled judgment, which confirmed earlier case-law, to explicitly apply a balancing test in this context (paras 7–8). Just to be sure, the dissent adds that the balancing test is applied wrongly as well, because the idea that Europe would be flooded if the Court would decide in N's favour is misconceived (para. 8).

We can see that the minority of the ECtHR, which argues for the radical position, does so by being legalistic. It insists that the criterion for the application of Article 3 is the usual real risk threshold (as opposed to the high threshold preferred by the majority). It argues that the possibility of socio-economic consequences of decisions about fundamental rights according to standard case-law are not a decisive factor against such decisions. It insists that in the context of Article 3, according to recently reconfirmed case-law, no balancing is to take place. The dissenting opinion rejects a context-specific approach and insists on application of the law. The majority, to the contrary, is context sensitive. It notes that the source of the harm which N faced was different from the source in usual Article 3 cases. It takes into account the socio-economic consequences of its ruling and rejects blind application of a formal rule, preferring one which takes into account the consequences.

D. Exposing the background

What if the Court had accepted N's claim, and had decided with the dissenters? Would it be reasonable to expect (as the dissenters say the majority suggests) Europe would become the sick-bay of the world, that the floodgates would be opened? The dissenters argue (a) that this is irrelevant, because balancing is not possible in the application of Article 3 of the ECHR. But it also argues that (b) this argument is 'totally misconceived'. However, to support this, they only refer to the number of applications to the ECtHR in HIV cases like that of N. That argument does not seem convincing, because the number of applications may be so low precisely because the ECtHR had not (and did not) 'open the floodgates'.

There may be reasons to go along with the minority on this point. After its *Salah Sheekh* judgment,[54] in which the ECtHR prohibited the removal of Somalians belonging to minority clans in Southern Somalia, there may have been an increase in applications, but even accepting that there was a causal relation between the Court's judgment and the increase (which has not been established), there was no flood. That does not confirm the idea that a judgment favourable to a group of migrants leads to a steep increase in migration.

But for a moment, let us accept the presumption that a decision in N's favour would lead to a steep increase in the migration of HIV-positive persons from, in particular, Africa to Europe. That may not be an unreasonable idea, because the life expectancy of the 50 per cent of HIV-positive Africans who do not have access to treatment would increase dramatically in this scenario. How would

[54] *Salah Sheekh v. The Netherlands, supra* n 21.

European countries respond? Of course, they would try to stop the flood by more restrictive migration policies. But we know by now that, even when we accept that such policies might have some effect, their influence would not be decisive. So there would be something like a flood. My guess, however, is that Europe would also respond by massive funding of HIV/AIDS programmes in African countries. Such an effort would not be entirely unrealistic. Universal access to HIV/AIDS prevention, treatment, and care would require 15 billion euros annually.[55] It could increase the life expectancy of HIV-positive people in Africa dramatically, and would do away with the central issue in *N*. And it would not be unaffordable, the more because substantial amounts of the investments would return to Europe, mainly through European pharmaceutical companies.

The issue at the core of the debate in *N* was: should Europe be prepared to provide 'free and unlimited health care to all aliens without a right to stay within its jurisdiction', regardless of how many might try to reach Europe if such a right is granted? It is very hard to answer that question affirmatively. In an immigration context, the ECtHR always begins by setting out that 'Contracting State[s] have the right, as a matter of well-established international law and subject to their treaty obligations including the Convention, to control the entry, residence and expulsion of aliens'.[56] So, contrary to what is usual in human rights doctrine, it is not the individual right that is put first (which states may legitimately infringe under particular circumstances), but the sovereign right of states (which individuals may infringe under particular circumstances). The ECtHR's majority is aware that, despite this tilt to the state's benefit, application of the normal criteria from the Court's own case-law will lead to granting N a right to remain in the UK. The Court allows for balancing by introducing, for the second time, the immigration context into its reasoning.

Table 7.5 Admit people who are HIV+? Yes/No

	Left	Right
Libertarian	Yes	No, it's not the business of European states
Statist	No, too large a burden on the public health system	No, too large a burden on the public health system by people who are none of our business

However, if the issue is reframed as suggested above (ie the issue is not about whether or not to admit HIV-positive aliens, but about whether or not to fund universal access to HIV/AIDS prevention), the positions could change. The dissenters could have pointed out that they addressed the immigration context by accepting the primacy of the right of states to regulate immigration. Applying the

[55] B. Schwartländer *et al.*, 'Towards an Improved Investment Approach for an Effective Response towards HIV/AIDS' 377 *The Lancet* (2011) 2031.

[56] *D v. UK, supra* n 49, para. 46; *Bensaid v. UK, supra* n 13, para. 32; *N v. UK, supra* n 53, para. 30.

ECtHR's own criteria to this case would have led to acceptance of N's claim, but not to unlimited immigration because European states can eliminate the crucial circumstance which was the ground for allowing N's claim: the poor state of HIV/AIDS medical care in Africa. The dissenters could have gained more support in this way.

Table 7.6 Invest in HIV/AIDS medical care in Africa? Yes/No

	Left	Right
Libertarian	Yes	No, it's not the business of European states
Statist	Yes, redistribution is OK if the financial burden can be managed	Possibly yes, provided that it can be established that good HIV care in Africa is in the interest of European countries

In the reframed setting, the minority position is not bound to be successful, but it has a better chance than in the setting as defined by the ECtHR in *N* and it does not require attacking another background rule—the primacy of states' rights (which is surprising in a human rights setting). It merely requires pointing out that the poor state of HIV/AIDS medical care in Africa is not, as the majority suggests, necessarily a given (naturally occurring illness and lack of sufficient resources, para. 43). Changing this part of the perspective would have allowed an escape route from the majority's complicated tinkering with the recently reconfirmed absolute nature of the protection provided by Article 3 of the ECHR. The change of perspective is brought about by not taking the inequality between Africa and Europe as a given. Where the Court in *N* (both the majority and the dissenters) took the lack of HIV/AIDS treatment in Africa as a given, the alternative perspective suggested here considers that as something which may be changed.

E. From law and ideology to law as ideology

How can it be that the dissenters got stuck with the immigration perspective on the case? Why did they argue that the floodgate argument was (a) normatively irrelevant and (b) empirically flawed—especially when combined, this kind of argument is unconvincing (I didn't steal a cookie, *and* I was so hungry). One might think that either the dissenters did not try hard enough, or that they were not smart enough. Both ideas can be dismissed immediately. The dissenting opinion displays unusual engagement, and is very thoroughly argued.

Until now, I have tried to show how the application of law to individual situations cannot be done without at the same time applying substantive, non-legal ideas about fairness, justice, and morality. Lawyers who believe that law and such substantive ideas should be separate might say—and every now and then do say—such an application of non-legal ideas is ideology, not law. In this way, they dismiss a reasoning as not being legal, because purely legal argument has been contaminated by substantive ('ideological') notions. My argument until now has been that law is always ideological in this sense, it is always linked to ideology; legal reasoning always has to rely on ideology.

But the ideas without which law cannot be applied are, in turn, influenced by law. So ideas influence the application of law, and the application of law influences ideas. The dissenting opinion in *N* is a good example of this. The right of states to control the entry, residence, and removals of aliens is simply posited by the ECtHR. There is no reference to a provision in the ECHR, or to any explicit rule of international law. It refers to its own case-law (which has indeed said this for decades), but for a non self-referential source it can only rely on 'well-established international law'. It is undoubtedly true that this is a well-established rule of international law. It is something like a political and legal axiom. This is well-established international law, because it evidently is so. The axiom holds, even in the face of contrary state practice. Asylum is an obvious example of a situation where states do not have this right. Theoretically, they still do have their full rights except for one option (removal to the country of origin), but in practice this implies the admission of considerable numbers of persons each year. Still, one might say, this is a tiny exception. But it is not the only one. In the European Union, states have, practically speaking, given up their right to control the entry, residence, and removal of citizens of other member states. European citizens have the right to enter and remain in the territory of every member state, and can be removed only in particular circumstances (Article 21 of the Treaty on the Functioning of the European Union; Directive 2004/38). But, one might say, this is a specific context, where states have mutually given up their migration control rights. A third case in which states act as if they do not have a sovereign right to control migration relies on Linda Bosniak's observation that states tend to give citizenship rights to both legal and illegal residents.[57] One may add that states also tend to regularize the residence status of undocumented aliens on account of their de facto citizenship.[58] In both contexts (grant of citizenship rights and regularization), states simultaneously emphasize the sovereign nature of their behaviour (ie it is grace, not entitlement), but the pressure to which they give in always partly relies on a notion of moral entitlement.

This is not meant to say that there can be no well-established rule of international law holding that states have the sovereign right to control the entry, residence, and removal of aliens. It is meant to say that it is not self-evident that this rule exists; its existence, and particularly its content, does not go without saying. Nevertheless, this rule is repeated like a mantra, its sources and its scope not subject to any serious debate. In *N*, we can see that it shapes our idea of how the world is. Even the dissenters in *N*, who were earnestly looking for arguments to prohibit the removal of N, found this sovereign right so obvious that they did not dispute its dominance even when it was introduced by the majority into its reasoning for the second

[57] L. Bosniak, *The Citizen and the Alien: Dilemmas of Contemporary Membership* (2008).

[58] For an overview of European practice in the 1990s, see P. De Bruycker (ed.), *Regularisations of Illegal Immigrants in the European Union* (2000).

time. It would have been enough for the dissenters to say that state sovereignty in controlling migration is the rule, but that the rule is not relevant when we look at the potential consequences of prohibiting N's removal. Apparently, the minority presumed that disputing the relevance of state sovereignty in a particular part of the argument would make it look unrealistic: would look as if they were disputing state sovereignty itself.

In short, I suggest that the moral and political ideas of the dissenters were dominated by the legal notion of state sovereignty. In their arguments, they go along with the majority in seeing the case as being about migration—one of the crucial markers of state sovereignty—and because they allow the argument to be so narrow they were unable to get broader support for their position.

4. Afterword: Scepticism and Activism

Critical lawyers—irrespective of whether they are conservative or progressive, leftists or rightists, libertarians or welfare state-minded—tend to 'use' law, ie to develop positivist arguments showing that the outcome which they prefer is right. This positivist style of argument requires a denial of the flexibility of legal argument. The core of positivist legal reasoning is that there can be only one correct answer. But this is hard to maintain. As lawyers, we know that legal issues can be dealt with in different ways, even if we strongly feel that one of these ways is the right one. Critical lawyers are doomed to be disappointed time and again by the fact that 'they' once again succeeded in winning cases, while 'we' were so right.

In this chapter, I have investigated some of the possibilities critical lawyers have in the field of immigration law: constructing consistency, exposing choice, and exposing background rules. This is not an exhaustive list of available tactics. It should be obvious that, in some situations, critical lawyers can get their way by insisting on 'applying the law'. In other words sometimes legal positivism, and insisting on the consistency and rightness of the law as it is, will be an obvious option and, certainly, there are other options. The effort in this chapter was to widen the scope of critical lawyers and to add to their arsenal. Instrumentalism is not the only available option.

To many, it seems scary to abandon instrumentalism and positivism. The fantasy which constitutes their main attraction is that, by acting as impersonators of the law, by pretending to be the people who come up with the right application of the law, we will share in the power of law. But this requires that we give up the other options, at least momentarily. When we formulate what follows from the law, we must act as if it is not us speaking, but the law. In that sense, we have to give up our subjectivity and act as functionaries of the law.[59] What I suggest in this article is that this is just one of the options we have, and if we use it now and then,

[59] I take this way of putting it from the—entirely different—context of Adorno's work on music, eg his 'On Jazz', in T. W. Adorno: *Essays on Music* (2002) 470.

it does not require us to believe in its truth all the time. Sometimes, we can argue that law is consistent (if it comes out our way) but in other contexts, we can argue that law is inconsistent and should be made consistent; or that there are several right options, and argue for one; or that what seems the only possible outcome rests on a presumption which is debatable.

Index

The manufacturer's authorised representative in the EU for product
safety is Oxford University Press España S.A. of El Parque Empresarial
San Fernando de Henares, Avenida de Castilla, 2 - 28830 Madrid
(www.oup.es/en or product.safety@oup.com). OUP España S.A. also acts
as importer into Spain of products made by the manufacturer.
Printed and bound by CPI Group (UK) Ltd, Croydon, CR0 4YY
14/09/2026
02216305-0002